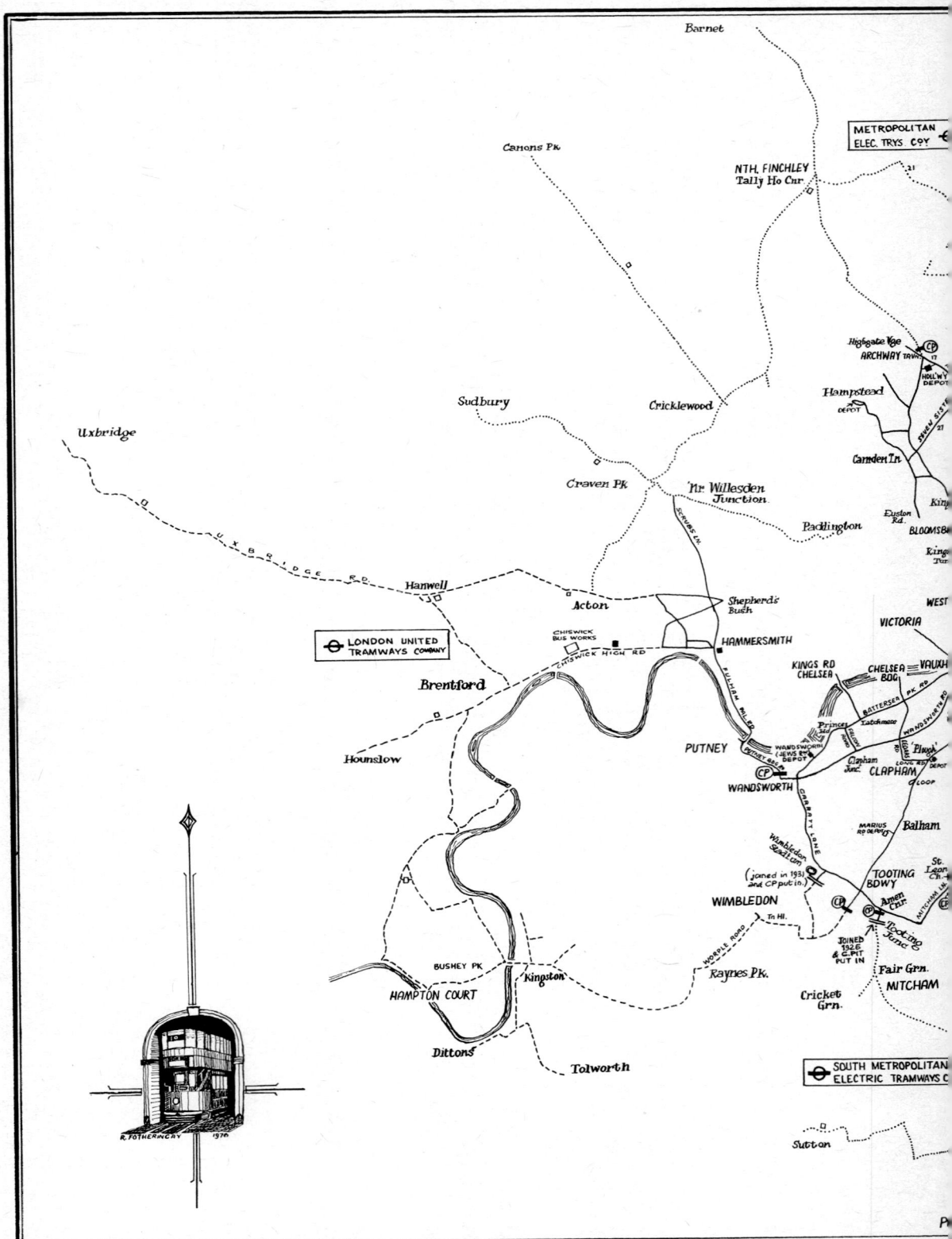

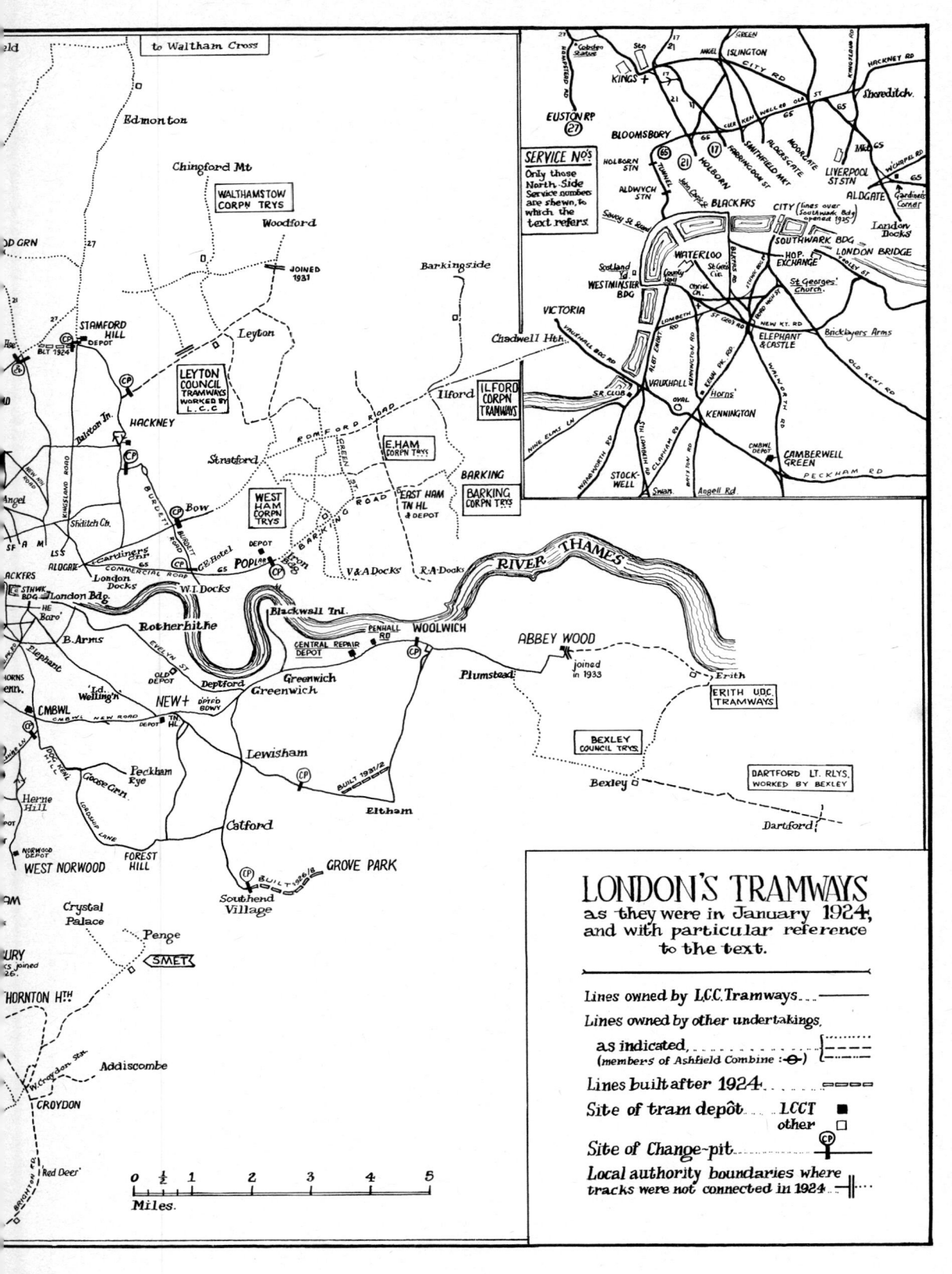

First published 1977 by Tallis Publishing, 35 Mooroaks Road, Sheffield 10.

Copyright : Terence Cooper

ISBN: 0 9505458 0 5

All rights reserved. No part of this book may be reproduced, stored or transmitted without the written permission of the publisher, except for the purpose of review or for other private purposes not connected with financial gain. The copyright in all illustrations herein remains wholly with the original copyright holders.

Editor's Acknowledgements.

Richard Berridge of Leicester designed and executed the cover, chapter headings and pen-and-ink drawings; Roy Makewell and Richard Fotheringay provided maps and diagrams.

Permission to reproduce their photographs was freely given by Mr. B.T. Cooke, Mr.F. Ivey, Mr. D.W.K. Jones, Lens of Sutton, London Transport, Mr. A.D. Packer, Mr. J.H. Price, Mr. T. Russell, and Mr. W.J. Wyse. The Greater London Council has also allowed some of its photographs to appear here. I have been unable to trace the copyright holders of certain photographs, and I can only hope that their reproduction gives no offence. A list of the known sources of all photographs may be had from the publisher in return for a stamped envelope.

Extracts from private London Transport documents are reproduced by special permission of the Executive, several members of the staff of which were especially helpful; Mr. R. Costa of the Industrial Relations Office, and Howard Butler and Jean Tuck of the Publicity Office, gave assistance beyond that which I had any right to expect. Similarly, I must acknowledge the helpfulness shown me by the Transport and General Workers Union in London, the Modern Records Centre at Warwick University, and the staff of the Sheffield Central Library. Indeed, many people have helped in the preparation of this book, but I must particularly mention John Gent, Mr. D.W.K. Jones, Roy Makewell and Albert McCall.

To all, I am very grateful, but it is to Stan Collins and his family, and to my own wife that I offer my most heartfelt thanks, for they patiently gave me their time, that most valuable commodity which I am sure they would rather have spent otherwise.

Printed by Hadfield Print Services Ltd., 41/43 Pikes Lane, Glossop, Derbyshire.

Bluebird's controller is shut off, and Stan Collins' right hand is operating the air brake, 1951.

CONTENTS

	Introduction	1
1.	Reared on tram-driver's dripping	7
2.	Military Service	19
3.	Holloway Depot	22
4.	Clapham Depot	34
5.	Trams and tramwaymen	52
6.	Telford Avenue and the Felthams	84
7.	Wartime	104
8.	Driving Instructor	114
9.	Last tram to Telford Avenue	126
10.	Bus Driver and Retirement	132

Appendices

1.	Some notes on the development of tram services in Streatham and Clapham	136
2.	Routes of Electric Services, 1903 - 1951	146
3.	A Short History of Services 16 and 18	149
4.	Wages and Conditions of LCCT and LT tram crews	160
5.	Some notes on labour relations on London's trams	162

Index 170

Bibliography 172

London County Council Tramways.

The Council requires of all employees:—

HONESTY, SOBRIETY, OBEDIENCE, PUNCTUALITY, CIVILITY.

INTRODUCTION

This is the story of a London tramwayman, Stanley Guildford Collins, who was born in Brixton in 1899, the son of a cable-tram driver. Except for a short break during and just after the Great War, Stan Collins worked on London's trams from 1913 until 1951, as a labourer and van-boy at the London County Council Tramways Central Repair Depot at Charlton, as a tram-driver from Holloway, Clapham and Telford Avenue Depots, and finally as a Driving-Instructor at the Clapham Motor School. In April 1951 he drove the ceremonial last tram through Streatham, and then drove tram-replacement buses until he retired in 1964, after almost forty-one years continuous service to the travelling London public. In 1973 he returned briefly to London Transport as a canteen-cleaner at Brixton Bus Garage, the building which had replaced the tram-depot from which he, his father and a brother had driven trams for so long.

It was there that I was lucky enough to meet him in the Spring of 1973, and on many occasions since then we have sat together, a tape-recorder between us, while he has told me of his life with trams and has patiently answered my questions, and I believe he has enjoyed our conversations almost as much as I have. In 1975 we went together to Syon Park and were allowed to board two of the trams in the London Transport Collection; that visit is the basis of Chapter Five of this book.

The words that follow have been transcribed from those conversations, and they are written just as Stan Collins spoke them, but with two general exceptions: his narrative is here arranged in chronological order, and I have therefore sometimes altered an original tense for the sake of continuity. So it must be remembered that what you will read is the spoken, not the written word, oral history rather than carefully composed biography. No man of 77 can be expected to remember with complete accuracy every detail of his working life — in certain circumstances he may deliberately choose not to — nor can he always fully understand the part he plays in the day-to-day operations of a large trading organisation. By any standards Stan Collins' memory is vast, detailed and accurate, but so that his narrative can be set against a broad background, and to occasionally amplify it, I have added certain notes and appendices. Where I have been able to check his statements, I have done so, but have found very, very few discrepancies with established or published fact, and these I have drawn to his attention. Some he has corrected, but where doubt has persisted I have left his words as he spoke them. He was there: Stan Collins was a part of London's tramway history.

The traditional approach of the tramway historian to his subject has been a rather dry, classificatory one, which has concentrated on the vehicles and the routes on which they operated and has too often overlooked the men who worked with trams and the political and economic reasons for their actions. This is a great shame, for not only has it limited our understanding of why London's trams developed as they did, but it has caused certain myths to develop and become commonplace. And all the while the number of tramwaymen, from whom we could have learnt so much, has been steadily dwindling. Stan Collins concentrates on the job of the tramwayman. You will find in his text no lists of constructional details, no complex tabulations of stock-numbers or dates; those who require such information will find it elsewhere. But a short pre-amble may help those who know little of the development of the London tram network or who are unacquainted with the cars that worked on it.

Between 1870 and 1901 London's trams were hauled by horses, except on two hilly lines where underground cables operated. For most of that period they were privately owned and operated.

Motorman Collins and a Standard E1 tram at Telford Avenue Depot in the late 1920's.

sometimes well, sometimes badly. The work was hard and ill-paid, the hours long: in the 1890's Sidney Webb contrasted the high dividends that certain companies paid with the wages and conditions of their 'tram-slaves'. From 1896 the new and Radical London County Council began to acquire all the tram companies within the County of London. As it did so, it increased the employees' wages and reduced their working day, and it gave them those most valuable concomitants of Muncipal Socialism, continuous employment and job security. In 1903 the LCC began to electrify and extend its new instrument of social welfare; working-class mobility was greatly improved, new jobs were created and new skills were born.

Many of the original horse-car lines crossed the LCC boundary or lay wholly outside it, and certain outer-London boroughs — most notably East and West Ham and Croydon — also electrified their statutorily acquired lines and laid new ones. To the North and West of London, however, and in one case to the South, municipal enterprise was wanting, and there came into being new companies to operate electric trams. Although certain of these smaller peripheral undertakings amalgamated, and there was eventually much through-running between most of them and the LCC, it was not until 1933 that all, municipal and company tramways, were brought together with the creation of the London Passenger Transport Board. Thus there existed in 1933 a vast London tramway network, with the LCC — by far the largest constituent — at its hollow centre, but it was a geographically mis-shapen network, which did not really penetrate Central London and certain suburbs and was fractured by the Thames.

The tramways that London Transport administered in 1933 employed almost 20,000 people; around 5000 of them were working tram-drivers who between them drove over 2600 trams along more than 300 route miles of track. But whereas tramwaymen had once enjoyed relatively good terms of employment, they had for some time been losing status. For many years busmen had been earning more money, often for slightly shorter hours, and this curious anomaly was to continue within London Transport for as long as it operated trams.

It is popularly believed that the new London Transport was possessed by an instinctive dislike for trams, for it lost no time in beginning to replace its inherited trams with other vehicles, generally trolleybuses before the Second World War and diesel buses thereafter. Certainly the new Board was plainly dominated by the bus and underground interests with which the LCC had competed — the Ashfield Combine — but it is foolish to imagine that trams were abandoned for purely doctrinaire reasons; prejudice alone cannot explain this policy.

After 1933 London Transport was legally obliged to make an overall annual profit, and it just could not afford to continue operating trams. The economics of tram operation were certainly complicated and socially unfair in practice — in much the same way as is claimed for British Railways today — but in the real market economy of the 1930's trams were a commercial liability which London Transport simply could not tolerate. Heavy capital investment was required elsewhere, and the trolleybus and diesel bus were fast developing as cheap potential tram-substitutes in their own right. Given the unfortunate terms of the 1933 LPTB Act, the political and economic climate of the 1930's and the inept urban planning notions of the time, the decision to replace trams was correct and inevitable.

London municipal tram operators generally had no powers to run buses, although such powers had been frequently sought. Had it not been for the known-to-be forthcoming Transport Board, it is likely that municipal buses or trolleybuses would have appeared in London before 1933. In many areas trams were not covering their costs and were being subsidised from local rates. In certain cases Combine buses had already replaced municipal trams, and the Combine had itself invested in both trams and trolleybuses shortly before 1933.

So it was, then, that the London tramway network declined progressively in size after 1933 — save for an interruption in the conversion programme caused by Herr Hitler — until, in 1952, the last metropolitan tram climbed on a wave of crocodile tears into New Cross Depot.

The 'Standard' LCC tram was a long, enclosed double-decker running on two four-wheel bogies. Most typically, the Standard car to which Stan Collins frequently refers was that type known as the E/1, of which 1000 were built to roughly the same design between 1907 and 1922. But the LCC tram was highly standardised and was quite unmistakable. In 1923 the LCC owned almost 1750 double-deck trams of varying ages and original designs, but their standard Charlton-designed top decks hall-marked their common heritage. Many E/1 cars continued in service until 1952, and one still remains, in the London Transport Collection.

All the LCC's electric trams worked at a line voltage of 550/600 volts DC. The whole network of tracks was divided into approximately half-mile-long sections, each section independently supplied with energy from a sub-station, and each isolated from its neighbour by a short 'dead' section. Each sub-station fed a group of adjacent sections with energy transmitted at high-pressure from the LCC Generating Station at Greenwich, rectified and stepped-down to line voltage before leaving the sub-station.

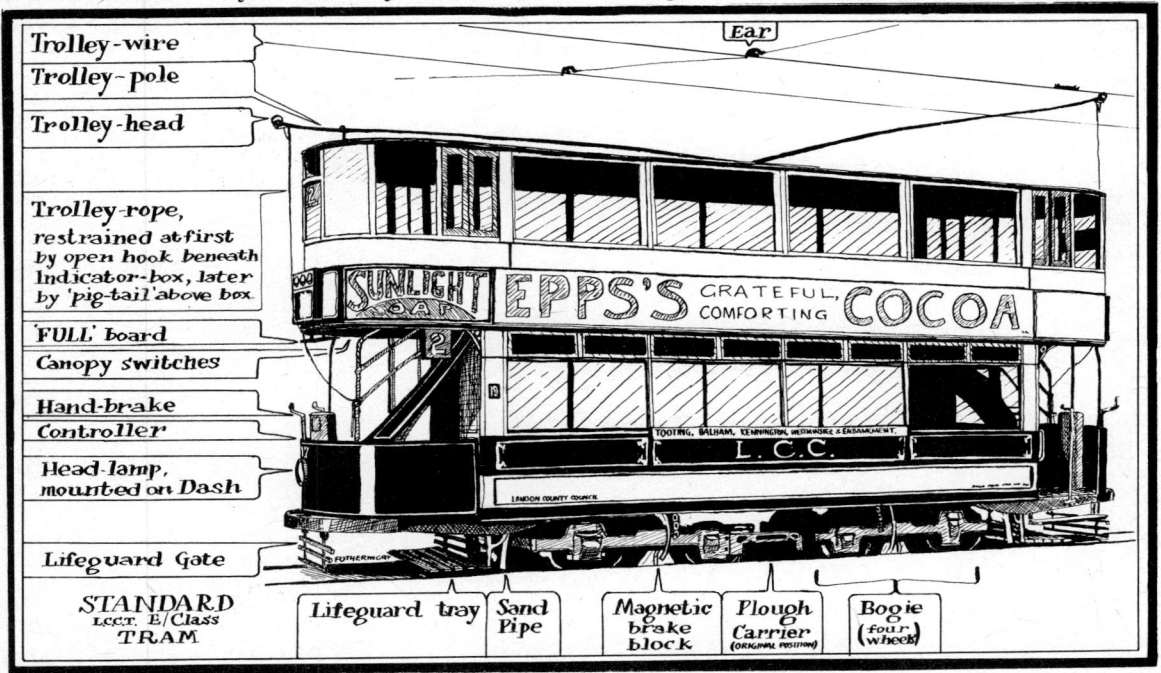

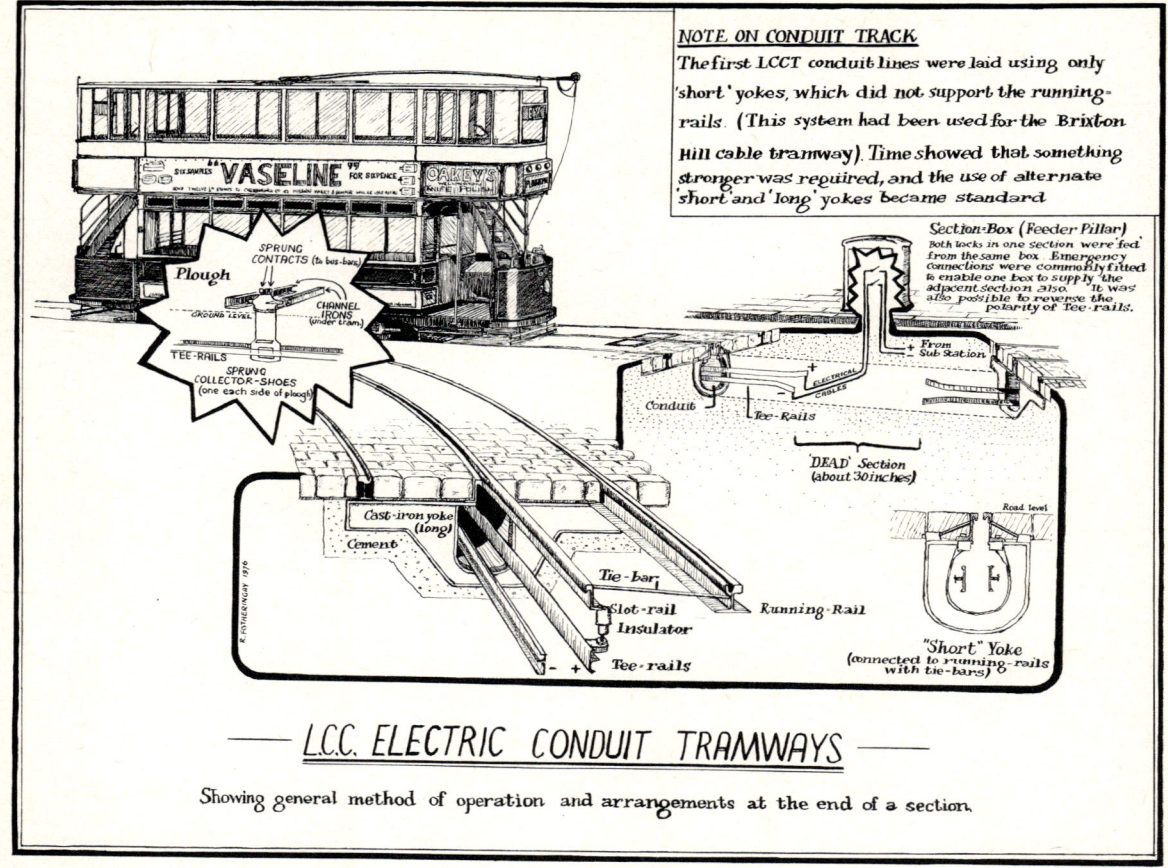

At each section break was a roadside feeder pillar — Stan Collins calls them 'section boxes', cast-iron cupboards, a few of which can still be seen in London — which contained positive and negative line-switches for both tracks in the section and, very often, a private LCC telephone. It was at the section break, that is at one end of each section, that energy was fed into either underground conduits or overhead copper wires, for collection by each tram.

In the older, generally inner-suburban areas of the LCC network, there was a continuous underground conduit beneath the centre of each track, inside which ran two horizontally facing T-section rails, placed six inches apart. One tee-rail was positively charged, whilst the other provided an earth return to the feeder pillar; the polarity of the tee-rails could be reversed if required. At the top of each conduit, mid-way between the running-rails, was a continuous one-inch gap, protected on either side with steel facings which together were called the 'slot-rail'. Running-rails, slot-rails and tee-rails were held rigidly together by cast-iron yokes set in concrete. Access to the conduit was provided at the dead sections through 'dead-hatchways' — manhole covers immediately above the gap in the tee-rails — whilst 'live-hatchways' were located at junctions and crossovers.

Hanging from lateral channel-irons beneath each tram — the plough-carrier — was a wooden plough, the thin shank of which passed through the slot and into the underground conduit. This removable plough was the means whereby the current passed from the tee-rails into the tram. On either side of the base of the plough was a sprung collector shoe, one bearing on each tee-rail. At the top of the plough, above two lugs which allowed it to move from side-to-side whilst hanging in the channel-irons, were two projecting terminals which bore against two sprung bus-bars fitted to the underside of the tram. Connected to the bus-bars were insulated leads which carried the current into the wiring on the tram. Above the bus-bars and plough-carrier, in the lower saloon floor of the tram, was a large inspection hatch.

Until the late 1920's, the plough-carrier was bolted to the inner end of one bogie. From about 1930 it was mounted directly on the underside of the car, as shown on the left. **Above right**, *the channel-irons and bus-bars can be plainly seen.*

Below: *The spare plough stands behind the tool-box, beneath the stairs of an E/3 tram; above it, on the bulkhead, is the police licence and the trolley-plough change switch.*

In the outer, more recent sections of the LCC network, and throughout the adjoining systems which came together in 1933 to form the London Transport tram system, positive current passed from the feeder pillar to a copper trolley-wire above each track. In this case the earth return was through the tram wheels and into the running-rails, which were in turn connected back to the feeder pillar. Trams operating beneath the trolley-wire were fitted with one or two sprung trolley-poles mounted on the roof. (The second trolley-pole avoided the need to swing the first pole from one end of the tram to the other at a turning point).

At the extremity of the trolley-pole was a swivelling globe — the trolley-head — in which revolved a grooved wheel which bore against the underside of the trolley-wire. From the trolley-head hung a trolley-rope, with which the trolley-pole could be raised, lowered or turned at ground level. Trolley-wire was suspended beneath insulated span-wires which ran diagonally across the road between pairs of tall road-side traction standards. Certain LCC trams were not equipped with trolley-poles and were thus confined to wholly conduit services.

Because of the two alternative methods of current collection, all London trams equipped for both types of operation were fitted with a 'change-over switch', to which was connected both under-body bus-bars and contacts at the base of the trolley-pole, selecting one or other power-source. From the change-over switch the power ran through automatic circuit-breakers to the tram controllers, one at each end of the car. The controllers fulfilled several functions. From

The controller on an open-fronted tram; to the right is the hand-brake. (Works car 012 in 1952).

the top of the controller projected two spindles. The right-hand spindle, operated by a large spanner-like key, selected 'off', 'forward motion' or 'reverse motion' according to its setting. The left-hand spindle, operated by a large brass handle, controlled speed by connecting the motors — one on each bogie — first in series (for maximum power) and then in parallel (for the greatest economy), and passing current to the motors through three or four variable resistances. These resistances were mounted beneath each platform.

Additionally, by reversing the polarity of the motors and converting them to generators, the main controller handle also operated an electro-magnetic braking system, whereby steel brake shoes were strongly attracted to the running-rails. A third spindle, also operated by the key, cut out one or other motor as required, but this was only used if a motor was damaged.

From the motors the negative current returned to the change-over switch, and from there to either the tee-rail or the running-rails. To the right of each controller was a hand-brake column which operated wheel brake blocks through a system of rods, chains and levers.

This, very simply, was how the LCC Standard tram worked. Certain later, more sophisticated cars were a little more complicated. This explanation — adapted from the LCC Motorman's Handbook of 1928 — and the sketches will hopefully clarify Stan Collins' narrative.

Although it is now almost twenty-five years since the last trams left London's streets, something of their spirit remains still, in the men who once worked with trams, and in the depots from which they once operated. This spirit has nothing to do with romanticism or any real desire to re-instate the tram, but derives from the tramwayman's background and from his attitudes, to his job, to his employers and to his workmates.

The London tramwayman had far more in common with a provincial transport worker than he had with the thoroughbred London General Omnibus Company or London Transport busman, and the LCC's operational practices were also more provincial than metropolitan. In some curious way, the tram and the LCC ethic — which continued within London's tramways and endured almost to the end of trolleybuses in 1962 — attracted or created a man who was recognisably different from his colleagues on London buses. Possibly because of his long-standing background of security, combined with the harsh discipline exercised by the LCC, he seemed more adaptable, less likely to question his management and more conscious of a sense of duty to his passengers.

The purpose of this book is to describe the tramwayman's life, and the conditions in which he worked, during a period in which London's transport underwent great changes, and to convey the attitude of one man, by no means untypical, to a job which he enjoyed immensely and remembers with great fondness.

T. Cooper,
Sheffield.
August 1976.

1899 to 1915

REARED ON TRAMDRIVERS DRIPPING

In December 1892 there was opened in South London a newly-constructed cable-operated tramway, which ran for two and three-quarter miles between Kennington and the top of Brixton Hill. The line connected at Kennington with horse-tram routes to many parts of what would now be called Central and South London. At the southernmost point of the line, on the site of a large house, was built a depot, to house part of the fleet of thirty gripper cars which operated on the line — there was a second, smaller depot at Kennington — together with a similar number of standard double-deck horse-trams which they hauled. The line was owned by the London Tramways Company, the second largest of the twelve horse-tram companies in London at that time, and it was reputed to make good profits. The Company also owned certain other lines in South London, on which trams were hauled conventionally, by horses.

There had been no previous tramway on Brixton Hill, for it was considered too steep for horses and the streets on either side were not developed until late in the nineteenth century, but an earlier horse line had linked Brixton, through Kennington, with Westminster and Blackfriars Bridges and the Borough. This route pattern continued after 1892, for when the cable-drawn trams reached Kennington, they were hauled onwards by horses.

The opening of the Brixton Hill cable tramway not only improved local communications, but it provided employment. Apart from Drivers and Conductors, artisans were required to maintain the line and South London's first mechanically powered trams, and skilled mechanics were needed to man the Power House beside the depot. It is likely that around fifty additional jobs were created when the line was opened.

Shortly after the new cable-tramway was opened, there came to Brixton Hill from Kent a young man, Horace John Collins. Born in Cranbrook in the 1860's, he had spent some time in domestic service before moving to the Metropolis to improve his prospects. He was luckier than many people who came to London at this time, for almost straight away he secured lodgings in Mill Lane and a position as a cable-tram driver at the nearby Telford Avenue depot.

In 1894 Horace John Collins married a local girl, and on 4th April 1899 there was born to him his second son, Stanley Guildford Collins.

Before she got married, my mother was lodging with her sister Carrie over her shop on Brixton Hill — it was a double-fronted sweet shop — and she took to waving at my father as he went past on his tram. Things being what they are, they got courting, and Mum used to take him out a bit of hot dinner sometimes, because in those days there was no meal relief and he could be working twelve hours or more straight through. He used to keep his knife and fork in the gripper box.

The cable ran at eight miles-an-hour along a conduit between the tracks, and if the drivers were running a bit late they would take the gripper off the cable going down Brixton Hill to run a bit faster and make up a minute or two. It was a very serious business running late, because you were robbing the car behind of fares, (1) and if you were caught at it you would be called into the office to see Miss Penman who controlled the men. The cable ran round a drum which used to be right up the back of the depot, which was where Telford Avenue Bus Garage is now.

1. This suggests that crews were paid on a commission basis.

From 1892 until 1899, special gripper cars hauled standard 44 seat trams between Streatham and Kennington on the Brixton Hill Cable tramway, **above**. Standard horse trams were then adapted to carry the gripper apparatus, **below**.

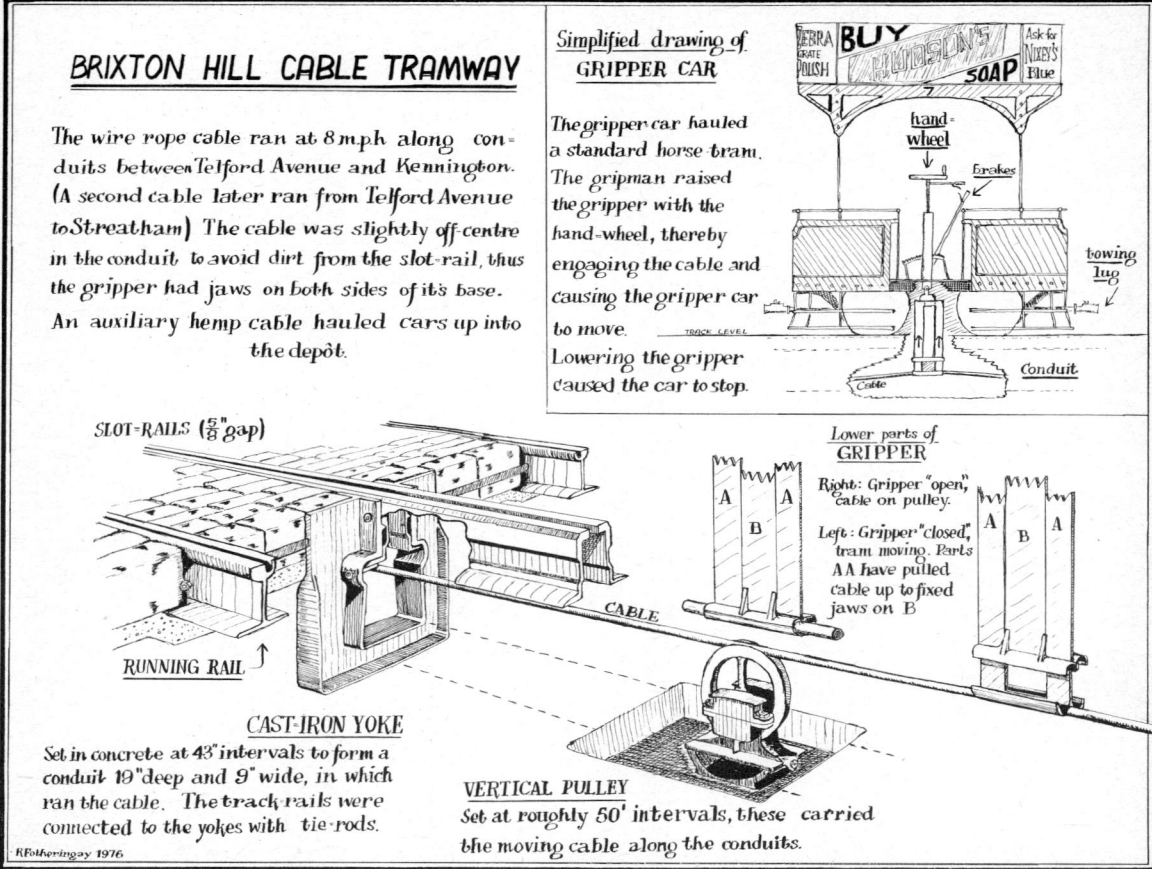

One morning in 1895 my father knocked the cable off the drum coming down Brixton Hill and put the line out of action for about twelve hours, and he was sacked on the spot. By that time he was married, and my mother was expecting her first baby, so she went along to the office and very near begged for his job back, and as a result of her pleading Miss Penman took my father back as a car-washer. Every night about half-a-dozen men would hang about the yard hoping to get taken on, and some did and some didn't, according to the weather and how dirty the cars were. Eventually he got on the wash regular. *(2)*

Horace Collins was later taken back as a cable-tram driver. In 1895 the cable-line was extended south, to Streatham Library, and on the first day of 1899 it was bought by the LCC. In 1904, the line was electrified, and five years later it was again extended, to the County boundary at Norbury.

In 1909 the LCC Tramways Department (LCCT) opened its Central Repair Depot at Charlton and, soon afterwards, Horace Collins became a stores-van driver there. Stan Collins habitually refers to the Central Repair Depot by its initials, 'the CRD'.

I was born in 1899 at 42 Wingford Road, just round the corner from where we live now, and you might say I was brought up on tram-driver's dripping. So was my elder brother, Horace, and he went on the trams as well. Horace died in 1969, but eventually I had four sisters and two brothers. Two sisters still live near — one's just round the corner — another lives in Kings Avenue and the fourth lives at Earlsfield. The other brother lives over at Catford.

As a youngster, even at school, I always had an ambition to be a tram-driver, always. At home, I can see it now, we used to have the old cane-bottomed chairs with holes in, and I used to bend a piece of wire like a tram handle, and stick it in a hole, and in my mind I was driving a tram. I was a boy at school, six or seven perhaps.

My father didn't take a lot of notice, he was away all day anyway. I don't think he mentioned trams to me much when I was a boy, not to realise my ambition, but I always wanted to be a

2. At that time a full-time car-washer was paid only 22s. a week, whereas a Driver earned between 32s 6d and 42s.

Installing the depot points for electric cars at Telford Avenue in 1904, **above**. *B class car 194 reversing at Water Lane in 1904* **below**; *the lantern slide from which this is taken is entitled 'the first car to Water Lane'.*

tram-driver. When he was on the stores-van, supposing he had to deliver some goods up at Streatham, he'd get the job done quick, then he'd hop on a tram and come down home, Mum would make him a cup of tea before he went back, then he'd pick up his bag again and I might go back with him. Then I'd sit inside the van, or stand on tip-toes peering through the little windows, trying to see where we were going.

He'd take me back to Charlton with him and bring me home on a service car. I don't know how he fiddled it but I know he never paid any fare for me, because he used to have the tokens then. Another time I might be out on Brixton Hill and I've seen the old van come along, and my Dad's spotted me and gone ping-ping on the bell and waved at me.

I went to New Park Road School, so I never had many miles to run. The girls were in the middle, big boys at the top and infants underneath. You went from the Infants into Standard One when you were little boys, and you gradually went up higher and higher until you finished in X 7, the top class, by the time you were nearly fourteen. When we left school we had to get a job where we could, errand-boys mostly, pulling a grocer's barrow and all that sort of thing.

When I first left school in 1913 I got a job as a butcher's boy. I heard it was going so I went down after it, but I wasn't there long, perhaps a month or six weeks. In those days a butcher's boy's job was bloody hard work, no aluminium rails like they've got now, all steel and they had to be emeried, and then you had to clean the windows inside and out, cut up paper, turn the sausage machine, you were never still. Right opposite this butcher's shop — down in Cornwall Road, it's Blenheim Gardens now — there was a place where you could get faggots, saveloys and that sort of thing. There used to be two schoolgirls, I can see them now, with their hair down their backs, and they used to go over to this shop and get a ha'pennyworth of pease pudding in a piece of newspaper, and walk along the street eating it. As they came past my shop they used to flick a bit of pease pudding onto my window. I couldn't leave my shop, I was the only one there, and if a customer came in I had to call the guv'nor to come and serve them, and I knew I couldn't run after them. Anyway, this kept going on, and one day I did run after them and they turned round and made faces at me, sticking their finger up their nose, poking their tongues out and all that sort of thing, and I said, 'I'll break your bloody necks one day when I catch you.' Well, of course, soon after that I packed that job up and went on the trams — my Dad had fixed up for me to start down at the Central Repair Depot at Charlton — but that particular story didn't end there, as you'll see.

Taken from the newly built Lambeth Town Hall around 1908; the tram is going to Water Lane.

Kennington, **right**, looking towards Camberwell, with Brixton Road on the right.

When the electric conduit was laid along Brixton Road in 1904, it incorporated a single-track crossing for the horse trams of the London Southern Tramways Company, which operated a service to Vauxhall. In 1907 the track was opened up for the insertion of special work for electric services on Stockwell Road and Coldharbour Lane, **below**. Beyond the unstable short yokes and tie-bars of the original conduit, car 510 approaches.

The lifting-gang at the CRD in 1932.

New mess-rooms being built at the CRD in 1915, **right**. Car 200 exhorts Men of the Empire to Join the Army today.

In those days the South-side cars were overhauled and repainted at the CRD, and almost everything that was needed was made in the works. The trams would come in off the road, shoot their ploughs out by the gatehouse, where there was a change-pit, and sometimes, if they had enough speed, they could get straight onto the traverser which was behind a big roller blind that they opened up early every morning. If not, the engine would come and push them, it was red if I remember. Then a gang of men — they were called the lifting gang — started stripping it down, body off straight away and down towards the paint shop. There were two traversers and a sort of dummy trolley which they used to swing out and put the body of the tram on it and traverse it down towards the paint shop. The remaining truck, or trucks, because there were a lot of four-wheelers in those days, remained on the traverser ready for stripping down. Trams came in and out every day.

On the gate were LCC policemen, and they'd stop you going in if you were late. They shut the gate and you had to wait outside till eight o'clock. I've been shut out and lost what we called 'a quarter.'

My job was to go round with an electric narrow-gauge trolley, picking up bits of surplus wood and iron and returning them to the stores. The hardest part was turning the trolley by hand on a turntable, but often one of the workmen would help me if he saw me.

It was a long day, though, because we were working a sixty-hour-week. I had to get up at four o'clock every morning to catch the four-forty-five tram from New Park Road to Kennington, where I got a connection onto a number 40. We clocked in at six o'clock, and if you were more than five minutes late you lost a quarter of an hour's pay, if you were more than fifteen minutes late you lost half an hour's pay, and if you got in after five-and-twenty to seven you lost a quarter of a day's pay, so it kept you on your toes. They were hard times, because they'd screw you right down to the minute. If you lost a quarter you weren't allowed in till eight o'clock, which was breakfast time, then there was an hour for dinner and another short break for tea. There was no canteen, just a mess-room, and there was an old boy up there — the Old Tosher we called him, I don't know whether it was his right name or not — and everybody had his own regular place at the tables. We used to take sandwiches, or Mum would make little meat pies for Dad and me to take in a saucer. Of a morning, if you had any food in a basin you wanted warmed up, you would stick it in the place where you sat. Well, Old Tosher knew just where everybody sat, and he'd warm their grub up in the oven and leave it in the right place ready for dinner-time. One day us kids ran up there at dinner-time before anyone else, and mixed them all up. There was hell to pay. All the men kept saying, 'Oi, Tosher, where's my grub'?, and moaning. They never

did find out who did it.

At six o'clock we clocked out, and I was usually home around seven, which only left me a couple of hours before it was time to go to bed. On Saturdays, though, we finished up at dinner time.

Spartan seating of this sort was the rule on LCCT trams until the mid-1920's; the upper saloon could still be enjoyed, virtually unchanged, in 1950.

Mind you, it was a long day, and I was only fourteen and a half when I started. I remember once I jumped on a number 40 one night, got a seat upstairs and fell asleep with my arm on the window-sill — the seats were all wood in those days, with low backs to them — and I woke up to find the conductor shaking me at Savoy Street, on the Embankment. We used to get really tired. After the War broke out the journey home got much worse. I remember one night in particular all the cars coming up from Woolwich were packed full of Arsenal workers, and tram after tram went through full. I stood there for a long time, and in the end I went up to a driver and showed him my badge — we were all supposed to wear an enamel plaque on our wrists, but I kept mine in my pocket — and he let me hop on the front and sit on the tool box. But it was cold up there. I've never been so cold in all my life.

When I first went to the CRD we used to be issued with tokens for one penny or tuppence and so on, for travelling to work, the exact number we needed each week, which were exchanged for tickets, but this stopped just after I started and they gave us the badges instead. These entitled us to travel free to and from work, duty passes they were called.

There were several of us kids at the CRD in those days, all doing different jobs, some of them apprentices, perhaps learning armature winding or something like that. In those days you had to pay so much to be an apprentice, and I never had the chance on what my Dad was earning. We used to have a bit of fun sometimes. We used to play around with the trams, learnt how to start and stop them, and that stood me in good stead later on. There was just one bit of wire at the CRD at that time, and it wasn't used much except by us kids. Later on, well after I'd finished, they put proper overhead up.

I was earning thirty shillings a week, very good money for me in those days, a golden sovereign and a half-sovereign. Friday was pay-day, and we used to line up at the gate, and as you got up to him the pay bloke gave you a tin with your money in it. It was all silver, no notes in those days. You just checked it and then dropped the empty tin in a basket outside the gates. I expect the tins had our numbers on or something.

After I'd been on that job for a bit, the foreman came up to me one day. His name was Old Dan Warnham, and if he told you to do a thing you did it. He was a gentleman, but he was firm, and you knew where you were with him and just what you had to do. He told me he was putting me on the 08 stores-van, behind Fred Shepherd. 08 stores-van was a single deck tram, wooden van body with sliding doors in the middle on both sides, on a four wheel truck. It had short driving platforms at each end, with a door off each platform into the body like the passenger cars had. I didn't get a rise.

My Dad was driving the 07 stores-van at the time, and he was a bit crafty, because sometimes he'd put his stores-van away in Telford Avenue at night instead of taking it back to Charlton, and he'd clock on there at six o'clock in the morning instead of at Charlton. Sometimes on the way to work, if I was a bit late — this was before I went on the stores-van — I'd jump off the tram at New Cross Depot, punch my time-card there, and go on to Charlton. The time-clocks were all the same, and they didn't know where you'd punched your card. You had to do these things.

With the stores-van we had to deliver armatures, axle-bearings, copper fingers, plough-carriers, controllers and all sorts of spare parts, taking them from the CRD round to the depots where they were needed. On Mondays we did the North-side, Holloway, Hackney and Stamford Hill Depots, and on Tuesdays, South-side, Camberwell, Clapham, Norwood, Telford Avenue perhaps. My job was to stand on the back platform, and for the first few weeks it went well, really. Fred was quite good, inasmuch as when we went on the North-side he'd give me a tinkle on the bell and then he'd stop, and I'd look, see some points just behind us and realise he's coming back here, and I'd have to get down and hold the points over while he ran back, then run after the van and jump on it while it was still going.

Going through the Tunnel, (3) I had to stand on the front platform to hold the trolley-pole tight down with the trolley-rope, out from under the hook in the middle, against the roof of the van, in case it hit the colour-light signals at Holborn. When we got to the top of the ramp at Theobalds Road I'd put it back under the hook again and go through the van to the back. There were lights down in the Tunnel, it used to make a hell of a noise, you used to hear the roar as you

3. Beneath Kingsway and Aldwych, from Bloomsbury to the Embankment, was a 1000 yard-long tunnel for trams. At this time the tunnel was suitable only for single-deck cars, although it was rebuilt for double-deckers in 1930. The first part of the tunnel was opened in 1906 and it was last used by trams in 1952. It was the only such tram tunnel in the UK. Both entrances remain, and part of the tunnel is now the Strand Underpass. Stan Collins refers to both 'the Tunnel' and 'the Subway'; after 1930 LCCT publicity used the name 'Kingsway Subway'.

Single-deck car 552 at Aldwych Station, **right**,*some time before 1929. New Cross Depot around 1906,* **bottom right.** *08 stores-van, still in use in the late 1940's at Camberwell Green.*

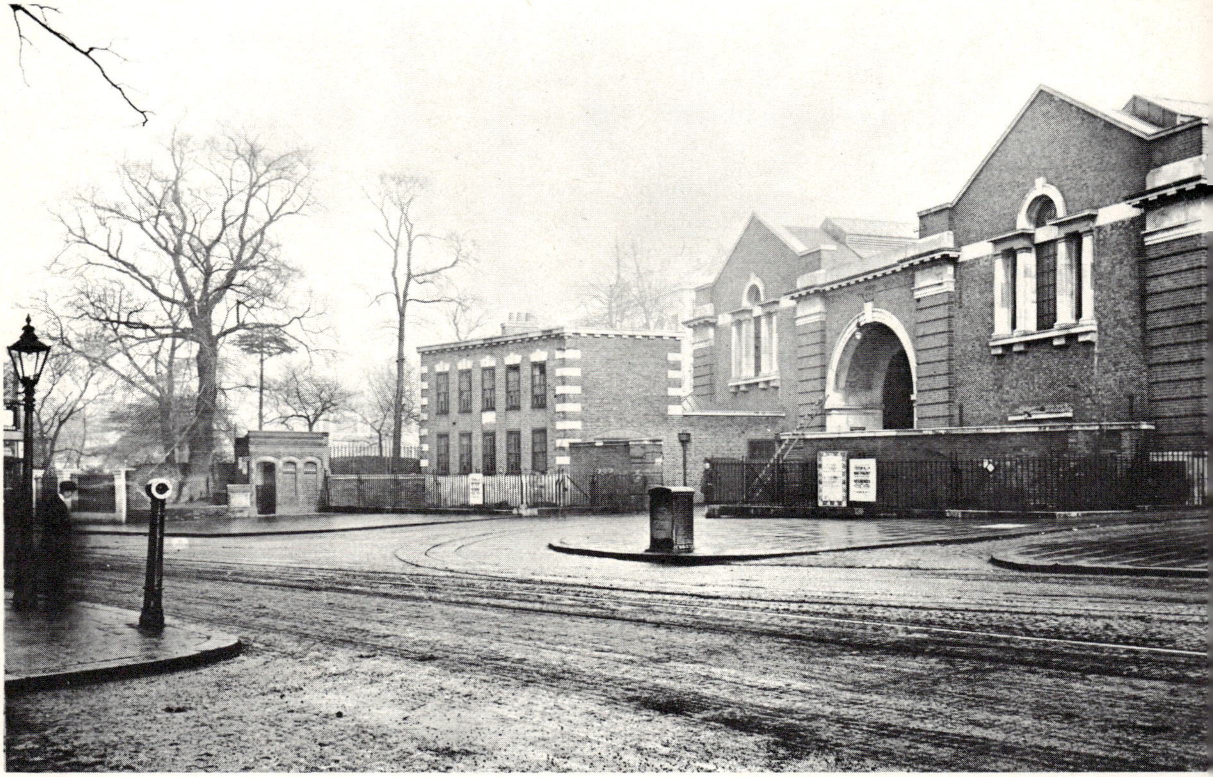

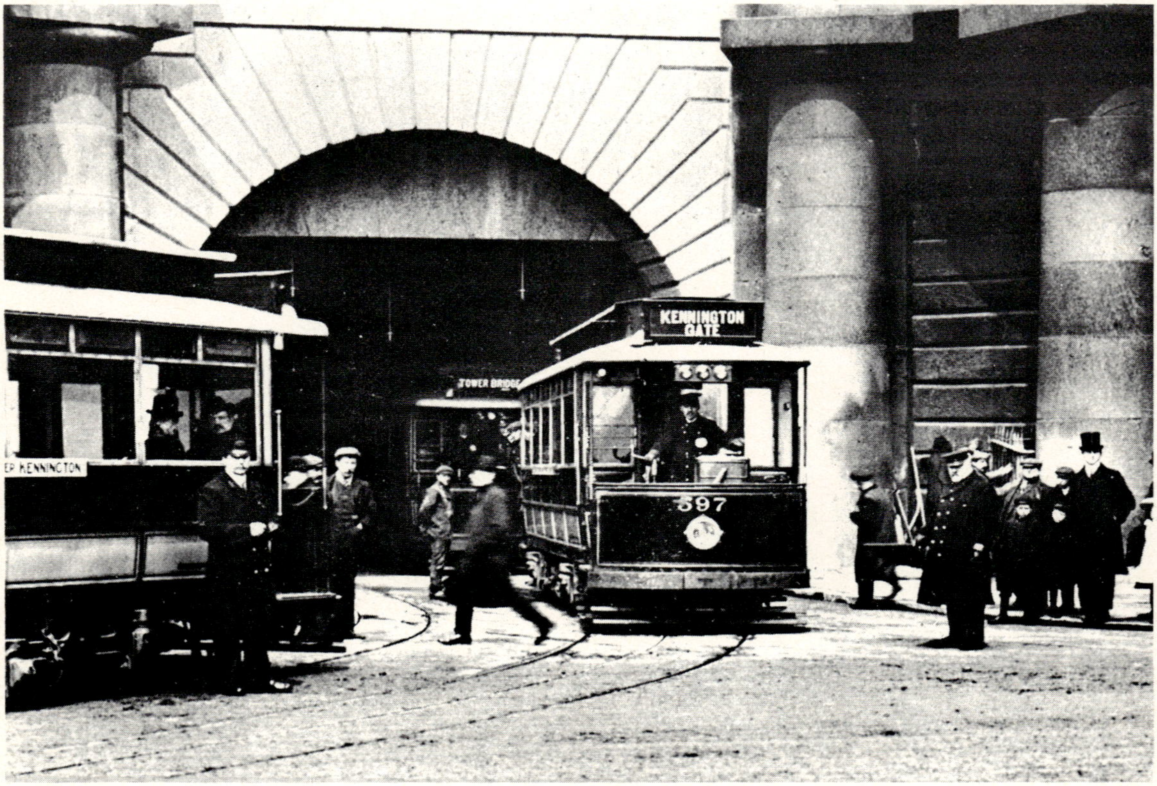
KENNINGTON GATE
TOWER BRIDGE
597
ER KENNINGTON

The LCCT owned 50 single-deck trams, most of which operated services through the Kingsway Subway from 1906 until 1930. The Embankment entrance to the Subway, **left** a fortnight after it opened in April 1908.

Telford Avenue Depot in 1913, **above**. On the left is the rebuilt cable-depot, on the right the new extension depot. Between these Roman and Egyptian tram-sheds is a private right-of-way and a rising water main over which the Metropolitan Water Board would not allow the LCCT to build.

went through. You went in off the Embankment just by Waterloo Bridge and went round to the right, then it went a little bit straight, then a left bend and you came to the first station, Aldwych, like a railway platform it was, in the middle of the tracks. Then it was dead straight up to Holborn, where the second station was, then you went down a dip and up the ramp into Theobalds Road, providing the lights were in your favour.

I loved that job, I really did, till we fell out. I hadn't been round London before, a proper eye-opener it was. My favourite was going through the Subway, holding that pole down and watching Old Fred Shepherd driving, going down at Holborn and then up the ramp. If I knew it was a day for going on the North-side I used to get really excited, I couldn't get that Subway out of my mind. I never thought that I'd ever drive a tram through there myself.

I didn't get on well with Fred Shepherd, I don't know why. By that time the War had started and I was a big lad for my age, and after a few weeks he started saying wasn't it about time I joined the Army, and that sort of thing, but I was too young. He kept on about it, and then one day on Brixton Hill a girl put a white feather on my shoulder, as if to say I was a coward, so that was that. A pal of mine at the CRD who was on the plough-van came to me one breakfast time and told me he was going up Deptford Town Hall to enlist, so I went up with him. I didn't ask permission, so I didn't get paid while I was in the Army. I knew that if I'd gone up to see Old Knight, the Superintendent, he would have said no straight away, because I wasn't old enough.

My pal walked in first, he was older than I was, he was nineteen, so the Recruiting Sergeant — he had a big moustache — asked what he wanted. They were forming a battery of artillery at the time. 'How old are you?' said the Sergeant, and my pal said, 'Nineteen'. So then I walked in. 'How old are you?' said the Sergeant. 'Fifteen', I said. 'You're no good to us son,' he said, 'go out the door and come back in and you'll be nineteen.' I walked out on the pavement, came back through to him, and he asked me how old I was now. 'Nineteen,' I said. 'Come and take the King's Shilling,' he said, and that's how I came to join up. It was the thirteenth of October 1915. A few weeks later I was in France. As things turned out, I think it was the best thing I ever did, because I did hear later that a lot of the kids at the CRD got the sack after the War, and I might have been one of them.

Old Fred Shepherd died soon after that. We didn't have a black-out in the first War, but a sort of half black-out, and he was in collision with another tram on the Kingsland Road and both his legs were squashed when the platform crumpled up underneath him. He died of shock a little while afterwards.

My dad carried on driving 07 stores-van until 1915, when there was a strike *(4)* for higher wages. They asked for volunteer Drivers while the strike lasted, notices went up all round. My Dad was a blackleg, and he came up to Telford. I'm not ashamed when I tell you this. A lot of them called him nasty names, and Dad told me that he very nearly hit someone on the head with his tea-bottle, and he turned round and told him, 'I've got two sons out in France, fighting for you and fighting for me, and I'm not coming out on strike'. There was no Union much in those days, and they gradually crept back. After the strike he got a letter of thanks from the LCC and he stopped on at Telford. Memories were short, fortunately. I admired him for what he did.

There used to be a tram, it might have been 1408, I'm not quite sure, but in the First World War a bomb dropped near it and a piece of splinter came through and stuck right through the middle of the brass handrail, halfway up the stairs. Well, it was such a souvenir that the LCC had it soldered in, and it ran for years like that. Conductors used to tell people that it was a very historic car.

At one time the LCC had some petrol-driven trams. My Dad drove one from the CRD to Marius Road Depot in the Fourteen War or shortly afterwards, when they put the trailers on. Marius Road, Balham, was the trailer depot, and they used this petrol-electric tram for pulling trailers in and out. Of course, it hadn't got a plough on it. I remember my father telling me that you couldn't get much of a speed on them, he didn't think much of them.

---

4. See Appendix 4.

1915 to 1923

MILITARY SERVICE

When I joined up with the battery of artillery — I was in the Royal Garrison Artillery — we drew our sixty-pounder gun from the Woolwich Arsenal, and we kept our guns and horses in the old tram-yard at Evelyn Street, Deptford. Our Captain was Captain Moore — a wicked old bugger he was — and day after day, day after day we were route marched with these blasted guns sometimes to Danson Park, but generally out Blackheath way.

One day we were going up Deptford High Street, people cheering us as they went by, in those days a soldier felt proud of himself; every man in the colours was a hero. The sixty-pounder guns were drawn by six heavy draught-horses, and at the rear of the gun there were two wheels that put the brakes on if you were going downhill. I was the brakesman on the off-side. One particular day we were going out on a route march and came out of Deptford High Street into Deptford Broadway just as a tram came along, a number 40. Our Sergeant, Glossop, a big six-foot man who thought a lot of himself, a real bastard he was, he started shouting out, 'Keep to your left, keep to your left,' passing it down the line. When this tram came by I looked up and it was my Dad. Proud little bugger I was, bandolier on, all highly polished, I wasn't half proud of myself. 'Wotcha Dad,' I said. Dad slowed up, 'Hello my son, where do you reckon you're off to ?, 'Plumstead Common,' I said, and no sooner had I got the words out of my mouth than Sergeant Glossop put me under arrest. Anyway, we went and did our route march, and directly after we got back, after we'd put our gun away, they slung me in the Guard Room, took my money away, took my fags, everything. I was really offended, I didn't know what it was all about. When the Sergeant had said, 'I'm putting you under arrest', I thought he was going to give me a rest or something.

Evening time came and I was still in the Guard Room. Not many yards away was a coffee stall where they used to sell cups of tea and coffee and hot cheese-cakes, and I asked if I could go up there, but the NCO guard told me I wasn't going out of there tonight because I was a prisoner. That made me sweat. I ended up staying in there all night.

Next morning Sergeant Glossop — he was the first one to get killed when we went over the other side — and two men, prisoner's escort, hauled me up in front of the OC, Captain Moore. They took my cap off and in I marched and stood there any-how. 'Stand to attention,' said Sergeant Glossop. Attention! I didn't know what attention was, we hadn't done any infantry training or anything. Then Sergeant Glossop gave his evidence and tells Captain Moore how the battery was proceeding down Deptford Boardway when a tram came along and he heard this Gunner call out to the tram-driver, and tell the tram-driver we were going to Plumstead Common — he'd heard it all — so he'd promptly put me under arrest. Then Captain Moore said he'd deal with it and he dismissed the Sergeant and the escort, then he asked me whether what the Sergeant said was true, so I told him it was. I was never one for telling a lot of lies. Then Captain Moore explained that we were at war with a very powerful enemy, and that when you were on a march you should never divulge to anybody where you were going, because the enemy had spies everywhere. He laid it down rotten to me. Then he asked me where I lived, so I told him, and he said that I'd better go home for the weekend, and he wrote me out a weekend pass. I don't know whether Sergeant Glossop remembered that, but he had his own back when we first got over to France.

Stan Collins then trained at Borden Camp, and early in 1916 embarked with his battery for France. On the 1st July 1916 was begun the Somme Battle, in which just over one million soldiers were slaughtered, around 400,000 of whom were British.

We went through the Battle of the Somme, which I believe lasted until about October or November time, when one day the Sergeant Major called for Gunner Collins to see Captain Moore. Captain Moore was down in a dugout. He asked me how old I was, and I had to do a bit of quick thinking. Nineteen when I joined up and I've been here almost a year.

'Nearly twenty, sir,' I said. 'I don't want any bloody lies, Gunner, how old are you?' So then I told him, near enough seventeen. Then he showed me a letter from the War Office that my mother had sent, to have me sent home, and he said I'd have to go home, but I would probably be put in prison for false attestation. That didn't worry me. So an NCO escorted me from there back to Havringcourt Wood where the horse lines were, and I had to go down to the railhead. Boulogne or Calais, I forget which it was.

Then I was handed over to the RTO — Railway Transport Officer — to leave on the boat the next morning. I had a pair of high legged boots, they pinched them off me and gave me another pair of boots to come home in. The next morning I was put on the boat, it was full of wounded, people groaning, hollering and screaming, and we landed at Folkestone. You couldn't go wrong there, anyone came off a boat and they'd give you a handful of fruit or cakes or something like that. Then we got on the train and I landed up at Woolwich, all on me Jack Jones I was. I got there about eight or nine o'clock at night and I went to the Shrapnel Barracks where the Royal Artillery were, to report to the Guard Room. The NCO of the Guard asked me who I was and where I'd come from, they didn't know anything about me. 'We've got no beds here,' he said, 'there's an old bed over in one of the rooms but we haven't got any mattresses.' I dumped my kit-bag on this old empty bed and then I thought, 'Sod this, I'm going home.'

So I walked all the way from Woolwich as far as Milkwood Road, Coldharbour Lane, then a tram came along and I saw my Dad. He nearly fainted. He'd only just pulled up at a stop and I went over and said, 'Wotcha Dad.' I can see my old Dad now, he let go of those handles and looked at me. 'What are you doing, boy, where are you going?' I told him I'd come from France and was walking home, and he gave me a couple of pennies so that I could get the tram the rest of the way. I got home and knocked at the door, and when my Mum came to the door and saw me she swooned. She soon came round and then got the old frying pan on the go. I had a wash and brush up and a good old scoff.

The next morning I borrowed some money from her and got back to Woolwich just before nine, went into the Guard Room, but still nobody knew anything about me. I couldn't even remember where I'd left my kit. Presently some lads started coming out, up came the bugler and they all fell in, one lot here, and one lot there, and the Regimental Sergeant Major with his red sash came over to me and asked who I was. I told him I didn't know what to do, I'd been sent home under age. They took me to an officer who asked if I was lousy, well I don't mind telling you I was, so he sent me off to Shooters Hill Hospital. I had to have a bath there, all my clothes fumigated — and there were lice in my shirt, we got them over the other side, we used to crack them over there — and they shaved my head, all down here, everywhere.

After I'd got new equipment and was presentable I was sent down to Coalhouse Fort, near Tilbury Dock, and I had a wonderful holiday down there. All these old boys were down there, and when they found out I'd just come back from France I was a little hero, and I got a job as a waiter in the Officer's Mess — I did well there, used to have some lovely grub — but the very day I was eighteen, in 1917, they sent me up to Catterick in Yorkshire. It was the wildest spot I'd ever been to, that water up there was so cold that it burnt you.

Then from there they sorted out five of us artillery men, and I was the senior soldier, I had to take them to Dover and report to the RTO there. Then when we got over to Calais they sorted us out and I had to go up to Ypres Salient to join Thirty-one Siege Battery, an Irish battery. From then on I just soldiered on until the Armistice. I rose up to Corporal, and was made up Acting Sergeant on the field because our number one gunner got killed. We had four guns in our battery, six-inch howitzers they were, and they made me up until they had another sergeant come out to the battery. I was in charge of eleven men and a six-inch howitzer, but I knew a bit about artillery drill by then and I'd learnt a lot. You've got to be so careful in action, especially on your dial side, because the slightest mistake and you could be firing on your own infantry. We carried on and we were at a place called Saint Jean in Ypres Salient. Ypres Salient went like a big horseshoe with Germans all round, so they could fire on us all the time from all round. We could only fire straight ahead. This is where I struck it lucky again! They wanted two guns to be taken up to Zillebeek Lake which was farther up into the Salient. They asked for volunteers and were one short, so I fell for it. Sergeant Botting was up there, we only had our guns and ammunition, no rifles or anything. One morning, just as dawn was breaking, all we could see was a lot of shining lights, they were coming over in hordes with fixed bayonets. We buried the breech-blocks and ran, we ran like hell, right back to a place called Goldfish Chateau and stopped for a breather. Our infantry stopped the Germans somehow, and it took us until September or October 1918 to drive them back again. When we did get Jerry on the retreat again we never caught him, away he went and we found our guns still in the same position, and the breech-blocks still buried, although they were as rusty as hell.

One thing they did learn in the '14 War was that buses were more mobile, and they always have been. In the '14 War they commandeered all the buses because they could shift the troops just as they wanted to. I know what I'm saying, because I've ridden on them when I was out in France. Suppose there'd been no buses in London and all trams, well, they couldn't have shifted the troops as well as they did.

When the War finished — the Armistice was in November 1918, and I came home on leave in 1919 from France — I went straight up to 23 Belvedere Road *(1)* to try and get my job back, but I couldn't get it then because I hadn't asked permission to join up. So I had a three month furlough and had a look round, and re-enlisted on a forty pound bounty and went out to India for four years.

We didn't do much in India. I was in the Artillery again, up on the North West Frontier near Afganistan, at Peshawar, near the Khyber Pass. It was a six day train ride, six days and six nights, from Bombay up to the frontier, over a thousand miles. All wooden seats to sit on and nowhere to have a walk or stretch, all you could do was to stand up. We used to pull up at different places for a bit of hot grub, a drink or something like that. It was all mapped out.

We used to get up at six every day, then an hour and a half's parade till the sun came up, then there was nothing else to do.

I was a Gunner again by then. I'd reverted myself, because I had a good pal in that battery, a real good pal, and he was a Gunner still. If I hadn't got a fag he'd break his last one in half for me, and I'd do the same for him. If either of us had a parcel from home, we'd share it. We were like two brothers.

But shortly after the War was finished and the Armistice was signed, the old Army order came out again that Gunners and Privates in the Infantry weren't allowed to walk with an NCO. I didn't want to part with my old pal, we'd been good pals in France and now we were good pals up there, so I'd reverted myself back to Gunner.

We never saw any action in India, but we had the wind put up us once or twice. There was no fighting out there then, what we were more concerned about was the bloody loose-wallahs coming over of a night time. That's what we used to call them, loose-wallahs, robbers they were, the Pathan, bloody great fellows they were, six-foot-six-inches, seven-foot, wacking great fellows, gor blimey.

We stopped up there on the frontier for three years until 1922, then we came home and I was finished with the Army.

A Great War scene at Streatham Library, looking north. E class car 529.

---

1. 23 Belvedere Road became LCCT offices in 1917; 19/21 Belvedere Road were also so used. In 1924 the LCCT quit No. 23, but repossessed it in 1928. It then remained the Head Office until 1933. County Hall now covers the sites of both these addresses, and Belvedere Road is the County Hall car park (wherein still lie plainly marked LCCT manhole covers).

1923 to 1924

HOLLOWAY DEPOT
via CLAPHAM MOTOR SCHOOL

At the end of 1922 I came back from India. I was 23, single, and out of work, so first of all I went up to 23 Belvedere Road — the Tramway's recruitment office — to see if I could get back on the LCC. They said there were no vacancies for Drivers, but to apply later. They said they'd put me on the list and let me know when something came along. They asked me if I had any relations on the job, and of course I had, because my father and my brother were both driving at that time — my elder brother had got on at the end of the War — but I don't think that did me any good.

Although there were over a million unemployed at the time, I was lucky and managed to get a job as a hod-carrier on a building site. Then one day in the summer of 1923 a card came through the door telling me to report to 23 Belvedere Road. They only had one vacancy for a Driver, at Holloway Depot on the North-side, and I acceped it straight away. Although it would mean a lot of travelling — I was still living at Brixton — I thought that if I got my feet in the door I could get a transfer later on.

There were one and a quarter million people out of work in the UK in 1923, although unemployment was neither as bad as it had been in the two previous years, nor as bad as it was to become. Throughout the 1920's and 1930's there was always at least one working person in every ten who was without a job. It must be realised that this effect of the post-war slump was never at its worst in the Metropolis, and particularly in the 1930's, when much new light industry developed in the London area.

Thus, employers who offered security, as the LCCT seemed to, could afford to be very selective in who they took on, and whilst Stan Collins does not think it mattered in his case, many tramwaymen have claimed that the LCCT did show preference to applicants with relations already on the trams.

In fact, the security that the LCCT offered was rather doubtful, for the Department was not in a sound state in 1923 and 1924. There was severe competition from buses — which remained unrestricted until 1924 — and traffic receipts were falling. The LCC trams were not operating efficiently, and it was said that morale was low.

The 1914 War had stretched the capacity of the LCC trams, and at the same time it had deprived them of the men and materials required to keep tracks and equipment in good order. It was only a combination of increased traffic and reduced car-mileage that had saved the Department from calling on the rates; as it was, a total of £195,000 was drawn from the General Reserve in the years 1913/1916, and less than £100,000 remained there.

The post-war world was governed by new economic rules, and inflation and scarcity continued until the early 1920's. Tram fares were raised in both 1919 and 1920, and for the first time the LCCT had to call upon the ratepayer; £19,000 in 1919/1920 and a further £591,000 in the following year. In 1921 tram fares were again revised, but this time downwards, for the cost-of-living was beginning to fall, and the LCCT was feeling the effects of bus competition and dole-queues, yet there was another dificiency: £89,000.

More fare changes followed in 1923, when workmen's fares were reduced, and in the year 1922/1923 — helped partly by wage reductions — the LCCT made a net surplus of £232,000. A policy was now starting to be evolved; by

Head Office of the LCC Tramways, 23 Belvedere Road, SE.

carrying them further, at the same fares or less, and at increasing speeds, the LCCT was managing to hold on to its passengers. (Excepting the year of the General Strike, annual passenger carryings remained within 2½% of 700 million for the rest of the 1920's).

But this was only half the battle; receipts were still falling, and the difference between working expenses and receipts was uncomfortably small.

So the next day I went up to see Sir John Colley, the LCC medical man, for an examination. He had a place on Bayswater Road and was quite a character. You waited downstairs, but the next person to go in sat at the top of the stairs outside his office to save time. If the front door bell rang, one of you had to pull a string to open it. That saved him having a butler. There were notices up about it. He asked me all sorts of questions and then passed me fit, except that he told me to have one tooth taken out, so I walked along Bayswater Road until I saw a large house with a dentist's sign outside. I rang the bell and a flunkey opened the door and asked me very smoothly if I had an appointment, because the dentist never saw anybody without one. Just then the dentist himself walked into the hall wearing an old fashioned smoking cap with a tassel on top, and asked what was going on, so I explained that I had to have a tooth out before I could start as a tram-driver. The upshot was that he pulled the tooth out for me there and then because I'd been in the Army. Although he didn't charge me anything he did suggest that I might like to put something in his hospital box, which was a bit awkward because I'd only got half-a-crown in my pocket and no other change, so I ended up walking home to Brixton. But it was worth it.

More or less the next day I went into the training school at Clapham Depot. Mr. Bancroft was the Superintendent in charge of the Motor School, with two Instructors under him, Mr. Webb and Juicy Baker. Of course, I had a good idea of driving by then, because of being at the CRD and watching my Dad driving, but I didn't let on. For a few days they trained us in groups in the School on half a tram they had in there, and they showed us various things on trams in the depot. Then they took us out on the road for three days on a Standard, on our own routes, taking it in turns. We were still wearing civvies then, there was no uniform until you'd passed, but they lent you a worn out old mac while you were driving. After three days were up, if Webby thought you were fit enough, you went out with a trained Driver on a passenger (1) for about a week — he got an extra shilling a day and an easy time if he had his wits about him — and then you finished up in the School again.

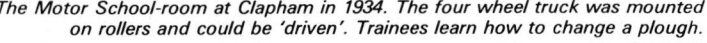

1. That is, a tram in scheduled passenger service, rather than a 'Special'.

The Motor School-room at Clapham in 1934. The four wheel truck was mounted on rollers and could be 'driven'. Trainees learn how to change a plough.

TRAINING DRIVERS 1934

Around the walls of the schoolroom were controllers and handbrakes; Trainees followed the instructions indicated on the side of the tram (previous page). **Below**; Mr. Banfield explains the working of the conduit system. **Opposite page**; Mr. Baker teaches trainees the motorman's stance in Clapham Depot, and Mr. Webb supervises a practice car on the Clapham Common turning loop.

Then came passing-out day. I took the car up to Blackfriars and along the Embankment to Scotland Yard where we picked up the Police Examiner. The Instructor stood away and I was on my own. 'Away you go, Driver,' said the Examiner. Driver! I'd never been called that before.

So I drove carefully over Westminster Bridge to County Hall and he directed me to keep straight on to Kennington. He watched me carefully for a while and then went into the saloon as we were going down Kennington Road. Suddenly he gave me five or six rings on the bell, the emergency signal. Pump sand out with the right foot, bring the left hand round so that the controller's on the brake notches — but not too fast in case the wheels lock — and bring it to a stop on the hand brake. It was a real test. Then came the questions on various aspects of driving, and I got one of those wrong. He asked what I would do if I broke down, and I said I'd get the next car to push me, but I forgot to mention the tow-bar or wire rope. But I was passed out, I was an LCC Motorman.

My first tram was driven out of Holloway Depot on 31st August 1923. Things had changed a lot on the LCC since I'd been at Charlton. We were doing forty-eight hours a week instead of sixty, a straight through eight-hour-day with no meal-break, scrounge a jug of tea along the road, eat your sandwiches on the staircase, no glass or anything else on, and we did that for six days a week, although on any day in the week they could give us up to ten hours actual work. Then there were spreadovers which could go anything up to thirteen hours with a long relief in the middle. The money was better, of course. I was on about ten-and-six a day at the start, going up to about twelve shillings a day after two years service, and you got three bob extra for a Sunday.

In 1923 Holloway Depot operated over 200 trams daily; it was the second largest LCCT depot. It operated single-deck trams on the Kingsway Subway services, and double-deckers on several lengthy routes between outer London terminals — Barnet, North Finchley, Enfield and Edmonton — and most of the northern Central Area terminals. Some of these routes were operated in conjunction with the Metropolitan Electric Tramways Company. Holloway also provided cars for services from Highgate Village and Winchmore Hill to Moorgate, and certain other 'local' services.

The shorter services from Hampstead and Parliament Hill Fields were worked from nearby Hampstead Depot.

A Standard E/1 heads south across Westminster Bridge on Service 2 around 1923.

I was trained for the 21 and 27 routes, and for the 17's from the Archway Tavern to Faringdon Street, and I was taken on as temporary staff. In fact I was still officially temporary when I left forty years later. I started off as a spare driver. Being spare meant that you were booked up to cover regular men's rest days or sickness, and you had to be a bit crafty because you were with a different Conductor every week. Drivers went down the seniority list and Conductors went up, so you'd watch out for the miserable Conductors and turn up late on the Monday so that the next spare man got him. I was lucky later on, when I got to Telford. I had a good regular Conductor for many years, old Alf Mole.

Even if you had a job, you never knew exactly what it was until the day before, unless you were given a 'temporary' regular service, to cover a man who was sick for any length of time. If there were no turns to cover, no-one went sick or came in late, you'd go out point-changing or scrubbing old time-boards or something, they always found you something to do.

There were four of us over at Holloway who lived on the South-side, and we thought we'd have to play up a bit to get transfers nearer our homes, so sometimes we used to sit in Old Gent's Coffee Shop in the Holloway Road and miss our job. Then we'd walk in late, one after the other, making excuses. The Chief Depot Inspector, Mr. Forian, was a thorough old gentleman and he used to say that he didn't know what he was going to do with us men from the South-side, he'd have to get us transferred. I used to make out that it was no fault of mine if I missed my connection on the way to Holloway in the morning.

Car 1109 loads at Grays Inn Road terminus in 1920.

Once when I purposely missed jobs twice in one week I was sent over to Hackney to see the North-side Superintendent, Old Cloney. He was a typical Irishman and he hated the English, as a lot of them did, especially at that time, and I told him how difficult the travelling was. He had my papers in front of him. 'We're not interested in where you live,' he said, 'we don't put trams on the road to get you to work. We didn't ask you to come and drive our trams, you came and asked us for a job, and if you can't get in on time, there's two million unemployed out there who can.' Little did I know when I walked out of his office without any suspension or anything what he was going to arrange for me.

Holloway Depot was built in 1909; functionalism has replaced the extravagant facade of Telford Avenue. This building is now a bus garage.

The following Saturday they gave me the last duty on the 21's, signing on at about five in the afternoon. You finished up leaving Tally Ho Corner at around half past midnight, then round through Wood Green and Finsbury Park to the Nags Head, and sign off at the Depot at about half past one. Then I had to walk all the way home, because the night cars didn't run on Saturday, and eventually got to Brixton at about half past four. Then they booked me up for another job on the Sunday at three o'clock, which meant leaving home again at around half past one. I didn't forget that in a hurry, and my Dad was livid, although I never told him that it was my fault for being late in the first place. But you couldn't do anything about it. The Union wasn't anything in those days.

My Dad was a Union man, and I was too, although there was a lot that never joined. But I thought to myself that you never knew if you might get into trouble, and you had the Union there to guide you and look after your interests. If you weren't a member and had a bit of trouble you were out, just like that.

Anyway, that little escapade was worth it, because soon afterwards we all got transfers, and I was posted to Clapham Depot which was only just over a mile from where I was living, so that was alright. But I don't think I was ever late again more than half a dozen times all the years I was on the trams.

The night cars were very useful to us Southside men. After the ordinary Tunnel service finished at around twelve-thirty, there was an hourly nighter to Bloomsbury and then it was just a short step down to the Embankment for the nighter to Brixton.

In the morning I used to more or less catch the first Tunnel through from the Embankment, and had to allow myself a good couple of hours to get from home to Holloway. If I had a spreadover — we never got paid for spreadovers in those days — say with five hours off, it used to just give me time to come home, have a bit of grub and then back again. Otherwise I'd go to Finsbury Park if it was in the summer time, and go and have a cup of tea in a café and a sandwich, a bit of fish and chips perhaps, then I'd go and lay down in Finsbury Park and have a sleep.

Another little comical story, really.

I had a job one day on the 21's, they used to run from Holborn to North Finchley. I'd done the first half and then I had about three hours off, I think, so I went and had a bit of grub. It was a lovely day, more or less a mid-summer's day, very hot, so I went into Finsbury Park just off the road, off came my jacket, made a pillow out of it. There was an old park-keeper walking around so I told him I was going to have a couple of hours sleep and would he wake me up at such and such a time. I tipped him a shilling,

Archway terminus, looking north, around 1923 To the left, at the foot of Highgate Hill, single-deck car 581 is about to set off on a trip through the Tunnel to Westminster To the right, car 683 has just left its plough at the change-pit before climbing Archway Road on Service 9. Beside the change-pit work is being carried out on the 'up' track. In the centre next to the lay-by is a Regulators hut, beside which can be seen (in 1933) spare ploughs dead-poles and sand.

the old bastard, but he forgot all about it. Anyway I had a good old sleep and when I woke up I thought, Christ, its only five o'clock in the afternoon and I was supposed to take my tram over at four o'clock.

So I went and saw the old Regulator in Seven Sisters Road, by Finsbury Park Station — that's where we used to take on and off — Temple was his name, and I said to him, 'I've done it all wrong guv'nor, I should have taken such and such a number on the 21's at four o'clock, but I was up at four this morning and had such a long journey that I went over the Park and fell asleep.'

'Driver Jackson's taken it on to Finchley for you,' he said. Well, I didn't know how to go on, I was only a young Driver, but he told me not to worry because the road was covered, but to see Driver Jackson when he came back. You see, I only had to go to North Finchley and back to Finsbury Park, and I'd finished my day's work then.

Old Jackson came back — he was a good old cock — and I told him what had happened. He never bothered about me, 'That's all right,' he said. 'Let me square you up, how much do I owe you?' I said, and I told him nobody had booked it, he'd done me a good turn. 'Give me half an ounce of tobacco,' he said. Half an ounce of tobacco! Tuppence ha'penny in those days. They were men then; you wouldn't get that happening now. I didn't go to sleep no more after that.

Us spare drivers generally worked on the 21 and 27 roads. They let us run over the roads once, only once, on a service car. Once you've been over the road you've got no get-out if you're in trouble. They were covered all the time; you were the bloke who was going to fall into the cart, if there was one to fall into. We stood on the platform and watched, or you might give the service Driver a break and he'd stand down and just watch you and tell you any little points about the road.

On the 11's which came out of Holloway and went up and down New North Road, I think you had to be driving for two years before taking them over, because of Highgate Hill. And the Tunnel cars were all single-deckers then, but if I remember right, even in those days you weren't allowed to drive through the Subway until you'd got two years service in.

Up at Wood Green Station on the 21's, there used to be an old Regulator with a big moustache. We always called him Old Hindenburg, because he was very much like Hindenburg of the First World War. I went up there one day, I was about five or ten minutes late, and he came over to find out why. 'A horse fell down in the Caledonian Road,' I said, but it hadn't. He went off. Two or three days after, I was up there again, and I'm still running late. 'Horse fell down in the Caledonian Road,' I told him. 'Again?' he said. 'Wasn't the same bloody horse, was it?'

Looking north, up Seven Sisters Road, at Finsbury Park Station in 1913; the park is in the right background. Between Finsbury Park - where there was a third, passing, track - and the change-pit at Manor House, was half-a-mile of line equipped with both conduits and overhead wires.

Sometimes we used to be sent out on what was called Foreign Service, when spare men were lent from one depot to another which might be short. You couldn't argue with it, you just had to go. One day when I signed on at Holloway I looked up on the list and saw: Monday, Driver Collins, Poplar Depot.

I hadn't a clue where Poplar was, not a clue. That night my Dad explained where it was and on the Monday I found my way over there somehow by way of Blackwall Tunnel, reported, and was given a job on the 65 road. I waited at the pub at the end of Aberfeldy Street where we took on and off, and a Conductor came up to me. 'Do you take 23 on the 65's ?' *(2)* he asked. I told him I did. 'Well, tell me when we reach the fare stages,' he went on, 'because I'm a stranger here.' He was from New Cross. Neither of us had been over the road before, and that was wrong we found out afterwards.

2. Every tram on a service (or group of services) from each LCCT depot was numbered sequentially, according to its place in the working timetable. This number was called the 'route number' (pronounced without the 'e'), and it was carried on small blue enamelled plates which hung on a lower saloon window pillar on both sides of the car. Where more than one depot operated a service, the route numbers were allocated in blocks to each depot. This arrangement was inherited from the London Tramways Company. Stan Collins occasionally refers to 'running numbers', but this was a busman's term. Here he is taking the twenty-third car on the schedule for Service 65.

Anyway, the tram came along on the other side of the road about twenty minutes late. 'BLOOMSBURY' it had on the front. I noticed all the Drivers had a big whistle hanging on the front of their coats. Not the ordinary Conductor's whistle, but like an elephant's horn. I didn't realise what they carried them for, but I soon found out. So we tootled along a bit until we came up behind a solid-tyred Foden on the tram tracks, making a hell of a row it was. I banged the bell but he wouldn't shift, then someone on the tram called the Conductor and told him that what usually happened was that both of us stood on the front platform blowing our whistles and me ringing the bell. So I found out why the Drivers carried whistles.

One thing about trams is that as long as there are no junctions you can't lose your way. I was alright at the Great Eastern Hotel because I could see another 65 on the down line ahead, but eventually we came up to Gardiners' Corner and I just hadn't a clue which way to go. There were points here, points there, and then some more points, and I was stuck, absolutely bamboozled. I didn't know which ones I'd have to take, except for the first ones which were set for me, or where the dead sections were, it was a shocker. Trams went that way and this way and across

Gardiner's Corner, Whitechapel, looking towards Spitalfields Market in June 1912. In the foreground, a Service 65 car moves across the junction on its way to Bloomsbury, while in the centre, car 664 is 'stuck on the dead'. Behind it passes a West Ham Corporation tram on the service from Aldgate to Ilford. This whole junction was re-laid in 1927.

Theobalds Road, near Bloomsbury terminus, looking east in 1913.

the front of me and right in the middle of it all was a copper waving me on. Then a big fat-gutted Regulator came over to me. 'Come on, Driver, the Policeman's beckoning you on.' 'I don't know which way to go, guv'nor,' I told him. Well, he just swore, told me to get out of the way, and took the tram across the junction himself into Commercial Street. 'There you are,' he said. 'it's a straight road right through to Bloomsbury, and DON'T GO DOWN THE BLOODY TUNNEL.' You see, at that time only single-deckers used the Tunnel. It wasn't high enough for Standard cars.

Eventually, after a bit of a struggle through Spitalfields Market — the road was all congested with handcarts and sometimes you had to cross over to the down line to pass them — we reached Bloomsbury, which I knew already from my journeys to Holloway. I got ticked off by a Regulator there for being late, so it was straight back. On my time-board it said 'Bloomsbury' then 'Green Street, Barking Road' and I was up in the blue again, but away we went. Through Gardiners' Corner alright, and bouncing along the East India Dock Road right through to Canning Town, shot the plough out at the Iron Bridge, pole up on the wire and I was beginning to settle, thinking to myself that I was getting on fine. Well, you know when you do something wrong, you get that butterfly feeling? I thought to myself, that's funny, West Ham Corporation cars passing me and I'm still going. Of course, I was looking out for a dead-end, where the tracks ended.

So, further down the road a chap steps out, uniform, gold braid round his hat. So I stopped. I wondered who he was. 'Driver, do you know where you're going?' he said. So I leaned over the dashboard and pointed up to the destination blind and said, 'Yes, Green Street, Barking Road.' 'Do you know where it is,' he said, 'because you're well past it, and try to be a bit civil.' Anyway he put me right, told me to turn at the next crossover and go back again. Presently we got back to the Blackwall Tunnel and we'd done a journey by then, although we were well out of pocket. The Regulator there was called Black Jack and he had the finest watch you ever saw, I'm sure he kept it on a horse's chain. He told me I was an hour late, and said to bring my tram back at Burdett Road so that I'd be on right time.

Now I didn't know where Burdett Road was, off we went on up the East India Dock Road and I stopped the tram and walked over to a copper to ask him where Burdett Road was. He looked at me as if I was a maniac, so I explained why I was lost. 'Alright, son', he said, 'go along the road until you see where the trams go across the road with their poles up on the wire, and that's Burdett Road.' So when we found Burdett Road we reversed and came back to the Blackwall

Tunnel and stopped to ask Black Jack where Green Street, Barking Road, was.

He told me to carry on for two miles after the Iron Bridge until I saw a lay-by round to the left. The points for the lay-by worked automatically. You pulled up just inside the strip, put two notches on your power and a hold on your hand-brake so that you just dribbled up, and your pole would touch a skate on the wire and this controlled the points. Then they re-set themselves behind you for the straight.

There were a few electric points like that on the system, but the LCC didn't go in for them much, so I wasn't used to them. Generally you coasted for straight on, and put your controller on a power notch to turn off to the left or right as the case might be. But I thought afterwards that I must have gone over those points on top notch on the first trip. If they had opened up I don't know what might have happened. Anyway, in we went, reversed, and came back out again.

All this time the Conductor still didn't know what was going on. If people asked him for a penny he punched them a penny ticket. He told me that we were carrying all sorts, every nationality under the sun, bar English.

I was over at Poplar for a week, on the same old road, but once I'd found my feet I didn't mind it at all, because I was getting an extra half-a-crown a day foreign service allowance. Half-a-crown! I was a millionaire.

Looking across the traverser-pit at Poplar Depot in 1936, **above**: *only the colour of the trams has changed since 1923. The LCCT brown-and-cream was replaced by deep red-and-cream after 1926, and LT red-and-cream after 1933.*

Gardiner's Corner, looking east in July 1934, **below**. *A Service 65 Extra comes across the junction towards Aldgate, its destination blind already set for the return trip to 'BLACKWALL TNL'.*

The LCCT operated fifty single-deck cars until 1930, mainly on services through the Kingsway Subway. At Vauxhall in 1912, two are delayed by horse traffic.

In the year after Stan Collins rejoined the LCCT, its General Manager — Aubrey Llewelyn Coventry Fell — retired due to ill health. Fell had come to London from Sheffield Corporation at the end of 1903, a few months after the first conduit services were opened. He was an electrical engineer by trade, and a good one, 34 and virtually at the top of his profession. For twenty years he managed the LCC trams with unimaginative competence, although it does seem that he found the post-war years a little trying. Fell's main lasting contribution to London — and it lasted too long — was the Standard tram, a robust and austere design which went into production shortly after he arrived in London, and was still being made shortly before he left. He also designed the CRD at Charlton.

Fell's attitude to his wages staff was ungenerous and autocratic. Most of the best remembered features of LCCT operation — the conduit, intensive rush-hour services, workmen's fares (for which he cared little) and the extensive range of cheap day-time tickets — were either inherited by him or developed by those who followed him. Fell was 55 when he retired, in 1924. When he died, in 1947, more than 350 of his Standard trams still remained in use in London.

There then came over the LCCT a distinct change, a change for the better. Cars and services were improved in many different ways, cheap day-time fares were extended, the CRD was extensively modernised and relations with staff improved. An efficient organisation developed, and although the trams continued to call on the rates in every financial year from 1924/1925 until 1928/1929, working expenses consistently fell, while receipts per-car-mile remained more-or-less constant. In 1929/1930, a surplus was made, and again the following year, when the LCCT contributed £129,000 to the rates.

It is probable that two men share the responsibility for this renaissance. The General Manager who followed Fell was Mr. J.K. Bruce. Bruce had been acquired by the LCC in 1899 with the London Tramways Company, and he worked under Fell, as Traffic Manager and Deputy Chief Officer. It was said that his plans for reforming the LCCT were prepared well before Fell retired. Twice during Bruce's management, the LCC rewarded him with ex-gratia payments of £2,000. Bruce retired in 1930, because of ill-health to which he had become prone. He died shortly afterwards.

In 1917, Fell had hired one Theodore Eastaway Thomas as Development Superintendent. Thomas was in his mid-thirties, and came from the Combine. His experience was considerable and varied, for his jobs had been of both a commercial and engineering nature, and had involved both buses and trams. In 1925 Thomas became Traffic Manager, and for two of the years that Bruce was General Manager, Thomas acted in his place. Thus it was not surprising that the LCC's General Purposes Committee unanimously decided that he should become General Manager in 1930.

The LCCT continued to operate efficiently under Thomas, although in its last two years it was in deficit. New trams were bought, the Kingsway Subway was rebuilt for double-deck trams, certain extensions were built, and an experimental tram was constructed at the CRD. Efficiency continued to improve, although in one respect it arguably fell. In 1931/32 (figures for 1921/22 are given in brackets) the LCCT operated 70 million *(59.5m)* miles with a fleet of 1712 *(1765)* trams, of which an average of 1422 *(1325)* were in daily service. Each car ran 135 *(121)* miles daily, at an average service speed of 9.94 *(9.13)* miles-an-hour. Total passenger carryings over the two years were almost identical - 689m - but as 18% more mileage was operated, the passengers carried per-car-mile, 9.8 *(11.6)* were down by the same percentage.

Without doubt, the hard years from 1924 to 1933 were the LCCT's finest.

4

1924 to 1936

CLAPHAM DEPOT

Early in 1924 my transfer came through and I moved over to Clapham Depot. Straightaway I was better off because it saved me about an hour and a half's travelling a day; I could walk through to the depot in about twenty-five minutes, there were no buses.

The trailer cars had almost finished when I started, but I remember pulling them a couple of times. They were used in peak hours between Clapham Common and the Embankment. They might just do one or two journeys. They parked them down in Marius Road Depot and you would run from the loop outside Cavendish Road and then up to London and back. A lot of people used to walk across the Common in those days and get on there. They were slow and heavy, though, and I don't think anyone was sorry to see them go.

Stan Collins worked at Clapham Depot from 1924 until 1936. During those years there were a number of changes to services on which Clapham trams operated. Details of these alterations, with maps, can be found in Appendix 2. Certain services which ran via Southcroft Road were operated jointly by cars from Clapham and Telford Avenue Depots, and it was to Telford Avenue that Stan Collins moved in late 1936. Therefore, the details of Clapham services given here are those operating in mid-December 1936, and in Chapter 6 you will find details of Telford Avenue's services for the same date.

In December 1936, Clapham Depot operated 139 trams in rush-hours and 70 trams on Sunday afternoons; all were Standard E/1's. In addition to these 139 trams, there would have been around a dozen spare trams allocated to Clapham. The Wimbledon - Embankment service required 28 trams throughout the day, with a further 49 trams operating in rush-hours as Extra's on this service and the allied Circular Services 2A, 4A, 22 and 24. (Telford Avenue also provided one tram for the 22/24 in the mornings, and ten in the evenings.)

Services 8/20 (Victoria and Southcroft Road) were also operated jointly with Telford Avenue; Clapham provided 11 of the 31 trams required. Clapham provided all the cars for Service 6 (Fair Green and City, 17 trams) and Service 32 (Long Road and Chelsea Bridge, 5 trams).

Service 28 (Harlesden and Victoria) required 12 trams from Clapham, with others from Wandsworth and Hammersmith Depots. Service 34 (Kings Road and Blackfriars via Brixton) was operated jointly by Clapham (17 trams) and Camberwell (14 trams).

An interesting feature of Clapham's workings at this time, is that there were three separate duty rota's: one for the 34's, a second for the 28's and 32's, and the third for the 2/4, 2A/4A, 6, 8/20 and 22/24. All the details above refer to the morning rush-hour, unless otherwise qualified.

There would have been few significant differences in 1924, save that Service 32 was operated with single-deck trams, whilst it is likely that Clapham also operated trams on Service 26 (Hop Exchange and Kew Bridge).

*The LCCT owned 158 trailer cars which operated between 1913 and 1923; all were open-topped. Most were used on the Embankment Circular Services 2/4 and 16/18. Car 1026, on Service 22, **right, above**, leads a trailer set under Waterloo Bridge in 1919.*

I was a spare driver for about eight years at Clapham until I got a regular service. They might give you a temporary service if a man was away sick, but directly he came back you were back on the spare list again.

It wasn't until 1929, when part of the 8 and 20 routes were transferred into Clapham from Telford Avenue, that I got a regular temporary service. But once I'd got a couple of years service in I became a spare emergency driver, and sometimes I'd be taken off my job because someone had gone sick or something, and sent over to Camberwell to work on the four-wheel-bumpers that worked on the Forest Hill Route. I believe we used to get just sixpence a day extra if we were sent to Camberwell.

About once a month, on a Sunday morning, we had to report to Old Webby at Camberwell and he'd take you out on a four-wheeler for a test. You'd never know when it was going to happen, but you might be halfway up Forest Hill when he'd knock the switches out without warning and you had to stop without letting the car run back, not even an inch. That was how they kept you in practice in those days.

At that time you had to have two years service before being allowed to take a car on the 58 route, because there were two dangerous hills on it. There was Forest Hill, just by Horniman's Museum, and Dog Kennel Hill, going up from Goose Green. When you got to the top of Dog Kennel Hill coming from London there were points leading into four tracks, two down and two back, and the points sent alternate trams down each track. Under no circumstances were two trams allowed to go up or down the same track at the same time in case of a runaway. Even then, the second car wasn't allowed to start going down until the car in front was half-way down, although they were on different tracks. Before you went down you had to stop at the top of the hill to screw your magnetic-brake-blocks down onto the tracks with a special wheel on the hand-brake column, and you went down that hill very steadily on your magnetic-brakes. It was a tricky job really.

They were really rough, those four-wheel-bumpers, and buggers to drive because they would rock and jump and roll. They used to say that there were more girls born in Camberwell

35

*Camberwell Depot, August 1934, **left**. The building on the right is 303 Camberwell New Road, once the Head Office of the London Tramways Company, latterly the Southern Divisional Trams Office. Camberwell Depot had a second entrance on Walworth Road.*

*Until 1930, only four-wheel cars were used on the Dog Kennel Hill services. Dog Kennel Hill in the 1920's, **left**. Car 1697 about to start the climb; the conduit insulator hatches are open for inspection, **below**.*

than boys because when their mothers were pregnant the babies would have the balls shaken off them on the bumpers. With a four-wheel-bumper you didn't know which end your plough was, whether you were standing on your plough or whether it was at the other end. On a Standard, your plough was under the middle of the tram but on a four-wheel-bumper it was under one platform. If you got to a dead-hatchway you had to think for shutting the juice off. If you didn't shut your juice off, and ran over the hatchway with your handle on the power, you'd blow the juice off in the sub-station. So you had to remember, is my plough back or front?

The Hilly Route trams weren't anything like as bad when they brought them in in 1930, and some of them came straight on the road with windscreens fitted.

36

A four-wheel C class car at Lewisham in 1922, bound for Savoy Street via Dog Kennel Hill, **above.** *Covered top buses did not appear in London until around 1925. Cedars Road,* **right,** *with Car 547 descending on its way to East Hill, around 1914. There is another photograph of Cedars Road on page 124.*

Sometimes I'd have to go to other depots on Foreign Service, but it was generally either Camberwell or Jews Row.

Another hill you had to be very careful on was Cedars Road on the 32 and 34 road. Cedars Road is a short sharp hill and it was a hard and fast rule that you started your tram and then put three notches on your magnet straight away so that as soon as you got a little bit of speed up your magnetic-brake would hold it. If you left it too late the magnets just wouldn't hold and you came unstuck at the junction at the bottom. Twice in my memory trams went into the baker's shop opposite, on the corner there.

Soon after I moved over to Clapham I got married.

At Easter 1919 I'd been home on three months furlough, and at the same time a pal of mine was home on leave from the Queen's, and on Easter Monday evening we were out on Clapham Common. Two girls came along, and I suppose we gave them the glad eye or spoke to them, and all of a sudden, before I knew where I was, my soldiers cap was knocked off my head and one of the girls was running off with it. Of course, I went after her in no uncertain measure, and that was the start of our romance.

Anyway, we'd got courting, so I told her that I was going out to India for three years and I said, 'If I make my mother's allowance over to you — she was drawing eleven and tuppence a week separation money from me — will you bank it for me?' so she said she would. I took a chance, but somehow I had the feeling that I could trust her. I mean, she could have gone off and said no more about it, but she didn't, bless her heart, so I went off to India for three years.

After I started on the trams in 1923 — she had near enough a hundred pounds saved for me, which in those days was a mint of money — we got joined and got married in May 1924. The wife was twenty-two and I was twenty-five. She had a friend, young Ivy, who used to come to tea every Thursday, regular as clockwork right up until the Second World War broke out. One day we were talking about the school days, and she reminded my wife of this pease pudding shop they used to go to in Cornwall Road. My missus turned round and said to Ivy, 'Do you remember what fun we used to have with that butcher's boy?' Of course I was all ears, but I asked what they were talking about, 'What butcher's boy?' Ivy said. 'You'd have laughed your head off if you'd known. We used to get this pease pudding in a paper, eat some of it and flick it on the butcher's boy's window, because he used to come out and try to chase us.' I got straight out of the chair and knocked their heads together, just gently, not so as to hurt. 'What do you reckon you're doing?' young Ivy said. 'I was the bloody butcher's boy,' I said, 'and I always promised I'd bang your heads together,' or words to that effect. They laughed so much, Ivy fell off her chair.

In 1925 our first girl, Bet, was born and in 1927 we had Ivy, our second. Then in 1930, we moved into the house we still live in. We started off renting the ground floor flat, then we moved upstairs instead. Eventually my daughter Bet moved in downstairs with her husband, and then we had the chance to buy the house as sitting tenants, which my two girls did between them.

Just after I got married in 1924 there were more horses on the road than there are today, and the old boys used to sit on the shafts sometimes. A good horse always knew his own way home. I was coming down Balham High Road, right opposite Marius Road Tram Depot that was, and this old boy in front of me was sitting on the shaft. I'm sure he was fast asleep. I gave a couple or three taps on my bell and the old horse is plodding along — it was only walking — and the front of my tram got past, but then the horse decided to pull out a little bit and his offside front wheel caught my rear axle-box on the nearside.

The wheel was just chipped, but they were so particular in those days. The horse kicked up, broke the shafts, the old boy fell on his arse, and the horse turned in front of me and ran into a bus. They had to fetch a vet and have him shot, poor old horse.

By this time I'd spotted something, so I said to my mate, 'You watch that axle-box, don't let anyone knock that off.' When the police came up I told him I was in the clear. 'You see the front wheel of that wagon? You see that little bit of wood chipped off it?' I said. Then I showed him the little chip still lying on my axle-box which showed that three parts of my tram were past before he hit me, and that cleared me. I was told to turn all my people off the tram, put them on the next car, and turn back at Marius Road and run my car back into Clapham Depot.

Then I had to make out a report and go straight up to 23 Belvedere Road, and I happened to see one of our Drivers, old Fred Hurley, and I asked him to knock at 33 Kildawn Road where I was living then, and tell my missus I don't know what time I'll be home, because I've had to go up to 23 Belvedere Road, but don't tell her why. I was about two hours late home. Horses were valuable in those days. It was a serious matter killing a horse, but I got out of it.

Around 1930 or so, they started putting signs on the dashes of trams to try and get cars to stop when people were getting on or off, and Conductors were ordered, when your tram stops and people are alighting, to put your hand out to stop motors. But a Conductor hasn't got the authority a policeman's got. If you were a decent sort of a person, well, naturally you'd stop, but

"Thank you. Mr. MOTORIST"

The LCCT produced this poster in 1932, in an attempt to 'educate' the growing number of private motorists. Similar posters were placed on the dashes of trams, and they were also used by other operators.

you always got the odd one that would toot-toot-toot and try to get through while people were getting on.

On one occasion while I was at Clapham, an old chap got knocked down getting off my tram up Scrubbs Lane on the old 28 road. I was looking through the nearside mirror, and I saw the old fellow getting off and watched a car come up on the nearside very fast and knock him over, and I never want to see anything like it again. The driver got nicked and I had to go to the West London Police Court.

There was an accident on Putney Bridge one Sunday, one of the worst I've ever seen. It was a wide bridge and the tracks were still against the kerb on the London side at that time. That part of the bridge was a right-of-way for trams, and all the traffic was supposed to keep to the other side of the bridge. I saw it with my own eyes. I was going over the bridge towards Putney, on the 28 road, when a motor bike passed me on the off-side and hit a tram coming towards me. Up went the bike, both the man and the girl on the back landed on the platform of the tram.

Fortunately it didn't have a windscreen. They couldn't have died, otherwise I would have been called as a witness.

I was coming up from Tooting Broadway one day on a Standard, and just up the road on the pavement was a copper with a load of kids just come out of school. Of course, I had my eyes open and just as I got up to him a kiddy suddenly ran across the road, right bang in front of me, and just on the tracks he suddenly put his hands up, scared, and I knocked him down. I only pushed him a couple of yards, I had my magnetic-brakes on and sand and what-not, I was trembling all over. It took a lump out of the back of the kiddy's head. Next day the copper met me and told me that the kid had seen his mother on the other side of the road. It wasn't my fault, anyway, and I was cleared.

I remember another case, the Driver concerned is dead and gone now, at Streatham Garage a bus pulled up and the Driver was getting out of his cab just as a tram was coming by. He put his backside out, and the tram just knocked him in the road. The tram-driver was in an awful state, and I always had that accident in mind when I was on the buses later on. They managed to keep that out of the papers. The papers used to pick up any little thing that was against the trams.

In May 1926 there was the General Strike. We came out in support of the Miners and there was hardly any transport in London at the time. The busmen were out and the railways had stopped as well. We all got the sack. A note came through the door saying, 'You are instructed to return your uniform to the depot where you were employed,' so we all went down to Clapham. I don't mind telling you, I had butterflies in my stomach. I was not long married with a baby to support, and there I was with the sack. The Union Secretary, I believe it was George Schofield, said there was nothing to worry about and he collected all the notices up, tied them up with a blue ribbon and put a nice bow on it, then someone jumped on a bike and went up to 23 Belvedere Road and pushed them through the letter-box.

We wouldn't let any trams run, although some volunteers and officials did try to take them out. One came out of Clapham but it didn't get far, and I heard of another that ran out of New Cross. You only had to go half a mile up the road, find a big bolt and jam it in the slot-rail. That would stop them. It would either break the plough or bring the carrier down.

That was what happened along the Old Kent Road, so we were told. At Clapham all the police were on horses, and a lot of the men jumped on the tram as it came out of the depot and started smashing windows. We had to run up a little court with the baby in the pram because the police went mad. They were coming right up on the pavement with their horses, they had long sticks and were just lashing out at anyone, women and all were getting hit, they couldn't care less. One of the coppers was on a big grey horse, and I heard later that he was done up at the Elephant and dropped down the toilet in the middle of Saint George's Road.

Churchill appeared on the scene, and in one of his speeches he said, 'If they won't go back to work, get the guards out and shoot them back.' I could never forgive Churchill for that. They say Churchill in the last war was a marvellous leader. Perhaps he was, because he had the voice, and when he was broadcasting to the Nation about, 'We'll stew them in their own gravy,' he was five and six hundred feet underground saying that.

We were only fighting for our rights. We'd come back from the War to unemployment and unhappiness.

At various times we had experimental cars at Clapham. One of the first came out of the CRD just after the General Strike, number 1817, the first Pullman car. This was an older Standard car which had been painted red and was fitted out with upholstered seats on both decks. The downstairs seats no longer faced each other — up to then they'd all been like two wooden benches, one down each side — they were done away with and new reversible seats put in, and they'd brightened up the insides. The passengers really liked it, in fact they used to queue up for it, because if it came along at a certain time on Monday morning, they would know it would come at the same time for the rest of the week, and they let the ordinary chocolate coloured trams go through. Conductors didn't like it because they used to get caned. It must have been a success, because they did up a lot more like it over the next few years. Then, with another lot of Standards, they took the old Westinghouse controllers off and put on a Metropolitan-Vickers, with a swan-necked handle on it. You couldn't half shift with them. They'd fly away. They were a different sort of a mechanism inside, the reverse of a round drum in a Westinghouse controller. The very first one of those Metropolitan-Vickers was 1406, I think, but either old Juicy Webb or Juicy Baker took it out on a test run and found they hadn't got a magnetic brake. It was wired up wrong. They soon put that right, and then they did them all like it.

The fastest tram on the road was 1814. It was fitted with German roller bearings, but one of the most controversial, as far as I can remember, was 1403, or it might have been 1506, which was the first to be fitted with a windscreen, not with glass all round as they were later, but with just one two-foot wide piece of glass in the middle of the dash. That was in 1930. What happened was that the wind just came round the sides and nobody liked it. Shortly afterwards they put full vestibule glasses on, and we started getting about two cars a week into the Depot like that. But even that wasn't too good, because nobody liked doing half a split turn on an enclosed car and the other half on an open-fronted car, especially in winter. By that time the Union was pretty strong, it was for the working person themselves, and if you went — I'm speaking collectively — and made a complaint to the Union Secretary he'd say, 'Right, I'll have that rectified.' There was no messing about like there is today. So they got onto the people in charge of London Transport, and before we knew where we were they were coming in like hot cakes and screwing them on. The police were a lot of trouble and delayed the installation of vestibules. We had to fight for them. They demanded that the Driver had to have 180 degree vision on the front.

Some of the older Drivers didn't like vestibules either, said they couldn't see through the glass, which to my way was a lot of tommy-rot, because they were a boon.

Although they were draughty, at least you could keep dry. I say keep dry, but a lot of the old LCC trams had been on the road for so many years that they had a touch of dry-rot, and the rain used to come in the roof and down inside, and of course it was the poor Driver who got the lot, but that wasn't so bad as having it all the time. Before they could put the glass fronts on, they had to shorten the hand-brake a bit, because Standards had long hand-brakes with a handle which stuck out over the dash. To my way of thinking that made it a jolly sight harder work, because with the long hand-brake you had a good lever on it. We got used to them after a time. With the old ones, if you felt like a bit of exercise, you could pull a car up on the hand-brake, but you couldn't do it after they shortened them.

The years around 1930 saw interesting changes in the LCCT vehicle policy, for there began to appear windscreens, mirrors and fog-lamps, without which tram-drivers had worked since 1903. In the same period the LCCT also experimented with air-braking and improved methods of power collection, as well as building experimental new trams.

Towards the end of 1929, the LCCT fitted three cars (1248, 1506 and 1539) with experimental windscreens of different designs. Car 1506 seems first to have been fitted with three vertical sections of glass, angled around the Driver, but without either windscreens or a mirror to his left. By February 1930, after all three cars had been tested in service, both ends of 1506 had been fitted with glazed sidescreens and mirrors, but with various interesting differences, as a scrutiny of the photographs will reveal. The design on the left, with the two glass panes beside the stairs replaced by a solid panel, eventually became the LCCT/LT standard windscreen.

The LCCT was in no apparent hurry to add windscreens to its existing fleet, for although some new trams entered service with windscreens fitted, by March 1932 only 71 cars in the existing fleet carried them, and there were still trams in regular service in 1940 without windscreens.

By March 1932, however, mirrors had been fitted to all LCCT trams, for the LCCT was concerned at the increasing number of accidents to passengers boarding and alighting. Fog lamps were fitted beside destination boxes from 1930, initially at the rate of 200 cars a year. Until windscreens were fitted, there had been no need for trolley-rope cleats on the dashes of trams, for trolley-ropes had previously been tied down to the stair-rails. From 1935, however, cleats were fitted to all trams, whether fitted with windscreens or not.

Vestibules did cause some problems in the rain, because they didn't have wipers. Some Drivers used to keep half a potato in their pockets. I had my own way, I used to use newspaper. For cleaning glass, a lump of newspaper is as good as anything, and once you'd cleaned all the dirt off the glass and the louvres — I used to hop out the front and give it a good wipe over with a piece of newspaper — it was a damn sight better than a screen wiper. The rain would just come down in one sheet, no drops, you were looking through clear wet glass. There wasn't much you could do about snow or ice though, except open the louvres. Vestibules were certainly draughty, the wind came in from the side and through the louvres, but in the summer you could get those louvres carefully adjusted and send a cool draught over your head. Before windscreens came in we were allowed to wear Union goggles, specially made by the Union, and if you'd been out in a fog you'd finish up with clean eyes but the rest of your face was as black as a sweep's. For a long time, though, the LCC didn't allow goggles to be worn and your eyes used to get so dirty that the only way to clean them when you finished was with Vaseline. Don't forget that there was a lot of muck on the roads anyway, and there were steam lorries throwing smoke and ash into the air.

The worst thing though, was the cold, because even though you were issued with a thick uniform and great-coat, you could get absolutely frozen standing there on the front for hour after hour. I remember one day my wife brought me out some tea when I was due past Clapham Common, and I just couldn't speak to her because my whole jaw was frozen. Sometimes when I got home she would have to pour that first cup of tea down my throat while the tears streamed down my face.

Those were wicked days, but I never caught a cold, not once. I didn't know what a cold was until I went on the buses.

Staff waiting to take-on at New Cross Gate in 1933, **above**. Although it is August, both Drivers wear great-coats; one also has goggles and a white choker. The Conductor wears on his cuff the recently introduced white band, part of a campaign to reduce step accidents. A propaganda exercise, **below**; the tram is from Clapham Depot, the van from the LGOC.

Hammersmith Broadway in 1933. Car 1045 was around 25 years old; it compared unfavourably in many ways with LT 1312, which had been on the road for less than a year.

On Boat Race days people used to flock to Putney, crowds and crowds, and we used to run Specials from Wandsworth change-pit — the top of Putney Bridge Road to Putney Bridge, just that little bit, backwards and forwards. It was a six-minute run, and I knew very well that my mate would only get his fares in if I took it very, very steady — you carried over seventy passengers on a Standard — but if I did that I'd be holding the service up. So we used to drive down Putney Bridge Road as hard as we could go and he'd be inside getting his fares in — he wouldn't hurry — by the time we got to Putney Bridge. Then I'd nip up the stairs and open the top door, 'Come on, this way down,' and I'd stand at the bottom of the stairs holding my cap while they showered the coppers in. You had to work it between you, half for me, half for him. We used to do alright. We knew that there were no Jumpers *(1)* about, they didn't worry about the Specials, and there wasn't the time anyway. They just wanted to clear the people away.

When there was dog racing at Wimbledon — I believe there were two meetings a week, on Tuesdays and Thursdays — they'd run sometimes up to a dozen Dog Specials. We ran those out of Clapham and Telford — generally it was about three cars from each depot — right up until the start of the War. The regulars all knew about them. Some used to pay their fares, and some didn't, as you might say. There was a Dog Special list at Telford with everyone's name on it who wanted one, and when you'd had one your name would be scratched out and you'd have to wait until everyone else had done one before you got another. Coming from Telford we used to put up 'TOOTING BROADWAY' and carry up to there, then alter the indicator to 'WIMBLEDON ROAD' and carry on up Garratt Lane. Then we'd do three or four journeys between the dog track and Tooting Broadway and when the first race started and people slackened off, we'd drop anchor round by the dog track until it was time to take them home again. Perhaps we'd sit in the tram and have a smoke, or go and get some fish and chips. Then one day a clever Inspector found us there doing nothing, and said that one of us had to work Tooting to Wimbledon, another Tooting to Mitcham and so on until the races were over, because we might pick up a few passengers. What we called him was nobody's business, because it had been a nice little job.

A Dog Special used to be worth three or four hours overtime, and that was worth about ten-bob which was millionaire's money to us. There wasn't much overtime before the War, because there were always men standing by, but if we thought that there was a bit of overtime going, I

---

1. A Ticket Inspector who moved unpredictably from tram to tram.

Feltham 2150 being towed into the CRD in the late 1930's, **left** *looking towards the gatehouse. Blackfriars Bridge in the 1930's,* **right**.

mean, when the kiddies were small and they perhaps needed a new pair of shoes — our money was only three pounds eleven a week — if there was a couple of hours going we used to try and grab it. Sometimes, if there was a lot of men on holiday, you might be able to work your rest-day, and that was all time and a half. When I was a young spare driver in Clapham, sometimes when I finished at perhaps ten or eleven at night the Night Inspector would say to me, 'Can you get up tomorrow morning, there's a tram to be taken down to the CRD?' So I'd have a few hours sleep, and get back at six o'clock to take the tram down to Charlton and get there about seven. If there was another one to come back I'd hang about down there waiting for it, otherwise I'd come back on a service car. A nice bit of overtime that was. We'd all jump for that. We were only too glad to get hold of overtime. They rarely had to cut cars out in those days.

One car that always ran without fail was the last one, on every route. It was an unwritten rule that the last tram always went through, fog, running late, snow, anything. Even if you were an hour late you had to go through, because there might be people still waiting for it. It never occurred to you to turn back, however late you were, that was one of our traditions.

One week everybody was paid ten bob short, the pay bloke said the cost-of-living had gone down. *(2)* They didn't even give us a warning,

and I had to come home and give the wife her housekeeping money, and by the time I'd put the rent by, it left me with nothing. We got through, I don't know how.

Newspapers were a ha'penny or a penny each in those days, and people would chuck them away. My Conductor would always keep those newspapers and put them in the locker, so he'd have a pile of papers. When we got to Putney High Street, while I'm nipping round putting the pole up on the wire and getting ready to throw the plough out, he's up a little alley-way there where there was a fish and chip shop, chuck them a load of paper and bring back fish and chips. We had it weighed up well. That used to be our perks.

It was while I was a Driver at Clapham that the London Passenger Transport Board was formed in 1933. We'd known for a long time that we were all going to be amalgamated, and wondered about our future, whether they would put the tram men off and bring in their own employees off the buses. The bus men thought the opposite might happen, but we got friendly after a time. We'd had our fixed stops for as long as I can remember, but in the days of the London General Omnibus Company they had no fixed stops, they'd stop anywhere, even at our stops. So we used to keep our eyes open, and if anybody on the pavement put their hand out the bus would stop, but while he was picking her up we were round and up to the next stop, because we wanted to pinch his passengers. It was more or less competition. Later, when they decided to

---

2. Throughout the 1920's the cost-of-living was falling and wage reductions were common, but from 1923 there were only two such on the LCCT, both of one shilling.

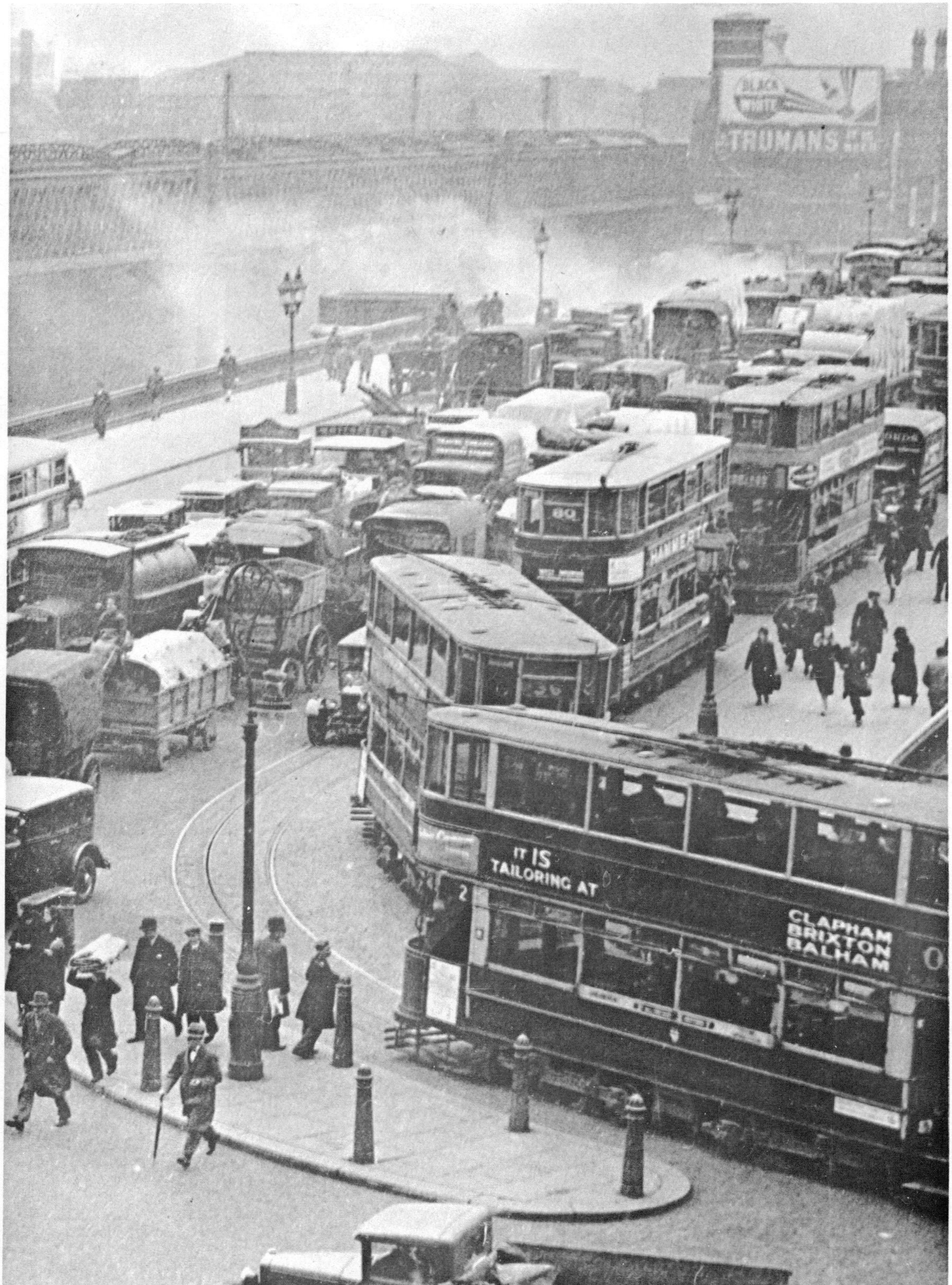
TRUMANS
IT IS
TAILORING AT
CLAPHAM
BRIXTON
BALHAM

scrap the trams, bus-drivers used to say to us, 'You wait till you, soldier's language, get up here,' but we could afford to laugh. I still say now, although I drove trams for twenty-eight years and buses for thirteen, providing he kept his loaf, a kiddy of twelve could drive a bus, but a tram-driver had to have a certain mechanical knowledge. You might be going along the road and your breaker would blow out. Put it back in, and it would blow out again, and that told the trained motorman — we were motormen in those days, not tram-drivers — that he'd got a motor going.

There was a lot of controversy over the pirates in the 1920's. What the London General Omnibus Company did if a pirate bus came along the road, was to check its time and put a General bus in front and another one behind so that he was sandwiched. But the General buses had fixed routes, a scheduled route all the time, and the pirates hadn't, so they just shot down a side turning, round another one and back onto the main road and got in front of the Generals. They just laughed at it. There was a lot of jiggery-pokery all the way through with those pirates. I can remember one case when I was coming down from London on a swing turn, or with 'EXTRA's' up, and a pirate bus pulled up right alongside me at Angell Road. His Conductor saw my Conductor. He went round the back and said he'd only got a few people on and could my mate take them on. The reason why he did that was that there was a big crowd of people on the other side of the road, so they just swung round, picked them all up and away they went. They were happy, so were we — he gave us something for a drink, I think, but I'll leave that out — and that's how they used to go on. If they saw a crowd waiting for a tram or bus they'd just dump their people — perhaps they'd give them their money back — turn round and take the others on. I believe they were more or less working on commission.

In those days trams kept traffic in order, you could shift a load of passengers from one stop, it was a sad day for London when they let the trams go. Apart from anything else, before the London Transport was formed the trams were run by the London County Council, which kept the rates down, as the trams had to pay their share of the rates. Then, when London Transport was formed I think it was Lord Ashfield's idea to get rid of the trams. He wasn't the type of man to buy a dying concern, which they said in those days the tramways were. He had his eye to business, he knew what he was doing. I don't think the LCC trams ever did run at a loss, (3) because we used to be packed out nearly all day long, especially when they introduced the tuppence-all-the-way and shilling-all-day tickets. We were carrying crowds of people where the LGOC buses were nearly half empty.

It wasn't until after London Transport came in that we were given compulsory meal breaks. Then we only got them after the bus men, and had to fight for it. The canteen at Telford was up at the back of the tram-shed. When I first started there were no canteens, there was no need for them until meal breaks were given, but the steward in the recreation room would make a cup of tea if you wanted one.

We didn't get free passes in those days, they didn't come in until after the London Passenger Transport Board was formed, and the only time you could travel free was going on duty or coming home. That's why you always saw a tramwayman wearing his uniform if he was going shopping; if you wore a suit you had to pay.

The 32 road was called 'the chicken run,' you were there and back again before you knew where you were. You used to do about thirty journeys in a turn. I used to love that road, nobody interfered with you, there was only one Inspector on that road and he never used to worry over us. There were only four trams on it and five in the rush hour. Cracking little road that was, a fish and chip road, from the Plough Clapham to Chelsea Bridge.

---

3. They did, in several years after 1920, given the inequitable local authority accounting system, but so did most London operators that provided intensive rush-hour services at substandard fares and also sold a range of cheap fares at other times. LCCT deficiencies were made good from the County rates, to which the trams also contributed when they made a surplus, as well as paying rates on their lines and premises. In the LCCT's five worst financial years, from 1925 to 1929, the contribution from the rates represented only 4% of total LCCT income (£860,624 from rates; total income from fares and other sources, £20m.) The whole question of transport costs is complex; one can either accept the traditional myopic arguments, or believe — as did the LCC — that good public transport is important.

Ashfield was the Chairman of the Underground 'Combine', with whose buses and trains the LCCT competed. The Combine also owned three tram companies, with which the LCCT co-operated. Ashfield became the first Chairman of the LPTB in 1933. He was a very shrewd man, and although he is often represented as the arch-enemy of the London tram, there is no real evidence for this. If any one man was responsible for the decision to get rid of trams, Thomas — the ex-LCCT General Manager — has probably just as strong a claim as Ashfield. Some interesting political manoeuvring took place within the LPTB in 1933, on which light could usefully be cast, but those who believe that an LCC-dominated Transport Board would not have abandoned its trams are deluding themselves.

I had a Conductor in those days who could always see the funny side of things. One morning during the peak hour, I pulled up at Long Road Clapham and walked through the car. Then an old boy got on and picked up a newspaper that somebody had left on. Now they were our perks, newspapers, so my mate came through and told me, he said, 'We'll look out for him tomorrow! Anyway, next morning the same old boy gets on and does it again, picks up a newspaper. Evidently, he's a regular rider, so my mate says, 'Right, we'll catch him tomorrow.' On the next day he gets a paper, opens it out, takes a couple of pages out and tears them into teeny pieces. Then he puts them inside the paper, folds it up and leaves it on the seat. Same old boy got on, picked up the paper, my mate collected his fare, and then he looks at the front page as if he'd just bought it and opens it up. He got off at the next stop, he knew what had happened. There wasn't half a mess in the tram because my mate had torn it into little pieces like confetti. Next morning when we got to Long Road the old boy was there, standing at the stop, but he didn't get on. He waited for the next one.

We didn't have to worry, time-boards didn't count a thing with us on that road. You knew you had to do about thirty journeys and you knew what time you finished, so I might leave the Plough Clapham two minutes late, but go like hell to Chelsea Bridge, get there on time. Then leave there two minutes late and belt back again. We used to have some fun there. It was a double-deck road. There had been singles on it at one time, but they only came as far as Lavender Hill then, they didn't come up Cedars Road. They were like the Tunnel trams, but then they lowered the road under the railway arch in Queenstown Road — it's Queens Road now — for the double-deckers to go through. You didn't get bored; time used to fly by lovely. Perhaps you'd shout out to another driver, 'How many more, mate?' 'Only twenty,' he'd say, or whatever it was. There was a separate roster for that road, with the 32's and 28's on it, one week you'd be on the 32's, the next week on the 28's and then back on the 32's again. It was twelve minutes from one end to the other, and I loved it. Nobody used to worry you, but it didn't half used to take some money. I've known my mate, before we went out of the depot, to pick up an empty old sandbag to put his coppers in. Everyone did it on that road. They'd walk in the yard with a sandbag full of coppers, then it was an hour's job to sit down and count them all out. They got rid of the 32 road in 1937, after I'd left Clapham, but I don't know why, it was a money making road. That road paid them much better than the 137 buses which took over. Cheap midday fares were a penny all the way, tuppence ordinary and the 'workman's' was tuppence return.

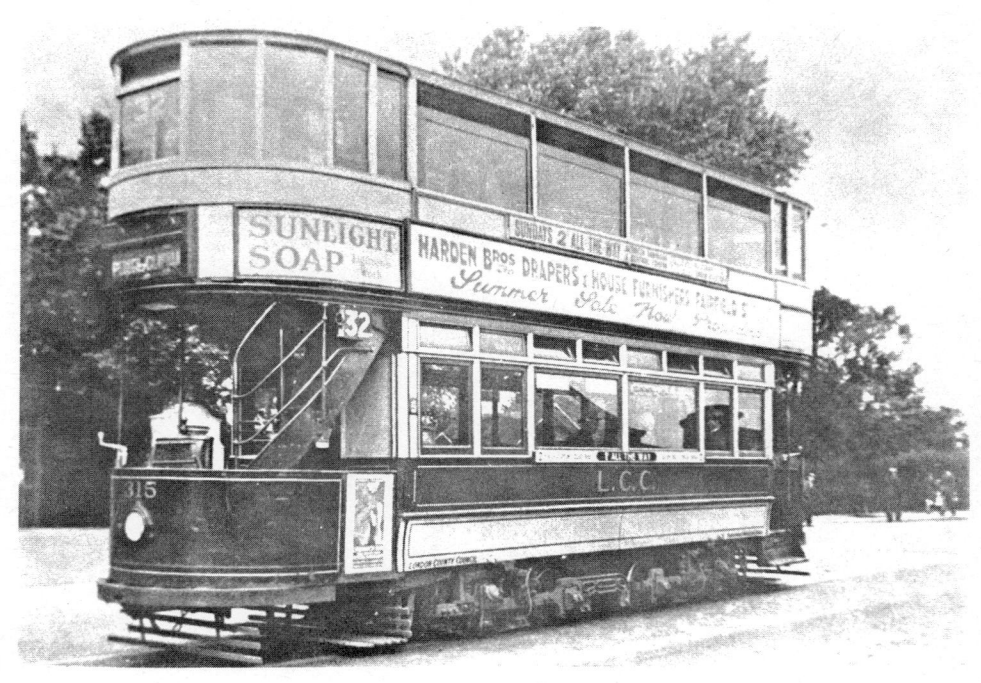

D class car 315 at Chelsea Bridge Terminus, towards the end of the 1920's.

There were two entrances at Clapham Depot, onto Clapham Park Road when you were running out, and from the High Street when you were running in. You could run right through the depot, same as you could at Holloway. Most of the time at Clapham crews used to change over at the Plough, and at one time there was a loop line on the up track which was used for stabling cars if nobody turned out for relief.

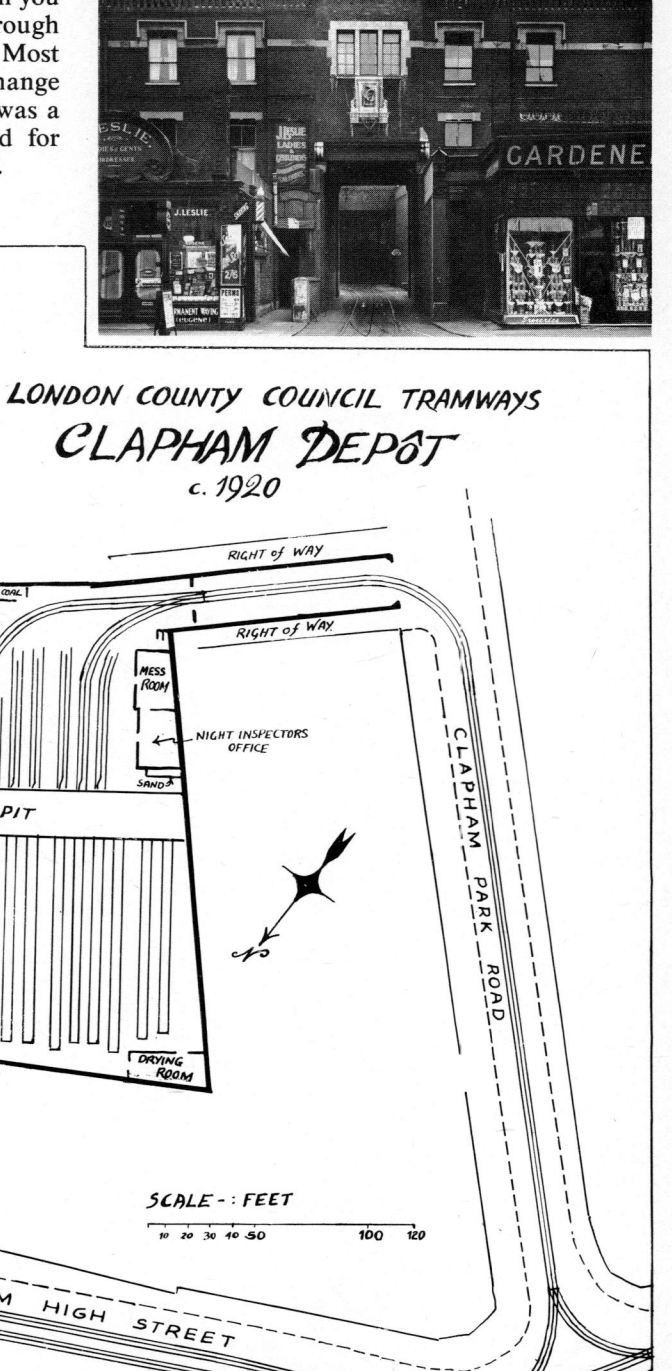

LONDON COUNTY COUNCIL TRAMWAYS
CLAPHAM DEPOT
c. 1920

SOURCE: L.T. RECORDS.
DRAWN BY R.F.M. 8/76.

**CLAPHAM DEPOT
1936**

The main entrance to Clapham Depot was through an arch built in 1904 through a row of shops in the High Street, **left**; the other entrance led onto Clapham Park Road, **below left**. In 1934 there was car-washing apparatus at this back entrance, but it was removed shortly afterwards.

Through the front arch, **right**, can be seen the entrance to the depot proper, where stand cars 1810 and 1826. Inside the depot, looking towards the front entrance, snowbroom 023 stands beside car 1820. At the side of the depot, **bottom right**, were offices.

49

I think it was towards the end of the 1920's that the LCC started the tuppence-all-the-way. You could go as far as you liked on one tram after ten o'clock for tuppence. On the 16 road, if I remember right, the first tram used to leave Norbury at about ten o'clock. Now people in those days would know, because the trams used to run to strict time, and if the last Ordinary went through at, say, four or five minutes to ten, they wouldn't get on, they knew that at ten o'clock the first tuppenny-all-the-way was coming along. So when we got to Norbury the Driver would jump down, turn his offside board to tuppence-all-the-way and the Conductor would do the same at his end. Then you'd see the crowds get on. *(4)*

It was about the same time that a lot of yokes dropped or went out of alignment or even broke, you got a dropped tee-rail and then the road would go dead, because your collector shoes, on either side of the bottom of the plough, weren't connecting with the tee-rail. A Regulator would have to find out just where it was dropped, but in the meantime, if the juice went off they'd spot it in the Sub-station and a breakdown gang would be notified, and they'd probably have a good idea where to look for it.

When we were on the trams we knew just where our tea-places were, where your mate could hop off for two jugs of tea at a convenient spot. This was more or less unofficial really, because if you were caught you were on a report, but we used to make sure we didn't get caught. When we were approaching a regular tea-place — not anywhere, because we knew where we could get a jug of tea for tuppence, and a cup on top — I used to bang-bang-bang, give him half a dozen bells. Then my mate would jump off, and the chap would come to the door with two jugs of tea all ready. He knew, he'd heard the bells. A pint jug of tea for tuppence, lovely cup of tea, too. There was one at Lessingham Avenue, just before you got to Tooting Broadway, that was when we were on the 2's and 4's. On the 34's it was just round the bend at Herne Hill, on Coldharbour Lane, and on the Purley road it was down at the Red Deer. On the 28 it was just round the corner by Putney High Street. There were so many of them. And every Christmas it was twenty fags, back and front, Christmas box from the coffee-shop. I was on the 34 road one early turn with a strange Conductor. He jumped off at the tea shop and off I went up Coldharbour Lane not thinking, round the corner into Gresham Road. Then I saw a car coming up in the nearside mirror, tooting, and there's my mate hanging on the side with two jugs of tea in his hand, I'd completely forgotten about him. Some Conductors used to take the precaution of knocking the breakers out at their end if they were getting off, then they couldn't be left behind.

---

4. Tuppence-all-the-way tickets were first issued in April 1920, between the morning and evening rush-hours. At other times 2d. would carry an adult for 1.8 miles.

Car 1780 in Worple Road, Wimbledon around 1929. The single track section here was controlled by signals mounted on the traction standard, left. Service 2/4 was extended annually to Hampton Court at weekends during the summers of 1926 to 1931, and on winter Saturday afternoons from 1926 until 1929.

On summer Saturdays, Sundays and Bank Holidays the 2's and 4's from Clapham used to pick up on the Embankment and run right through to Hampton Court. It was a lovely run and I used to enjoy it. I'd look on my time-board and say to my mate, 'Look, Hampton Court this time.' It was a marvellous run, right down through Wimbledon, Worple Road, Raynes Park, over Kingston Bridge and then through Bushey Park.

Beyond Wimbledon on the Hampton Court road we were on the London United tracks, and we had to watch our points. There was one left hand bend which was so acute that the front of our LCC tram would touch the sides of one of their trams on the other track. If I remember, there was a warning board up, trams must not pass on this bend, and you had to wait. Their track was rough. You couldn't let it out, but had to go very, very steady, more or less half power. The track was so bad that they had more running time on their tracks than we had on ours. You couldn't speed along. That all stopped when they trolleybussed that Hampton Court Road.

One Bank Holiday I was on the Hampton Court road with old Jack Hills. He would never blow his whistle. If he was on the top deck he'd just whistle through his teeth. Sometimes on that road you'd fill up going round London and then perhaps not stop again till you got to Hampton Court — the Conductors used to like that — but we picked people up all the way along if we had room, and this particular time I pulled up at Haydons Road and a load of fellows got on. One of them asked Jack to hold on while they bought some beer from an off-licence. Of course Jack didn't mind that, he couldn't half neck it, so they brought these four crates of beer out and loaded them on the tram. When we were down near Raynes Park, in a very quiet country part, Jack came through to me. 'Alright,' he says, 'I'll take the handles, you get down under the stairs and have a drink.' He'd pinched this quart bottle. When they got off at Hampton Court they left all the empty bottles on the tram. I can see Jack now, when we got back to Haydons Road, running across the road to the off-licence with two crates in each hand. We did alright out of that one, fifty-fifty.

5

TRAMS & TRAMWAYMEN

In this chapter are placed those parts of Stan Collins' narrative that are concerned with the day-to-day operation of trams. In general he is speaking of the years between 1924 and 1939, and the atmosphere he conveys is, hopefully, pure LCCT.

This period was a strange one for the LCC trams. From 1924 onwards, the Department greatly improved its operations, and it became efficient and competitive, but it was well known throughout the 1920's that some form of unification of London's passenger transport was inevitable. The question was 'how' and 'when', and while politicians procrastinated, the tools of urban transport — particularly the bus and trolleybus — underwent considerable improvement. Unfortunately for the LCC, the answer was far too long in coming, and it was the wrong one when it came.

The new LPTB began functioning on 1st July 1933. It was not directly controlled by an elected body, and its only political link with the LCC — a fragile one, which seems to have been of little practical value — was through one of the Board's part-time members.

The management of all London's trams was at first divided geographically between Mr.C.J. Spencer — from the Combine — and Mr.T.E. Thomas from the LCCT. Spencer was the man who had recently introduced both new trams — the Felthams — and trolleybuses to the Combine tramways, and although his trolleybuses were very successful, Spencer still believed that the tram had a place on London streets. Thomas seems to have been a 'transport' man — probably the best in London at the time — rather than a 'tram' man, and it must be remembered that he had hitherto had no real option but to run trams; in a sense, he had worked with one hand tied behind his back. Thomas is known to have been impressed by Spencer's trolleybuses.

Spencer resigned in October 1933, allegedly after a disagreement with Ashfield — the LPTB Chairman — and Thomas then became the General Manager of the whole London tram system. Within one month, the decision to replace London's trams with trolleybuses was implicitly taken, for how else can one interpret the proposal to operate trolleybuses to Euston ? (This had not been present in the outer-suburban trolleybus plans announced just before Spencer resigned.)

Beneath Thomas was then developed a supervisory hierarchy in which ex-LCCT men predominated. This, together with the fact that the LCCT had, of necessity, already imposed many of its own operating practices on the previously independent tram systems, ensured that it was the Belvedere Road method of running trams which continued and spread throughout London during the 1930's. It was also applied to trolleybus operation, for both trams and trolleybuses were administered by the same section of LT.

Thus the 1930's had a unique quality. The Belvedere Road ethic remained strong, and although London's trams were being replaced by trolleybuses, the remaining cars continued to be well-maintained. Indeed, certain valuable improvements were made to them after 1933.

Car 97, one of the original A class cars built for the 1903 Clapham services, loads at John Carpenter Street in July 1919. The signs over the entrance to the shelter were linen blinds, which could be adjusted to show other destinations.

Suppose you're loading up, say at Lambeth Town Hall. You've just had two bells to start, or if your mate's up top he's given you two blasts on his whistle out of the little window at the top of the stairs. He'll have looked to see if it's all clear behind, but you had to look round to see that nobody else was getting on at the last minute before you started.

Right. Touch the dog on your hand-brake with your right foot to release it, then one, two, three, four, round with your controller handle through the series notches, slight pause while you picked up speed, then five, six, seven, and onto top notch. You worked your controller with your left hand, and you always brought that handle round smoothly, away from you for power and back towards you for braking. If you built up on your controller too quickly, out would go your switches and you'd have to shut off, knock them back and start again. *(1)* It often happened climbing a hill. On a Standard you had two canopy switches at each end. Suppose you were going along the road on top notch and your controller locked — you couldn't shut off — you'd have to knock those switches out at your end and stop it on the hand-brake.

Then you got the bell to stop, or you could see someone at the stop with their hand out, so you shut your power off, slight pause, and brought the handle round onto the brake notches, gradually increasing the braking until you'd almost stopped, then bringing it to a halt on the hand-brake. If you had the time you'd shut off the power before you got the bell and you'd coast, gradually losing speed, but we didn't often have the time to do it. You had to keep going.

Back in the LCC days we used to get what we called our 'juice money', coal bonus. All our juice came from our own generating station at Greenwich, which used coal, and we were instructed to coast as much as possible to save coal, and about once a quarter you'd find five, six or even seven bob extra, juice money, on your money. *(2)* London Transport soon knocked that on the head.

---

1. These 'switches' were main circuit-breakers, set to automatically cut-out if a fault developed, or if the Driver attemped to overload the circuit.

2. The price of coal rose considerably during and after the 1914 War. In 1914 the LCCT was paying an average 16s 11¼d per ton; in 1920, 44s 7d. Prices then fell but rose again in 1926 as a result of the Miners' lock-out, but by then the LCCT was using coke, and price comparisons are not simply made. More relevant, and perhaps explaining why the coal-bonus was knocked on the head, is the fact that raw fuel costs in 1911 represented 6% of LCCT revenue expenditure, whereas in 1926 they were down to 4%.

If you had a Feltham it was a bit different, because you had a booster notch when you got onto top notch. You pressed the handle down and you heard it click — that was the booster notch going in — and it gave you an extra three or four miles-an-hour. We only used that if we wanted to shoot past something quick. When you got the bell on a Feltham you shut your juice off just the same and put your air-brake on — the air-brake was worked by a little handle on the right of your controller which you moved to the right — and sometimes, if it didn't seem to be pulling up fast enough, you brought the controller round onto the brake notches as well. Just before you stopped you eased up on the air-brake so that you stopped smoothly. When you stopped you opened the front air-door — there used to be a little key and when you pushed it forward the air-door shut — but you had to be very careful because people would try and get on that way. The main doors on a Feltham, at the back as it were, folded back and slid into a sort of cavity. They stayed open all the time according to which direction you were travelling, but if you were full you had a rope to pull across the entrance.

One thing you always tried to avoid and that was stopping on a curve, because you didn't seem to get that grip somehow when you started off again, and it used more juice than starting on the straight. It was always best to coast round a curve if you could.

You might start off and suddenly feel the wheels slipping — perhaps the rail was a bit greasy or there were wet leaves on it — so you'd shut off straight away, foot on your sand pedals and bring the handle round again nice and steady. As you were going along you kept an eye open for dead-hatchways or section insulators — where your gap was — and always shut off as you went over them. If you didn't you might blow out the sub-station. But you got to know where they were and it became habit. Same with junctions, there were various dead sections on junctions, so you coasted over them nice and gently — five miles-an-hour was the rule — a little bit of power, then shut off, a little bit more, shut off again, then you were on the straight and could bring that handle round again. You never stopped on a junction. You could be stuck, waiting for someone to come and give you a nudge to get you moving again.

If you were stuck on the dead you had to wait until the next bloke came along to push you off. People up top would start stamping their feet,

A crew manhandles around twelve tons of M class car which is stuck on the dead at Vauxhall in 1920.

might call you a bloody fool for getting stuck, fidgety lot they were. Although you lost all your lights at night, the streets were well lit up and the tram would show up as a black object in the middle of the road. Some places were worse than others. If you were stuck on a straight someone could just come up behind you and push you straight off, but on a bend or at the Elephant and Castle it could be a bit awkward. Suppose you came up behind someone stuck on a bend, you had to push him a little bit and let go, he'd swing round a bit and you would too, you'd push him a little bit more and so on. You'd keep touching him, touching him, gently, until once he'd got his plough on the live again, away he'd go. You had to be careful if you were pushing, not to get stuck on the dead yourself. That could happen up at the Elephant. On some bends, like at Saint Leonard's Church, there used to be a long wooden pole strapped to the railings, and if you couldn't get right up tight to the other tram, buffer to buffer, your Conductor would hold the pole — it had a handle on it — between you both and you'd push him off with it. We used the old

pole many a time. Over the North-side, over Poplar and all that way where the traffic was very very heavy, nearly every tram carried its own pole because, if a horse and cart broke down on the track with a load on, the Conductor could get down and put the pole onto your axle-box and then onto the cart and you gradually pushed him off.

Many a time I've helped people up Brixton Hill like that. There was a hole in the middle of our buffer where you fixed your tow-rope. If there was a horse and cart stuck there on the track we'd say, 'Driver, bring your nose-bag round,' and you'd stick your pinch bar upside down in the hole, put the nose-bag between the pinch bar and the headlight so that you wouldn't smash your glass, then you'd creep up behind him and gradually give him a push up the hill. We used to say, 'Get hold of the horse's head and run him up the hill,' and he'd get the horse on the trot up to the top. A lot of things were done unofficially.

On the overhead you didn't have to worry

A Clapham E/1 waits in Newington Causeway in 1936 before crossing the junction; the Driver leans on his controller, the Pointsman on his lever. Ten years and a war later, a Feltham waits at the same spot.

about dead sections, because they were so short, and there weren't many junctions. Of course, the pole always trailed behind you, and there was a rule that if you had two poles it was always the offside one that was up and the nearside one that was tied down at the front.

Sometimes you could do ten solid hours stuck on the front, no glass, no meal-relief, eating your sandwiches as you went along and putting them on the stairs beside you between-times. I used to put my time-board on top of them to stop them blowing away. Ten solid hours, even longer in my Dad's day. When I look back I think, how did we stick it? But we had to, there was always someone else would take your job on if you didn't want it. Before vestibule glasses went in I've been soaked to the skin, but then when they gave us the Felthams we used to laugh at the rain. Mind you, even with vestibules, if the louvres were loose the wind would blow through, but in the summer we could open the side windows on a Feltham, or even give signals through them.

We couldn't give proper hand-signals on a Standard, and we were never instructed to, but we used to keep our eyes open. At the Plough Clapham, for instance, if you were turning right into Long Road on the 34's you'd put your right hand out if there was any traffic about, but you couldn't signal a left turn because of the staircase. If you were turning left your mate might put his hand out on the back.

After I'd been driving for a few years they put a mirror on the nearside of the Standards, but they wouldn't stick open as a fixture in case they got knocked off by passing vehicles. There was a little handle screwed on and the Driver could just put the mirror out to check behind him and then it would close up again. A lot of blokes used to put a match-box behind the handle so that it always kept open, but the mirrors were always getting knocked off. If an Inspector saw you with a match-box cocking that mirror out you were in trouble. He'd book that straight away. But we more or less had to have a disruption to have those mirrors put on. In the old days you put one foot on the staircase and looked round the hand-rail if you wanted to see if anyone was getting on or off. We fought for mirrors and we got them in the end.

We used to get horrible black fogs, pea-soupers. I remember the time when we had a big fog coming down from Kennington, and I was just creep-creep-creeping along the road, you'd go two or three yards along the road then, bang-bang, the bell. A few yards more, bang-bang, and so on. If you stopped and wondered just where you were, you'd find you had a load of motors and horse-vans behind you and you had to lead them along the way. But trams kept running in the densest fog, when everything else packed up. We couldn't pack up, we had to go on, because people relied on us. Well after I started on the trams they gave us fog lights, up beside the destination box, but we used to forget they were there, they weren't very effective, not in the sort of fog we had in those days, when you couldn't see more than a few feet sometimes.

When I started driving in 1923 there weren't any traffic signals or pedestrian crossings; we watched them grow. I think it was through me being a bit cheeky over a pedestrian crossing that I got pinched up at Streatham in 1936. Two women were standing about a foot from the offside kerb, on the crossing, talking. They weren't walking across, I didn't take any notice of them, but I saw they were standing there, jawing. I didn't know there was a copper behind me on a motor-bike. When I got to Crown Lane

Fog on the Embankment in December 1920.

this copper got off his bike, out came his book, and he said he was reporting me for failing to give free and uninterrupted passage to pedestrians on a crossing. He said I should have stopped my tram to let the women cross over, but I told him they were just standing there talking. Of course, I'm arguing a point with a copper, aren't I, and I'm losing my temper. My mate's getting a bit hooked, because he's got a load of fares on.

Anyway, he reported me for a summons and I had to go to court over on Lavender Hill. I saw the Union solicitor, explained everything to him, and he told me my case wouldn't be coming up till about three o'clock. 'Shan't be long,' he said, 'I've got to pop over the road.'

I watched where he was going, he went over in the pub. A little while afterwards he came back. 'I've been considering your case,' he said, 'I think you're on the wrong side of the fence.' 'You're a bright one to come and defend me,' I said, 'I haven't even been in yet and I'm being accused already.' When I went into the court I never said a dickey-bird, the Union solicitor said it all, and the magistrate asked if anything was known about me. The Clerk of the Court said, 'No, but he holds so-many safety-first medals,' I forget how many. Then the magistrate said to the copper, 'Do you know everything about these pedestrian crossings?' 'Oh, yes' said the copper. 'Well, you're a lucky man,' said the magistrate, 'because I don't.' I got away with it, ten-bob costs, that was all. Anyway, I made ten-bob out of that, because I got ten-bob out of the Union and ten-bob out of our Wheel Club, so I was ten-bob in pocket. Mind you, I lost a day's pay over it, and that was more than ten-bob.

We used to pay about thrupence a week for what we called our Wheel Club. If you got pinched, they paid your fine. If a Conductor took a bad half-a-crown he'd keep it in his pocket until pay-day, then he'd get the bloke who ran the Club to break it or bend it. Then he'd get his half-a-crown back from behind the counter. Often, though, a Conductor would get rid of them. If ever you had a bad two-bob or a dud half-a-crown in your change, you could always get rid of it. Give it to your mate! *(3)*

As far as I can remember the tram never

---

3. Thrupence, 3d, converts to 1.25 new pence
 Two-bob, 2 shillings, converts to 10 new pence
Half-a-crown, 2s 6d, converts to 12.5 new pence
Ten-bob, ten shillings, converts to 50 new pence
A basic day's pay in 1936 was 13s. or 65 new pence

altered the lights when they first started. If you were stuck on a red light you had to wait for a motor or something to come by and go over the strip. Late at night, when there might not be any motors about, the Conductor might run along and jump on the strip, and I've often jumped on it myself.

A fitter works on the roller-bearing axle-box of an E/3 tram in October 1937. The E/3 was a development of the E/1, introduced in 1930. Between the wheels can be seen a magnetic brake shoe.

Our service brake was the magnetic-brake, and there were four on each tram. Your magnetic-brake worked off your motors, and when you shut the controller handle off and came round on your brake notches the juice generated in your motors went straight into your electro-magnets and forced them down on the track. The pressure of those magnets was four thousand pounds on each shoe, a terrific pressure, and if you got cut up a bit and had to jump on your magnetic-brake and your sand I'm not going to say where your passengers would end up, but they'd be shot out of their seats in no uncertain manner. On a Standard you could be travelling along at forty miles-an-hour and you could very near stop the tram in its own length. In those days there wasn't the motor stuff about, just horses and carts mainly, but even so there were times when you had to put your magnetic-brakes on heavy.

As your magnets came down onto the track they pulled the brake blocks onto the wheels at the same time, but your magnetic-brake was no good under about four miles-an-hour, so you had to use your hand-brake to finish it off. This was a handle on a column on your right hand side which you worked with your right hand. It had a ratchet to hold it while you tightened it up, and a dog to release it at the bottom. This worked on chains underneath the platform, which were connected through rods and levers to brake blocks on each wheel.

A magnetic-brake on the track should be sufficiently above the rail for you to put three penny pieces in underneath the magnet. Now, if you had that magnet too high, when you brought your controller handle round they'd go down with a plonk. We'd have to phone up the Depot from a section-box, and a man would come out with a spanner when we got to Clapham and lower them a shade. Then you could get what we called 'twisted magnets.' Somehow you'd know your brake wasn't working properly, and you'd get down and have a look round and you'd spot a twisted magnet. This was often caused by a Driver putting his magnets on going over the points, or it could be a bolt in the track or a dropped joint in the lines, you couldn't always find the cause of it, but the shoe would get twisted as it came down. You'd get half your magnet going down onto the rail, trying to make a brake, and the other end of the shoe would catch the stone setts. It was dangerous, it could pull you off the road, so you always changed your tram straight away, and took it very slowly until you did. It often happened. Another thing we used to get sometimes was what we called a 'slack block,' when the brake shoes were worn so thin that you had a job to hold your tram still on an incline with the hand-brake.

If the track was a bit greasy, perhaps a bit muddy or dead or wet leaves on it, you used your sand-pedal to help the wheels grip, because if you started skidding with the wheels locked the magnetic-brakes cut out straight away and then you were in trouble. I remember I had a collision many, many years ago, an old boy with a horse and cart with one of the very high dickeys they used to have in those days. I was on a Standard coming down from the Elephant towards Kennington and there he was, on the track in front of me. I gave him several bangs on the bell, then put my magnetic-brake on, but there was nothing there, nothing at all, the leaves were all squashed on the track. I walloped into the back of the van and the old boy disappeared off the seat into the back of the wagon. It didn't hurt him a lot, but I got away with that, then while I was taking particulars another car came along and hit the back of me. There were five cars in all in collision that morning. The Inspector who was on duty at Kennington had come up by then. All he did was to just get his knife out and he scraped the dead leaves off the running-rail for evidence, and that was what cleared us all. You see, even if your wheels didn't lock, dead leaves could build up on the rail under your magnetic shoes and stop them gripping. It was an impossible situation, really.

Sand was carried in hoppers under the end seats in the lower saloon, one on each side, and you always checked before you took your car out to see that you had enough. At the bottom of each hopper was a shutter, and when you pressed your sand-pedal it opened and let sand down the sand-pipe so that it fell onto the rail just in front of your wheels. You had four sand-pipes and four hoppers, two at each end. If I thought I was going to need a lot of sand I used to take two or three extra bags out with me in the morning, because you relied on that sand sometimes.

Back in the wartime, when they took the clippies on, if they wanted to go to the toilet some of the clever Drivers used to say, 'Don't worry over that girl, lift the seat and do it in there.' True. Then you'd come to a tight corner and the sand wouldn't come out. There was nothing worse than wet sand, and it stank like blazes. It really got so bad that we had to complain about it. We knew what was going on, and you don't like shopping your mates, but in the end we had to do it, it was so dangerous, especially in wet weather, because it could isolate your magnetic-brake.

Just before you got to a terminus you'd nip up and change the indicator to show 'EMBANKMENT' or wherever you were going, and your mate would walk through turning the seats back upstairs, closing the door at one end and opening it at the other. When you got to the terminus your mate would hop off and take his pole down while you put yours up. He'd swing it round if there was only one, and that could be dangerous at times. Of course, if you only had one pole, at night all the lights went out when you were swinging it round. If you had two poles you were supposed to put the second one up on the wire before your mate pulled his down.

Then you let your step down, slid your door back and locked it open, dropped your sand-pedals and put the hook on your hand-brake, otherwise people would start playing with it, the handle could swing round and give them a nasty knock on the elbow. It was a crime if you forgot that hook. Then you took the controller key up to the front, pulled the step up and put the chain across. It was another crime for a Driver not to pull the step up at his end, in case someone got knocked down. Then you'd pull your sand-pedals up and give them a twist, there were two at each end on a Standard.

Some of the gong pedals were so worn that they used to sink below the floor, and you had to heel it. We used to get an old rubber heel, put two nails through it, and drop that on top of the pedal so that you could get a good old punch on it. Often you'd forget to take it with you when you came off, many's the one I made. At one time there were so many about that the chaps used to leave them on the table in the ticket office so that you could take one if you hadn't got one.

Crowds board a Service 4 car on the Embankment in August 1934, **right**. *The hand-brake is correctly restrained, and behind the controller lean a point-iron and pinch-bar. The trolley-rope is tied onto the stair-rail, as rope-cleats are not yet fitted to all cars. Beside the destination box is the fog-lamp.*

With a deft flick of the wrist, **below**, *the Conductor slips the trolley-rope into the retaining pigtail after raising his trolley-pole. From the top of the traction standard to his left, there runs a feeder cable to the overhead wires. Purley, March 1951.*

59

Then you were ready to go. At night-time you had a red change-over switch to switch over your lights. Up until the War we didn't have a red rear light, *(4)* and all the change-over switch did was to put the front light on at one end and the canopy light on at the Conductor's end, ready for the return journey. A rear light wasn't necessary before the War because a tram was well illuminated, anyone could see it going along the road. Then they put the wartime masks on the headlights and incorporated a flap on it that gave you a red light, so they altered the wiring so that both headlights were on at the same time, one showing a white light, the other the red light, according to how you set that flap. They left the masks on after the War.

During the Second World War, when the clippies were on, they used to go up in the air with the trolley-rope until they got the knack of it. The springs were very powerful. Many's the time I've had to say, 'Come down out of it, girl, let me do it.' We used to just let the rope slip through our fingers putting the trolley up, but they didn't know this and gripped it, and up in the air they'd go.

A tram-driver had to be a skilled man on the job. People used to think that all you had to do was turn two handles, but you had to be electrically-minded to a degree. If a tram broke down you had to be mechanically-minded enough to know where to look for the fault. It could be in your controller, it could be in your motor, it could be in your plough or even your plough-carrier. If your tram broke down you had to do your utmost to keep the service going. If a bus breaks down you can just leave it in the nearside of the road — and a good bus-driver always breaks down near a coffee shop — but you couldn't do that with a tram.

A good tram-driver always carried a copper nail in his pocket, always. I don't know where we got them from, but we always carried one. If you had that plough-lead burn out, your tram would come to a stand-still, so you'd get the rubber gloves from the tool-box, open up the hatch in the lower saloon floor, cross the two broken plough-leads over, and drive the copper nail right through so that you had your connection. That would carry you to the Depot. That was an old tram-driver's wrinkle.

Another time you might be going along the road and suddenly you'd hear a rattling from underneath the tram. Your tram would come to a stand-still, and there would be your plough-carrier down on the tracks. Straightaway you'd phone Control at Kennington for the breakdown gang — there was a section-box with a phone in it every half-mile along the track, and we knew where they were — then you'd do what you could to help the gang before they got there. You'd get out the rope with the two hooks on it, ready to pull out the channel-irons from underneath.

---

4. This isn't strictly true, for illuminated stencil number holders were fitted beside the stairs on all LCCT trams during or just after the 1914 War; these holders incorporated a small rearward facing red lens. The fittings were removed in 1939 and the stencil numbers placed beside the platforms.

Car 120, with a broken plough-carrier at Streatham Hill Station in March 1951. It was pushed thus to Brixton Hill Depot.

179K was one of several Karrier breakdown Tenders bought by the LCCT in 1929/30. Here it is seen at Holloway Depot in 1948, fitted with a tower for attending to the trolleybus overhead.

When the gang came along, they'd get the flare on the plough, cut it through and let it drop into the conduit pit, then you could pull the channel-irons out.

Or you might be driving along and all of a sudden, bang-bang-bang-bang from the wheels. So you'd stop and have a look and there was a bolt or big nut jammed in the running-rail and you'd just been over it. You had to try and dig it out with a pinch bar or point iron, but if you couldn't shift it, it was on the blower straight away to Control and get the gang out, and they'd take a sledge-hammer and chisel to it. Those breakdown blokes weren't fussy with the old sledge-hammer. They'd give it a whack and that was that. I heard that a bolt shot out that way once and went straight through someone's window.

There were breakdown gangs at Camberwell, in Clapham and over at New Cross, and it was amazing how quickly they could get to a breakdown. They'd come all round the back-doubles, they used to shove along, the police didn't take any notice of them. The lorry'd hardly stopped and the chaps were down having a look, trying to find the quickest way out of the trouble. If they saw they couldn't sort it out as quickly as they should do, out came their sledge-hammers, bang-bang-bang, didn't matter what they broke so long as they could get the tram away. (5) Then they'd get the tram behind to push you to the nearest crossover, stop another tram coming the other way, get him to back over, and then he'd tow you home. It was all well thought out. If there were no trams about, they'd push you with the lorry to the nearest crossover, then wait there for a tram to tow you in. Some Drivers didn't like doing it, although they had to, but I didn't mind it myself, it was all experience.

When you were in training as a tram-driver you used to be told, 'Use an eye and a half for where you're going, but keep half an eye down on the track,' but we couldn't, except when there wasn't much about. In those days, of course, there were steam lorries and horses and carts, and tools and all sorts of things would fall off them, and this caused us a bit of bother sometimes, because if the road surface was bad the other traffic used to follow the tram-tracks. But often I did spot things. I daresay I've still got tools in my shed that I picked up off the tracks.

Every now and then a plough would catch fire. As often as not some rubbish in the conduit would catch in a collector-shoe, arcing would set it alight, and the fire would quickly spread to the plough which was wood. All along the lower saloon floor were various hatches, for fitters, wiring, getting at the motors and such, but the middle one was over the plough, above the channel-irons. When you opened it you could see the two bus-bars faced with copper strips, with insulated plugs at the ends to which the car-leads were attached. The plough came in automatically from the off-side at the changepit, sliding on the channel irons, with the two contacts at the top coming in between those bus-bars, which were sprung, and making

5. The sledge-hammer was an essential item of LCCT equipment, and for very practical reasons. One tram disabled for ten minutes on Brixton Hill in the rush-hour could delay fifteen following trams, or up to 1200 people. It was in everyone's interest that disabled trams be made towable as quickly as possible.

In depots equipped with conduits, the tee-rails were placed at the sides of the pits. Here can be seen the greased channel-irons, from which hangs the plough. Wandsworth Depot, October 1937.

contact. If the fire was in the top of your plough you put sand on it there and then, but if it was down where you couldn't see it you were in trouble. You had to get to a dead-hatchway as quickly as you could. They were across the slot-rail, there was a break in the tee-rails there, and you had special keys to open them in your tool-box. Then you'd get the hatchway up, put the car over it, pull the bus-bars off and pull the burning plough out with the ropes from your tool-box. At one time, with the old type of plough, you had to disconnect your car-leads too. You chucked the plough on the platform at the back — you could put it out with a bit of sand — and put the spare plough in from under the stairs. Then you got the tram behind you to nudge you onto the live tee-rail, put the hatches back and you were off. You might have a line of trams behind you by then, so of course, you'd got the road. It was a hell of a job to change a plough, and I always hated it. If it happened at night you hadn't got any lights. An old driver who'd done it a time or two before could change a plough in about ten minutes.

In those days tram-men were pals, you'd help one another. A chap would come up behind you, he wanted to get you out of his way, perhaps he'd be finished when he got to Telford. They'd all come and give you a hand, and you'd do the same for them when they were in trouble. I only had a burning plough once, but I was fortunate inasmuch as it was just this side of Kennington, between the Horns and the corner of Brixton Road, where we used to turn out. There was a hatchway there. I had a burning plough coming down from the Elephant, and I'd got as far as Kennington when old Regulator Jones — he was one of the finest old gentleman on the road — he came over just as I pulled up at this hatchway, because he'd had a phone message from the sub-station that there was a tram coming down knocking the juice off, which it would do. 'Are you the one in trouble ?' he said. 'Yes, guv'nor, I've got a burning plough.' Up came the hatchway, in and out, he was down on his hands and knees wriggling about. Up came the bus-bars, out came the plough, in went the other one, 'Give us a little touch, Driver, very gently, right, away you go.'

Another thing that could go wrong was the motors. Each Standard had two motors, one on each bogie, number one motor and number two motor, and every now and then one might burn out and you had to cut it out. On the Dick Kerr

62

A controller being tested, Wandsworth Depot, October 1937.

fingers for number two motor. You pulled them back and gave a nut behind the fingers half a turn to stop the fingers flying back. On an older type of Westinghouse controller you had to double up a dry ticket to break the contact. On later controllers there was a sprung lever which held the finger back to cut a motor out. Mind you, with one motor cut out, the car would start with a jerk because you had no series notches, it wouldn't start until you got round to the fifth notch, which was parallel, we'd have to warn the passengers, especially because the magnetic-brakes would come down very fierce then. If you did lose a motor you'd put your passengers on the car behind if you could, put up 'SPECIAL', take it out of service and run it into the Depot, but if you had to change ends you had to remember to cut the motor out on the other controller as well.

controller all you had to do was to shut your controller off and use the key on a stud round the back of the controller, turn it one way for number one motor out, the other way for number two motor out. A very old type of tram had a Westinghouse controller. We used to have to knock our breakers out, take the shield off, find out what had gone wrong, and pull out three fingers for number one motor and four

So let's suppose you've tried everything — you can't even drive it from the back end — and you can't get it moving again, you'd get the next tram to push you, but the first thing you'd do was to put the tow-rope on the back of your tram and the front of his. That's where I went wrong on my test in 1923, because I forgot to mention that. While he was pushing you, you had to do the braking for his tram and yours. In another case, if the breakdown was on the opposite track, an Inspector might stop you at the cross-over beforehand, tell you to pull over and run up wrong line — transfer all your passengers first, of course — and then you'd put your tow-rope on him and pull him back to the Depot. Now this time he does the braking and you're working the juice and doing signals. You'd leave the doors open between you so that he could see

A broken plough-carrier — one of the angle-irons is missing — at Streatham Hill in 1950; the breakdown tender has shunted a disabled tram into a position where it can be attached to the following car, which, in its turn, will push it to the nearest depot. The disabled car — from Purley Depot — correctly displays SPECIAL.

Removing the wire tow-rope, Telford Avenue, July 1948.

through your tram, wave him down if you wanted him to brake, and wave him on when it was clear again. If you did the braking he might run into the back of you, although you weren't supposed to do more than six miles-an-hour using the tow-rope. The wire tow-ropes had been made out of the old original Brixton Hill cable. When they electrified the road, the cable was chopped up into four-foot lengths with a big eye on each end. There was one on every tram.

After a breakdown you had to let one tram get away, twenty or thirty yards away, before you started your tram, and the same with the one behind you, in case you blew the breakers out in the sub-station. If you had a big breakdown on one track, something they couldn't shift quickly, they had to work a single-track on the other track while they were sorting it out. For instance, there was a crossover at Water Lane and another at New Park Road, and you might work single-track with an Inspector at each end. You'd wait at one end until the single was clear, then you'd reverse back over the crossover — there might be two or three trams together — and you'd all go through on the wrong line, past whatever it was that was causing the hold-up. The Inspector would give the last Driver a bit of wood or something, and then he'd give it to the Inspector at the other end. Then, when you'd gone through and had crossed over onto the double-track again, that Inspector would send another two or three trams back with the bit of wood again, and so on.

Very often we used to have trouble with hot axle-boxes, and they used to really stink. Lack of lubrication caused it. The axle boxes were packed out with cotton waste and then flooded with thick oil, but if one had been overlooked it would start squeaking. If it was squeaking too bad, we used to get a Regulator to phone in to change the car at Telford Avenue. Then a foreman would come over, 'What's the matter, what are you changing for?' 'Can't you smell it?' we'd say. It used to make us feel sick. Even the passengers would moan over them sometimes if you had one that was too bad. They might even catch fire, nothing serious, because the truck was all iron and steel and they wouldn't catch the bodywork, but they used to smoke — thick black smoke — and you might get a little flame come out sometimes. Then you'd get motorists going by, toot-toot-toot, but we knew about it, we could smell it.

I only once had a derailment, down at Magee Street, Kennington, on the crossover. We were working a single, I was relief on the nighter, someone had gone sick. The front truck went over the points, but the rear one didn't, I expect it was caused by bad points or taking them too fast, but it was nothing serious. I told the passengers what was happening, told them we'd have a lorry down presently, and turned them off while they pulled it back on. The gang soon came down, hooked the breakdown lorry on the buffers and pulled me back onto the track. Then we picked up the passengers again and away we

Trouble on the road could mean anything from a minor mishap to the occasional major incident. Outside New Cross Depot a faulty destination blind is given attention, August 1950, **right**. Hilly Route car 120, **centre**, derailed at the Elephant & Castle, about to be attached to a towing car; 120's plough rests in the slot rail beside it. Car 770 impressively derailed, **below**, in Lewisham High Road, September 1911.

went, hoping for no more derailments. I never heard any more about it. On the report we always put, 'Reason unknown,' everything was unknown.

You used to get quite a few derailments on the bend at the end of Southcroft Road. They used to take that bend too fast. I was always cocum on that bend, four miles-an-hour was quite fast enough for me. Years ago one turned over there, just after the Mitcham Lane had been opened. I remember them laying the tram-track on Mitcham Lane, when I was a boy at school. In our summer holidays us kids didn't know what to do with ourselves, we used to walk to Streatham and watch them laying the track. All I can remember was seeing the little trenches where they were putting the cradles in to take the lines, little dreaming that I'd ever drive a tram down there.

Streatham change-pit, looking south, on the last day it operated. The Conductor of the Standard car is putting his pole under the trolley-hook. Behind him, the Conductor of the Feltham is flicking his trolley-rope to free it from the pigtail before lowering the pole. The plough-shifter waits, ready to fork the plough under the Feltham as it rolls past him.

On a lot of routes there was a change-pit, where you threw your plough out and put your pole up on the wire. We had one at the entrance to Brixton Hill depot — the old trailer shed — there was another down at Gleneagles Road on the 16 road and one at the end of Effra Road by Saint Matthew's Church for the Norwood routes.

When you got to the throw-out, coming from London, you'd have to stop just this side of it to change the change-over switch. On a Standard it was under the stairs at one end, and you had to take your controller key out to operate it, so everything was switched off while you did it. Sometimes the change-over switch might be at the other end, so I'd have to take the controller key back there to operate it, but if you had a Conductor with a very strong grip he'd call out, 'OK ?' and do it himself. The change-over switch on a Feltham wouldn't operate unless your line-switch was out, and there were different positions for number one pole and number two pole. If you tried to change over without your line-switch out, you could lose it. Sometimes you might lose your line-switch — it might burn out or something — but then you had two wooden blocks, up in the cab, and you could open the line-switch cupboard and slip a block between two brass terminals and that would keep you going. The line-switch cupboard was out on the platform behind the cab, down near the floor, and it could be awkward if you had a crowd of people on the platform and you had to move them out of the way to put your blocks in. If anything went wrong you'd shout out to your mate, 'Put the blocks in the other end,' and he'd do his while you did this one. If you lost your line-switch — which very often did happen — you put the blocks in and still had your connection.

So, while you're operating the change-over switch your mate would be out the back putting the pole up, or if you only had one pole he'd be swinging it round on the rope. Then he gives you a bell and off you go, but you're on your trolley now. The plough shoots out as the slot-rail crosses over the offside running-rail, because the plough-carrier was well greased.

Going the other way, say, coming up from Purley, you knew from experience just where to put your buffer, then the chap would put the fork with the plough in it, the ends of the fork resting on your channel-irons, he'd bang your side-board, then you'd go forward, very, very, gently. When the plough was in you'd hear his fork tap on the ground as he got it out. Then you just stopped again to change over from trolley to plough, your mate would pull the pole down, and you were on the conduit.

The change-pit was worked by light-duty men, someone who was sick perhaps, and no more fit for driving, but if it was his day off they'd send a spare driver down. I've done it often, it was a piece of cake, all you had to do was to take the ploughs out and put them back in. Any spare ploughs, last thing at night, you'd chuck on the front of trams as they came through on their way to the Depot. You'd put a plough in, 'Hang on a minute, Driver,' you might chuck one up on the platform, that's the way to get rid of them. You never left anything there overnight, even took the fork back with you.

Then in the morning they'd all come out again. You didn't necessarily have to get on the first tram, as long as you were there for that first one from Croydon that needed to be ploughed. You'd get the first Driver going through to Purley to drop one or two off for you, and so on, he'd shoot a plough out for you anyway, but it would be an hour before he got back, unless there were any Croydon Corporation cars coming up in the meantime. You always had to keep a few ploughs in hand, because although in theory you gave one out and got one back alternately, you might get a hold-up coming from London — particularly in the rush hour — which meant you weren't getting them in. Don't forget, each tram was supposed to carry a spare plough as well, so you were never really stuck. You dropped them into the pit through a hatchway at the end of the slot-rail where the tee-rails were dead. They used to have an old cupboard at the change-pit sometimes, to sit on when there weren't any trams. You might keep an old pair of gloves in it. The regular plough-shifters used to make them themselves.

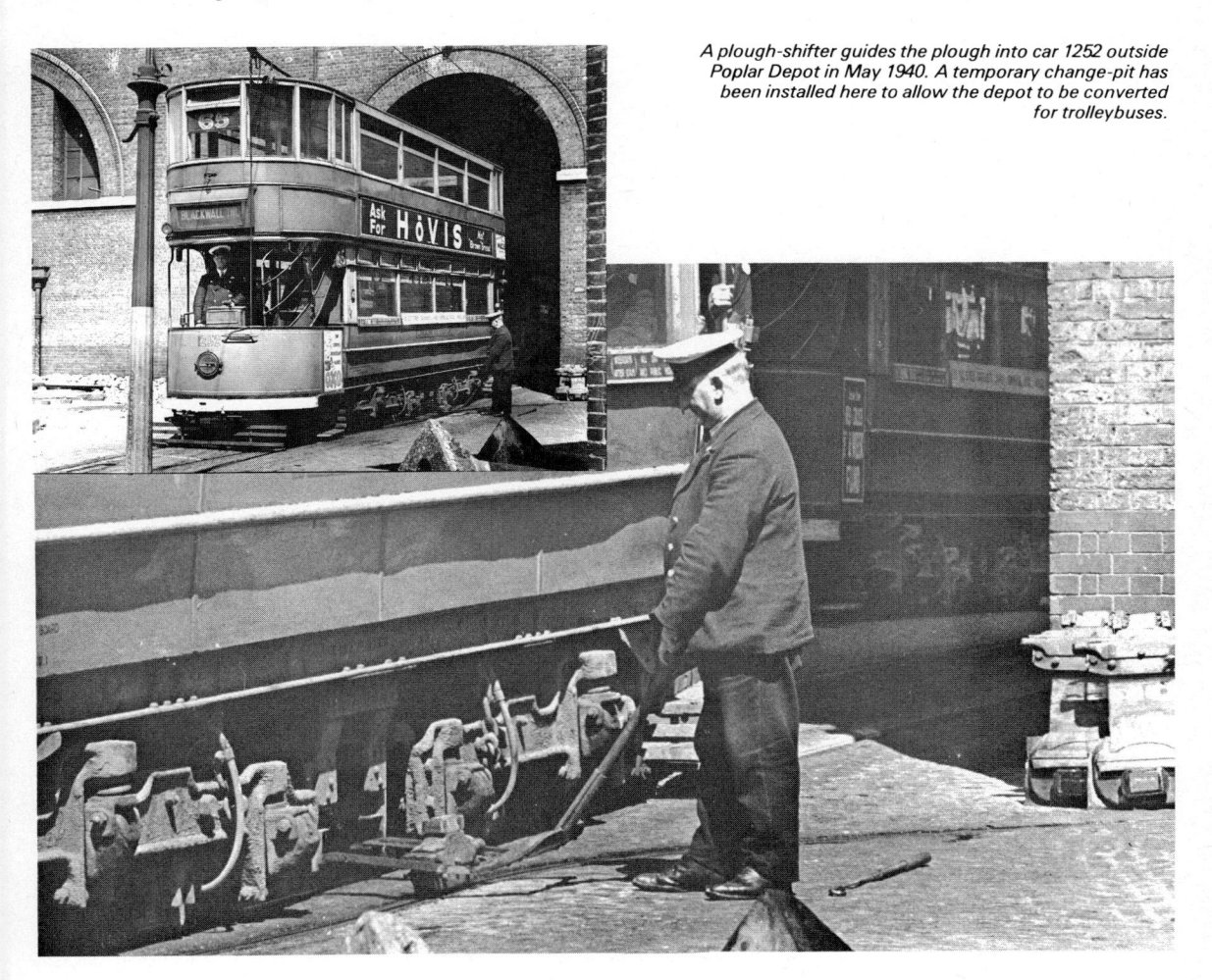

A plough-shifter guides the plough into car 1252 outside Poplar Depot in May 1940. A temporary change-pit has been installed here to allow the depot to be converted for trolleybuses.

The LCCT method of operating trams was labour intensive, and as time went on and wages increased, this became increasingly disadvantageous. Throughout the working day, every facing point at every conduit junction was controlled by a Pointsman. At Vauxhall in 1936, there were three Pointsmen, two of whom can be seen here, and a Regulator who stands beside a section-box and dead-poles. Inset at the top, looking south at Camberwell Green in late 1939. Inset at the bottom, the Elephant & Castle in 1930. Pointsmen were often platform staff transferred to 'light duties' for health reasons.

68

At most junctions there was a pointsman who stood on the pavement pulling a lever and changing the points, according to where the next car had to go. At some complicated junctions, like the Elephant, say, you might have several pointsmen, each with his own set of points. They worked right up to the last car, and we rarely had to change points ourselves except at crossovers. When I was a spare driver I was put on points sometimes. They might say, 'Points, you, tomorrow, Stockwell Road.' You could get soaked right through to the skin on points, because you were working in the open all the time, unless you were able to shelter in a shop doorway between cars, but eventually somebody gave us tarpaulin huts. Before that we used to have an old box to sit on on the pavement, and we had to provide that ourselves if I remember.

My Dad ended up as a pointsman. He had his finger chopped off round about 1930 under Charing Cross Railway Bridge, when a piece of the bridge fell down. He'd stopped to let some people cross over the road in front of his tram from the island onto the pathway, and had his right hand on the hand-brake. There wasn't a vestibule on the tram — in those days the hand-brakes had handles that stuck out over the dash — and it just happened that his hand was over the edge of the dash. Just as he started off again, down came a piece of the bridge, a big lump of iron, and chopped his finger right off. It was just bad luck. They took him off driving straight away, I don't know why, because it was his left hand that did all the work, and put him on points. He dropped ten bob a week over that, although he got four hundred pounds compensation. He was at Saint Leonard's Church mostly, but sometimes they put him at other places, like at County Hall where the 14's used to turn off onto the Albert Embankment. He died in 1936. He'd always enjoyed his job.

Not until 1946 was the first canvas shelter for Pointsmen introduced. It was placed outside County Hall, **right**, *where around 1914,* **below**, *a pointsman leans on his lever.*

When you went into the Depot in the morning you went into the office, the Depot Inspector signed the sheet, and you picked up your board and plates. *(6)* Then you looked down the list to see what number tram you were taking out.

Of course, some duties took-on on the road. At Telford we changed over outside the Depot, and it was the same at Clapham, except for the 28's when you were taken off at the bottom of Cedars Road, and then you were allowed travelling time up to the Depot, a quarter of an hour I think it was. You were paid for that. At one time you lost a day's pay if you were even one minute late on duty. As you went into the Depot you might see another Driver taking your tram out — there were always spare men waiting — and you were told to go home and get a good night's sleep. Two lates in the same week and you were up in front of the Divisional Superintendent and given a dressing down.

So let's say you're starting from the Depot in the morning. Once the Driver had found his tram, first thing he did was to make sure nobody was working underneath it, and he'd look up to make sure his four switches were out — on some trams there were five — before he opened up his controller to try it. There had been cases where cars had gone down the traverser pit while a Driver was checking his controllers. It was a terrific crime if that happened, and both Drivers were in trouble, the one who put it away the previous night for not knocking the breakers out, and the one who'd taken it out for not looking to see that they were out. I don't remember it ever happening at Telford Avenue, but it happened twice while I was at Clapham, and of course it blocked trams in the Depot until the breakdown gang got it out.

So you'd try your controllers — the key was left on a seat just inside the lower saloon — to see if they were running easily or stiff, and you'd pick up your life-guards at both ends. Then you'd put your indicators right, PURLEY, NORBURY, WESTMINSTER or wherever you were going. Then you'd put the switches in, because if you had a Feltham you had to turn on a big switch up under the canopy to get your compressor going. *(7)* You'd hang about, you'd hear it building up, until it switched itself off. You'd look at your sand, make sure your hoppers were full and your sand-pedals working. If the hoppers were empty you filled them up and put three or four spare bags of sand under the staircase, or more if it was inclement weather. In the summer we didn't worry so much, but an experienced Driver knew that his sand was his best friend.

Then you'd have a last look round, raise your front step and lower the back one, make sure your pedals were at the right end, and onto the traverser. You never moved your tram off the

---

6. Time-board — with all one car's times and routings for the day — and route plates, the blue enamelled plates referred to in Chapter 3.

7. That is, the air-compressor; Felthams were fitted with air-brakes and air-operated front doors. The only other air-braked tram in London (not counting temporary experiments) was the LCCT's Bluebird.

Telford Avenue Depot — the old cable-tram shed — in 1947.

The traverser ('trav' as in tram, and shorten the following syllables) was a railed platform which carried trams sideways along a traverser-pit between entry and depot tracks. It saved both space and complicated conduit point-work. This is Wandsworth Depot in October 1937, where there are already signs of precautions being taken against possible future air-raids.

traverser until the traverser driver gave you a bang on the side, then away you'd go, out of the Depot — check your magnetic-brake, and your air-brake on a Feltham — and then you just followed the instructions on your time-board. At Telford, as you went out, the Conductor had to hold back the lever for the catch-points because it was a bit of a slope. At Brixton Hill you had to stop on the way out to pick up your plough. Running into Telford, and Clapham if I remember, if you had a car with two poles, they were supposed to be both over the back of the tram as you went in.

When you put the tram away at night, you'd put it over the pit, shut the controller off and knock the breakers out, then you'd put the controller key on the corner seat inside, where the driver next morning would find it. Then you'd get down and just give the pilot-gates a kick to drop the lifeguard trays, that was orders, to make sure that they worked. If you had a Feltham you knocked the compressor switch off. When I was a young driver we were taught how to do things. If the night foreman went round and saw a tram without its trays lowered, the Driver would be traced and disciplined. All these things had died out by the end, although they were still a habit with me, it was drummed into us, we did it automatically. During the night, down under the pits, they would clean the tray, oil it and grease it, so that it just needed a touch to release it. On a windy day we used to get a bag of sand and put it on the pedal, because sometimes the wind used to blow the pilot-gate back when you were going along, and trip the tray. Sometimes that would stop it and sometimes it wouldn't.

We knew a lot of tricks. On the old-fashioned Standards the pilot-gate was a bit wide and sometimes something would catch the top wooden slat, break it and knock it off. So you'd keep it carefully in your pocket, and when you were putting the tram away in the Depot, nobody looking, just put it back on and give it a couple of taps with the controller key. They always broke splintered. When the car examiner came round he wouldn't notice it. If you got a scratch mark on your paintwork — perhaps something might cut you up — when you got to the other end you'd just dip a sand-bag in the mud and rub it on the scratch so that it looked old. You had to do these things, because it saved writing out a report.

Car-cleaners at New Cross Depot around 1906, when labour was cheap and plentiful, **above.** *In the Second World War, men were scarce and their jobs were frequently taken by women, although there were no female tram-drivers in London as there were in certain other parts of the country. A car-washer at Abbey Wood Depot,* **below.**

At one time they used to wash the trams on the pits at night. There were tower wagons which ran backwards and forwards beside the pits. One man did the downstairs outside of the tram and another did up top, with buckets of water and leathers. Even the windows used to sparkle in those days. Then they brought the automatic washers in, and directly you ran in on the wash the Driver had to be pretty slippy in stopping it and get inside and shut the door quick, otherwise he'd get drowned. The chap up the top there would pull the lever and the water would spray out. Then, after he'd turned the water off, men would come out with long brooms, they'd dip their brooms in what we called pickle — it smelt like vinegar — and they used to rub it up and down. That used to dry of itself, it left no smears, it was very good. Then you'd pull onto the traverser and drive it onto the pits.

Up until the 1914 War they had brass-boys, young lads of seventeen, eighteen and nineteen whose job was to keep all the brass clean. That was night work. At the top of the hand-rail on the platforms was a smooth collar they had to keep it clean, and the tops of the Westinghouse controllers — in those days they were solid brass tops and even they had to be polished — the hand-rails all the way up the stairs and the coin tester at the top. If there was any dirt anywhere they were for it. There was an old Driver I knew at Norwood who started off as a brass-boy, it used to look smashing in those days, but time went on and the brass-boys left or got the sack on economy purposes, and after that the brass all went black. Then they had an idea of staining some of the rails black, but passengers complained that they were getting their hands dirty as they went up the stairs. A lot of things deteriorated after the 1914 War.

On Armistice Day, at eleven o'clock in the morning, we used to have to stop our trams, put our hand-brakes hard on and stand down in front of the tram, stand to attention. The conductor would do the same. It was orders. What we were worried over was that you might not hear the guns go at eleven o'clock, but we sort of fumbled through it, you'd see other Drivers looking at their watches. Everything stood still in those days, everything, even people crossing the road would stand in the middle of the road. People would even stand to attention inside the tram, and if men didn't take their hats off they'd get them knocked off. It seemed a long two minutes, standing in front of your tram. When we started again we had to go very steadily for a few minutes, otherwise you'd blow the switch out at the generating station. You knew all these instructions, though, they were pinned up and you couldn't go wrong. That's all dead and gone, that sort of thing. It didn't last for many years after the Second World War started, and they moved it to the Sunday afterwards. Nowadays they don't want to know, but I still stop what I'm doing at eleven o'clock on Armistice Day, and it all comes back to me, there's so much to remember about that War.

The rosters always ran from Sunday to Saturday, and once you had a regular service you did early turns and lates on alternate weeks. Then there were middle turns, and I used to hate those, but I never had any trouble getting up for an early turn. I could go to bed at ten o'clock and get up at half-past-two, it never worried me.

When I was at Clapham there was one Driver, old Dusty Miller, who couldn't get up in the morning, so I used to watch out for his early turns and swop with him for my lates. My regular Conductor used to get so annoyed, but you couldn't blame me, I liked early turn, didn't like lates at all, especially in the Summer when the evenings were hot. You might be coming up from Wimbledon about ten o'clock and men would be coming out of the pub with a smirkey smile, wiping their lips, and I used to think to myself, 'You lucky blighter.' My tongue would be hanging out. But shifts never worried me really, and my wife married into shifts, so she didn't worry about it. She knew I liked my work and never interfered with it. I don't think she ever complained about my working shifts.

We used to have single-road schedules and married-road schedules. With a married road you might do the first part of your day's work on the 16's and 18's, and come back and do your second half on the 8's and 20's. We'd been doing it like that from the start, it was what we were used to, although there were times when you might lose your thoughts for a minute, say up at the Elephant, thinking you were on the 18's when you were actually on the 10's. When we went over to buses, all our routes became single-road schedules, you'd do your whole shift on the 109's say, but then that was the way they'd always done it on the buses.

If you were spare and they hadn't got a job for you, they might put you on 'show-up.' Half-past-three was the first show-up, 'half-past-three gate' we used to call it. You had to be there by half-past-three because the first tram went out at twenty-to-four, and if he slipped up you were on it. We used to hope he wouldn't turn up. We used to watch that clock, 'Twenty-to-four, guv'nor, he's late.' We used to fight for it, and it was hard luck because he might walk in two or three minutes after, but he wouldn't get his job, we wouldn't part with it. Everyone liked an early finish. Then they had another show-up at four o'clock, one at half-past-four, five o'clock and so on. There was a Conductor on each show-up as well, of course. After about five or six o'clock the spreadover duties started, and some of those might not finish till seven o'clock in the evening. We didn't half used to swear over those blokes if they missed it, and when they did turn up we used to choke them off.

I had a four o'clock show-up one Sunday morning when I was a spare driver in Clapham, the blokes were coming in and all the trams were going out on time, and I thought to myself, 'I'm sitting pretty here.' At eight o'clock the phone went, from Camberwell, and Webby called me over. 'Camberwell,' he said, 'there's a 34 in the yard, should have been out at such-and-such a time. Get over there and take it out.' I went over to Camberwell and the tram wasn't in the yard at all, it wasn't due out till half-past-eight. I took that tram out, I did four rounders on the 34's,

The Embankment in 1913, when many cars still reversed at various points along its length.

Car 1235 in Camberwell Depot.

Kings Road to Blackfriars, about two hours each rounder, and I finished at half-past-four. Then I had to get back to Clapham. I'd been away since four o'clock in the morning. My missus wondered where the hell I'd got to, we hadn't got the phone in the house then. Twelve solid hours straight through!

If all the Drivers turned up they'd always find you something to do. They'd give you a broom and tell you to sweep up, scraping the old labels off time-boards, or they might send you down to relieve a man on the points at Brixton for half-an-hour. They'd always find you a job, even if nobody missed it. When you were on show-up you never knew what you might end up doing or what time you'd finish. We used to have an Inspector down at Clapham, the cashier behind the counter, old Wally Holland. He didn't half used to like his old drop, and anybody showing-up who didn't get a job, he used to say, 'Nip down the corner and get me a pint, there's the bottle.' As you ran and got him the pint you knew what was going to be next. Directly you gave him his pint, 'Go on, hop it,' and you were finished.

We used to have Summer Schedules and Winter Schedules, you could always depend on them. One season's schedules would be more or less the same as the year before. They might alter a few times here and there, and there were some special Summer services, like the through run at weekends to Hampton Court, but there was very little change from one year to the next.

From the first of May to the first of October it was compulsory to wear a white cap cover. I expect it was to make us look smart, or to let people know the Summer had come. Some of our Drivers used to cut the tops of their caps off underneath that cover, especially if they perspired a lot. When the bomb dropped down

Victoria Embankment, opposite New Scotland Yard in August 1934. The Driver of the 'EX' car — operating a short working on Service 26 from Hop Exchange — wears Union goggles and a white cap-cover. This summer headgear had been worn by LGOC's staff for some years, but was not adopted by tramwaymen until 1933.

the road one Sunday morning, a friend of ours, a tram-driver who used to live down there, came up here. Poor Harry had put his cap on ready to go to work, of course it had no top on, he'd cut it off, and he hadn't put the white cover on yet, his wife had it ready ironed for him. As he came up the road I heard someone say, 'Poor bugger, he's had the top of his hat blown off.' I never bothered to cut the top of mine off, but those that did wore another hat in winter, we always had plenty. I've had as many as two or three indoors, but we used to like to stick to our old caps, you get a new cap on and it hurts your forehead. Once your cap was broken in you didn't like parting with it.

When I first started you had to pass out before you got your uniform, then all you were issued with was a cap, jacket and great-coat, no trousers, you had to wear your own. That's how it had always been on the LCC for Drivers. Soon after I started they began issuing trousers, they were made of Melton, and that first pair was so thick that you could stand them up on the floor by themselves. There was a clothing issue every year, and as our clothes wore out we used to chuck the old ones to the blokes on the permanent way, they always knew when there was a clothing issue coming round. The great-coats were lovely and warm, big double-breasted coats they were, you could put the flap up under your collar and button it down in cold weather, or if it was warm you could undo it and show a collar and tie. We always wore gloves driving, but we had to buy those ourselves. Before we had the glass on the front we used to get mackintosh hats. You put it on top of your cap and there were two little buttons — like boot buttons — to button it on, and the flap went down your back. It stopped the rain going down your neck. We used to have any amount of them, I used to give them to the milkman.

At one time you didn't dare go to work without your full uniform, including cap, collar and tie, or a white choker. You weren't allowed to have a black or a blue or a pink one, it had to be white, but you could only wear it the one day because it used to come home filthy black from the dirt on the road and the dye on your coat. Buttons needed polishing every day — the brass soon tarnished if it was damp or foggy — and often I'd do mine twice if I was on a spreadover. If you didn't take a bit of care over your appearance you could be in trouble. When you walked in they might say, 'What's the matter with you this morning, you haven't shaved. Go home and have a good shave.'

When I first started we had to get a new licence every year, and that lasted up until about 1933, but after that we paid three shillings for one that lasted three years. Our licences were always deposited at Belvedere Road and we had a copy which we had to carry on us, because in those days a copper could pull you up and ask to see it. Or when you reported in the Depot in the morning they might ask to see it, and if you hadn't got it you had to go home and fetch it. Up till about 1933 we had the old enamel badges on a six-inch strap, and if you were hobbling along the road and a car came past you on the other track, the wind would catch it and the badge would lift and give you a good smack on the chin. I've had many a clout from my badge. Then they changed them for the small one like they have now.

It was a crew job, the trams, and you got to know each other's way of working. For instance, if I ever had to pull up dead short over anything, my Conductor would know very well that he couldn't blame me. Not that I'm praising myself up, but I was always well known for giving a smooth ride. I've had Conductors behind me on a rest-day and they'd say they wished their mates could give them a smooth ride like that. I never had a driving complaint all the years I was driving, because I studied my work. I always found out that if you gave a Conductor a fairly smooth ride he wouldn't care two hoots how much money he took or how many fares he had to take in. But if he got chucked here and chucked there, and he was just going to put a ticket in the punch and you suddenly put your magnets on very hard or something like that, he punched on the line. Then if an Inspector got on and saw that ticket of his punched on the line instead of in the section, he booked the Conductor for it. But it wasn't the fault of the Conductor, often it might just be the sway of the tram, but they didn't accept that.

In the peak hour, for instance, leaving Waterloo Bridge, if your mate gave you three bells you were full up and you'd know he hadn't got his fares in. Well, I'd slow down a bit until he cleared the inside deck, and then he'd give a knock on the front door behind me, he was going upstairs. I knew what he meant, and I could bounce along a bit then. It was between ourselves, we all knew these little things, but in those days, if an Inspector got on and found one uncollected fare he'd book the Conductor for it.

The motorman of car 461 pulls down his 'FULL' board as he leaves Vauxhall with a car-load of cricket enthusiasts in 1912. These boards continued to be used until around 1930, when the first windscreens appeared.

It was an amicable arrangement between us, if he gave me those three bells, by the time I got to Westminster he could have the inside in.

We used to carry passengers' luggage on the front platform, for instance, boxes of flowers coming down in the morning from Covent Garden. Now a good Driver always carried a long piece of string with him, because each parcel that was put on was tuppence, but if we put a piece of string round a whole load of parcels it was still one parcel, still tuppence, and the rest was ours. You can talk about these things now because nobody's interested in what we did in those days and what we didn't do, but that was our tea money. They'd pay the Conductor, and then he'd come through and stick a little white label on. You could have a whole pile of parcels and they'd be only tuppence as long as that piece of string was round them. I've had so many boxes of flowers on the front sometimes, that to stop them coming forward I've had to hold them with my back, If an Inspector came through and had a look, as long as a label was stuck on it never got queried. Then, often, when they got to their destination, the passenger might offer us tuppence. 'No, we mustn't take tips,' we'd say, 'put it down there and we'll pick it up,' and they'd put it on the platform.

In those days we all realised that if we didn't do our job, there were three men out there waiting who would come and do it — they didn't hesitate to remind you of that, either — so we always studied our work, and we studied our passengers. In those days passengers looked up to you, you were something, you were taking them to work and you were bringing them home. But today, they tread on you now. Before the War the public at large was vastly different, they behaved themselves. We never had any real trouble and we had our own ways and means of dealing with them. The only people who sometimes gave you trouble were drunks, but a good Conductor knew how to pacify a drunk, and if you couldn't pacify them, you got them off straight away and ran off. I remember a drunk got on the nighter once at Charing Cross Station — he was well boozed — asked to be put off at Tooting Broadway and then fell fast asleep. Well, there's nothing worse than trying to wake a drunk who's in a really deep sleep, they can turn quite nasty sometimes, so we went two stops along the Embankment and then put him off, telling him it was his stop. He was still there, fast asleep draped over the parapet, on the next trip round.

The LCC was very strong on discipline, from the top down. When I started Aubrey Llewellyn Coventry Fell was the Manager and he was red-hot, although I never met him personally, but he had his understudies all the way round. When Mr. Geary took over as Traffic Superintendent in the 1920's he said he was going to have his men looking like a regiment of soldiers, nobody under five-foot-eight and nobody with glasses, and he got them, a standard quality of men. They could afford to pick and choose in those days, but as time went on they did lower the standard quite a lot, and even men with glasses started coming on. The LCC had a small office up at 23 Belvedere Road where they recruited, and they used to start queuing up at five o'clock in the morning for jobs. We were told all this, we got to know about it, the grapevine talks, doesn't it ? You realised that once you were on the trams you'd got a job for the rest of your life as long as you behaved yourself, you didn't have to worry any more. The LCC was a fair employer at the top, but the CDI's and Inspectors were bastards, they were harsh, and you worked under constant fear of losing your job. They'd make something of the least little thing, and you couldn't afford to answer anyone back, they'd even book you for dumb insolence, and that was one day's suspension or just a choking off up the road if you were lucky. You used to think, 'I'm in work, so I've got to stick it out.'

---

8. Charge Depot Inspector: he was in charge of traffic arrangements at a depot, but not mechanical matters.

Car 406, bound for Southwark Bridge, is watched by the Regulator as it passes Telford Avenue Depot around 1914

The LCCT — like the railway companies — was organised rather like an army, and uniforms tended to reflect military fashions. **Above**, in December 1913, a Regulator stands before a tram fitted with a tow-bar for hauling trailers on the Embankment to Merton service. His youthfulness is explained by the rapid growth of the LCCT in the previous decade. The Driver's hands are gauntletted, but he is not yet allowed to wear goggles.

In 1933, **top right**, a Regulator with a distinct military bearing holds his 'book' of tram passing times at Catford. London Transport softened the cut of the LCCT uniform, **right**; note the various white painted blackout aids at Kennington early in the Second World War.

There were two grades of official who mattered to us on the road, Ticket Inspectors — what we called 'Jumpers' — and Regulators. There was one Inspector to each section, early and late turn, and their job was to move about checking tickets, time-keeping and everything. In this area the sections ran Kennington to Brixton, Brixton to Saint Leonard's Church, and then either down to Norbury or round to Tooting Broadway. They used to watch out for all sorts of things, smoking, your appearance, close-poling, boards and blinds, whether your trolley-rope was tied down properly, and anything that came into their minds, and if they caught you they booked you. They might get on your tram and the first thing they'd do was to look at your sand-pedals at the Conductor's end to see if they were up. If you hadn't dropped them down you were in trouble, but a good mate would check that they were down before you left the terminus. Then the Inspector would peep through the front door while he was checking tickets inside, to make sure you had them up at your end, and to see that you'd got your chain across the Driver's platform.

Every Sunday morning before the trams came out it was the Inspector's job to walk along the track in the section he worked looking for bolts in the slot or obstructions in the running rails that might have been dropped in the night, because there were no nighters on a Saturday night. He would walk along in the middle of the road checking both lines at the same time, but it was quite safe because there wasn't much traffic about in those days.

A Regulator was always at a fixed point, he was there for his eight-hour job, he never moved, he'd stand there with his book. In this area we had a Regulator at Brixton, another outside the Depot, one at Saint Leonard's Church, and their job was to check on passing times, crew-changes, and that sort of thing. They had to see that the service kept going. An Assistant Regulator more or less worked with a Regulator, and if there was any trouble on the road, say you hadn't had a tram up for five minutes, the Regulator would send him down the road to see what had happened. An Assistant Regulator was only a man that put in for a Regulator's job, but he had to go out with another Regulator, sort of learning the ropes, on probation, three months, six months, it would just depend.

Regulators used to have books with all the times in of all the trams that passed their point, with the running numbers, although we had a Regulator at Saint Leonard's Church — old Bill Humphries, lived not far from me — and he was never known to pull his book out to see what time a tram was, he knew every time, he had it all up here. Marvellous old fellow he was.

Sometimes you might get a chap who'd just been made up as an Inspector or Regulator, and he might push his nose up in the air a bit, well, we didn't take a lot of notice of them, but the average Inspector and the average Regulator we got on very well with them. They had their job to do, you knew that. You might stop at the Plough and the Regulator would walk over to you and say, 'You're a couple of minutes sharp, slow it down a bit before you get to Tooting Broadway.' Well, if you were anything of a decent sort of bloke, you'd do what he told you, because although he didn't say as much, we knew that if we were two minutes early at the Plough Clapham, we'd still be two minutes early at Tooting Broadway, and we'd get booked there. Then the guv'nor would want to know why old Stringer, the Regulator at the Plough, hadn't booked us as well. So we used to ease the road down a bit and arrive at Tooting Broadway right on the dot.

They used to book you for the least little thing in the old tram days. If you were booked for running early you had to go and see the Guv'nor on Friday — pay-day — and he'd want to know why. We always used to put it down to lack of passenger traffic, it was always the same old excuse, but he knew, he knew so well. 'Just watch your step in future,' he'd say. If you were a minute late back off your relief you'd get booked, they'd get on the phone straight away to Tommy Tilston at Vauxhall, he was the Superintendent of the South-side, the big pot in charge. If you had to go up there you went up in your own time. He'd give you a rollicking, 'If you come up here again,' he'd say, 'I'll give you the sack.' I never went up there, I managed to scrape out of things, but there were so many pitfalls.

Sometimes you might get a Regulator turn you back. Suppose you're going to Purley, you get to Telford and they've had nothing come through going up to London for quite a little time, he'd hold you there for a moment till another tram came up behind. 'Put your's on the one behind,' he'd say, 'and nip back and do a London run.' That very often happened. You'd go round London, put up 'TELFORD AVENUE' coming back, and see the Regulator there. He'd put you right then. You might go down as far as Streatham Library, might go as far as Norbury, and then you'd look out for your running number coming up from Purley. Let's say you were number twelve, you'd look out for number eleven, then as soon as you saw him you'd turn back at the next crossover and jump in behind him, so you always put yourself right.

Although it did happen sometimes at other Depots, I don't recall ever being put on another route by a Regulator. It meant taking all your numbers down, your 16's and 18's, and we didn't keep spare numbers, say if he wanted you to work a journey on the 10's. And don't forget, we had Felthams, and they were restricted.

CLOSE POLING IS A PREVALENT CAUSE OF TWO-CAR COLLISIONS.

Extract from Traffic Circular dated 1937, **above.** *London Road, looking north from the Elephant & Castle in July 1934,* **below.** *Car 1665 on Service 2 leads ex-Croydon Corporation car 384 across the junction into Newington Butts. Signs of a 'window-order' can be seen. Further back, the rule on close-poling is being carefully observed.*

The windows on the top deck of a Standard used to move together on a ratchet. We had a huge great window winder, and the Conductor wound them up or down, but he only opened the windows when he was told to, when a window order came out. You might go past the Plough Clapham and the Regulator would hold four fingers up, that meant wind the window four inches down. Two fingers meant two inches, and so on. If he waved his hand right down, that meant wind the windows right down, or waving his hand another way meant no windows open. You had to understand these signals.

The worst crime of the lot was smoking on the front. We used to get threatened with two days suspension for smoking, so that we could 'sit at home and have a good old smoke.' Once in 1924 I had to go and see the Superintendent. He kept me waiting outside his office for a long while and then asked me why I'd been booked for smoking three times in one day. There was nothing I could say. It was strictly against the rules to smoke on a tram. He told me to get out, but I told him that there was one more report on his desk, because I was actually caught smoking four times that day. He hollered at me to get out before he lost his temper. I don't think I ever got caught smoking again. I'm not saying I didn't smoke, because when it was quiet I'd often have a crafty roll-up, but I made sure I never got caught for it. Nowadays, though, they sit in the cab smoking and don't care who sees them.

I was on the old 8's and 20's one day, and when we got to Amen Corner I was dying for a smoke, so I rolled a fag while the people were getting on. Old Inspector Johnson walked over. 'Hello, Driver,' he said, 'smoking ?' 'No, guv'nor.' 'You are,' he said, 'what's that in your fingers ? 'A cigarette,' I said, 'but it's not alight, so I'm not smoking.' 'Hop it,' he said, 'get out of it,' he thought he had a case.

I well remember one Sunday morning, I was on a very early tram out and it was pouring with rain when I left home. It was still pouring when I finished work, it hadn't stopped once. I remember I was going along Blackfriars Road and I was soaked to the skin and I thought to myself, 'To hell with everything, I'm going to have a smoke.' So I got down behind the controller, lit up a fag, and blimey, there's an Inspector right in the middle of the road in front of me. 'Smoking, Driver ?' I said, 'Yes'. 'Why?' So I told him, I was fed up to the eyebrows and soaking wet through, I'd had as much as I could take. He said he'd let it slide this time, but not to do it too often, and told me I was the first Driver who'd ever told the truth when he caught them smoking. 'Will you tell me one thing ?' I said. 'Where did you come from ? Before I lit this fag up there wasn't a sign of anyone about, not a fly.' 'That's my secret,' he said. I've got an idea he was hiding behind a lamp-post or a tree, they used to do that, they came out on you from nowhere. Anyway, I never heard any more about

Car 1806 on Service 20 at the Swan Stockwell, around the mid-1930's.

that, he was quite good, we were good pals after that.

Then, when they relaxed the no-smoking rule and allowed us to smoke at a terminus, well of course, hardly anyone wanted to smoke going along the road then, they didn't bother. They knew they could have a jolly good old smoke when they got to Purley or Wimbledon or wherever it was. If you had a three or four minute break, or a five minute turn, well, you could smoke a fag in five minutes and thoroughly enjoy it, although I will agree that if we used to pinch a smoke on the quiet it didn't half used to go down well. I think I must have broken all the rules in my time, although one thing I never did was to drink on duty, I never had any sympathy for a Driver who was caught doing that, because it wasn't fair to the passengers. And you only had to have a hint of beer on your breath if you had an accident and you were for it.

The Rules and Regulations covered all sorts of things, and we were all issued with a Rule-book which we were supposed to carry around with us all the time, but some of them we observed and others we didn't. We've all taken a chance. Take close-poling for instance. The rule was that Drivers must not get closer than fifty yards of the tram in front unless you were at a stopping place, but we got bunched up sometimes, you had to take a chance, you'd never get the job done otherwise. Then again, on single-track, 'up' cars were supposed to have priority before noon and 'down' cars afterwards, but we didn't bother too much about that rule. If I was a couple of minutes early, I'd wave him on whoever had the right of way.

We all had our own little signals, for instance, at the Horns Kennington one tram would go straight on for Blackfriars and the next would go left for Westminster. You'd both go opposite ways round London — it was the same on the 2's and 4's out of Clapham and the 16's and 18's out of Telford — until you got back to the Horns again, and you had to get back in the same order for running down to Purley or Wimbledon. And if you came down Kennington Road to the Horns, there might be a number 10 waiting there in Kennington Park Road. He wouldn't know whether he was in front of you and you wouldn't know if you were supposed to be in front of him, so what we used to do was this. Suppose it was ten o'clock and your time was two minutes past ten, well, you'd hold two fingers up in front of you. Or if you were running sharp, you'd just look over to him and, holding four fingers up, you'd rub your hand up and down in front of your chest, four minutes in front, four minutes early. But if you were two minutes late you'd hold two fingers up, and then you'd do the same thing behind your back, and so on. It was one of our little dodges, something you had to learn for yourself. They all died out, though, as the old drivers packed up and retired.

Of course, there have been times when I've had to jump my leader at Kennington. The copper on point duty would wave you on and you

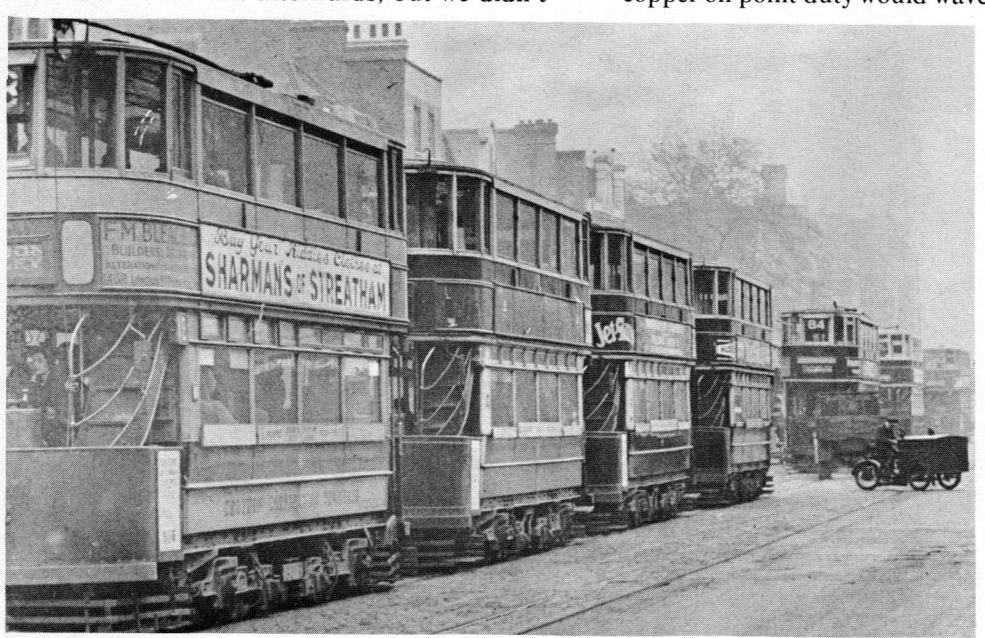

Kennington Road, approaching the Horns Tavern in the early 1930's. The Croydon Corporation car, to the left, still has its plough-carrier mounted on a bogie.

Vauxhall Cross, mid 1936. Service 8 ran the anti-clockwise Victoria — Southcroft Road service; Service 20 operated clockwise.

had to go, even if you could see your leader on the other side of the junction. We'd go down Brixton Road with him keeping pretty close to my behind, then, when you got to Water Lane, I'd shoot back over the crossover, let him go through, then I'd come back again. That was very unofficial, but we did it scores of times, you had to, but if you got caught doing it you were for the office.

I never thought of becoming a Regulator or Inspector, because I'd done everything that a tram-driver shouldn't do, smoking, running early, running late. How could I be an Inspector and book a man for smoking when I've done it myself? I never put in for that job, never. I was very happy with my driving. It was my Dad's living, it was my brother's living and it was my living.

6
1936 to 1939

TELFORD AVENUE & THE FELTHAMS

Telford Avenue Depot was treated as two 'allocation' units in December 1936. The two adjacent sheds at Telford Avenue made up one (which LT called Streatham), whilst the 1924 'trailer-shed' was the second (LT called it Brixton, although the Charlton blind-printers insisted on Brixton Hill).

In 1936, the combined rush-hour output of Telford Avenue was 109 cars; 31 of these came from Brixton Hill, which only put out cars in the rush-hours (and it must be remembered that there were in those days two Saturday rush-hours, in the morning and at mid-day). Of the scheduled 109 trams, 42 were Felthams and 67 were Standard E/1's, and both types were allocated to operate together on several services. There were only two crew duty rota's at Telford Avenue, one for each type of tram. Thus it will be realised that operations from Telford were rather complicated at this time, although they became less so when the rest of the 101 Felthams arrived there in 1938.

The Purley - Embankment service required 50 trams throughout most of the day; 21 came from Purley and 29 from Streatham, although Streatham ran two additional cars in the evening rush-hour to allow for a slight increase in running-time. Ten of the Streatham trams were Felthams. 16/18 rush-hour Extra's came from Brixton Hill (24 Standards and 6 Felthams) and Streatham (2 Felthams and 2 Standards, but only in the mornings)

Service 10 (Tooting Bdwy and City) required 25 cars, all of which came from Streatham, 16 of which were Felthams.

Services 8/20 (Victoria and Southcroft Road) and 22/24 were both operated in conjunction with Clapham Depot. Brixton Hill put out one Standard car on the 22/24 (ten in the evenings), and Streatham ran 8 Felthams and 12 Standard cars on the 8/20.

All the details given refer to the morning rush-hour, unless otherwise qualified. It may be found useful to refer to the maps in Appendix 2. In addition to the 109 scheduled trams, it is probable that there were about ten spare cars allocated to Telford Avenue, to cover breakdowns and accidents.

Joining the tracks of the LCCT and Croydon Corporation Trams at Hermitage Bridge, Norbury in 1925. For almost twenty years only a few inches had separated them.

My brother started at Telford Avenue in 1919 just after the War finished. They were asking for Drivers then, he went straight up to 23 Belvedere Road and got a job. He was at Camberwell for about the first six months, I think, then he transferred to Telford. He did forty-one years, same as I did. Around 1925, I think it was, I'd got a transfer over to Telford, so there were three Collins' up there. Old Johnson, the Regulator up at Telford, used to say, 'There goes old man Collins, now you see the two boys coming along behind.' There would be my Dad, he might go to Westminster, then my older brother, he'd go to Blackfriars, and I'd be the next one, I'd be going to Westminster.

Now at one time the Croydon Corporation line from Purley only used to come as far as Hermitage Bridge, Norbury, and there was a gap of about eighteen inches between the end of their line and the beginning of ours. Then they joined them up, but they found that the original Croydon Corporation Tramways had their own particular gauge of track which was very very slightly narrower than ours. When we first went through to Purley we could feel our wheels grinding, they couldn't run on Croydon track as well as they did on our own. You could hear the wheels labouring, if they could have spoken they would have said, 'I am not satisfied with the way I'm running.' So they decided to lay a new track right through to Purley. How they got over that without interrupting the service was to put a temporary track out beside the old one, then that piece of track would be pulled up. We had to take it ever so steady over the temporary points, along the temporary track, and back onto the proper line a bit further along. Now, when they'd relaid the piece of track they'd pulled up, they moved the temporary track further down, and so on like that all the way to Purley and back again. On the temporary track you were running nearly in the kerb, it was just laid on the surface of the road, and you could feel it jump up as you went over it. Two or three trams got derailed on it, but not seriously. It was a long job. *(1)*

---

1. According to written records, the Croydon Corporation tracks between Norbury and Purley were relaid between April 1924 and March 1925 expressly to allow their safe use by the relatively heavy cars of the LCCT. The operation was just as Stan Collins describes it, although the 'labouring' to which he refers was probably caused by the different profile of the Croydon track, for the CCT and LCCT were both laid to standard gauge. Thus there is a mystery here, because through running began only after the relaying was finished.

A likely explanation is that either Stan Collins or his father were involved in the test runs that were undoubtedly made over Croydon tracks before 1925.

I wasn't long at Telford then. I had a bust-up with the CDI, but I can't remember what it was over. I remember saying to him, 'I'm not wanted here, I'm going back to Clapham.' So I slung my service in and went back to Clapham.

Then towards the end of 1936 we heard that the first batch of Felthams was coming over from the North-side to Telford Avenue, and my brother heard a whisper that one of the Telford Drivers, young Bert Leonard, didn't like the thought of going on them, so he fixed up for us to change over. I jumped at it. I'd been trying to get back to Telford, but I could never find anybody to change with me. I'd been happy enough at Clapham, but I preferred working at Telford because it was so near — I could get up there in ten minutes from home — and I was on my home road as you might say. I knew Brixton Hill from a kid, and Streatham, but the other Clapham roads seemed so far away from me.

The Felthams came across in two batches, first towards the end of 1936 from the old London United, and then the rest in 1938 when they trolleybussed the North-side. Up as far as Putney Bridge Road they came on the wire with North-side Drivers, and we took them over at the change-pit. Sometimes one Driver would fetch two or three down from Putney in a day. We weren't used to them. Old Juicy Baker brought the first one over and we went out for about an hour with him on the 16 road getting instruction on the air-brake, but the rest we had to pick up for ourselves, we learnt it in service as we went along. We thought they were fine, just loved to get out and drive one of them. They were so modern compared with the Standards that we had. Drivers used to be disappointed if they looked up on the car numbers and saw they had a Standard. I remember one morning I went to work without my overcoat — I thought I was bound to have a Feltham — but they gave me a Standard and I froze until I was able to come home on relief and get my coat. They were a beautiful tram to drive. I can't praise them too much. After standing up all those years, and then suddenly being able to sit down, it seemed impossible. And you had a cab heater. At first the passengers used to let the Standards go by just so that they could ride on a Feltham, they were that new. Conductors liked them too, although they carried more people.

The centre-entrance car was brought over too, but it never went out on passenger service and was just stored for a couple of days in Brixton Hill. I heard that the police didn't want it to be

One hundred production Feltham trams were built in 1930 and 1931, for use on the London United and Metropolitan Electric Tramways; both companies were members of the Ashfield Combine. The Felthams were very modern and sophisticated for their time, and brought new standards of comfort and design to London streets. Together with one of the prototype Felthams, 2167, they were all transferred into Telford Avenue Depot in 1936 and 1938. 2069 operated from Wood Green Depot until May 1938; shortly afterwards it was photographed, **above**, reversing, into 'DEPOT TELFORD AV' after working as an evening rush-hour Extra. An extract from the November 1936 Traffic Circular, **below**.

1224.—FELTHAM CARS.

The attention of all employees is called to the transfer to Streatham Depot of Feltham cars, which will operate on the undermentioned routes.

Employees must not stand between tracks on these routes whilst cars are passing.

Routes 8 and 20, Victoria to Tooting Broadway.

Via Vauxhall Cross, South Lambeth Road, Stockwell Road, Brixton Road, Streatham Hill, Mitcham Lane, Tooting Broadway, Tooting High Street, Balham High Road and Clapham Road.

Routes 16 and 18, Purley to Embankment.

Via London Road, Norbury, Streatham High Road, Brixton Road, Newington Butts, Elephant & Castle, London Road, St. George's Circus, Blackfriars Bridge, Victoria Embankment, Westminster Bridge Road and Kennington Road.

Route No. 10, City to Tooting Broadway.

Via Southwark Bridge, Marshalsea Road, Borough High Street, Newington Causeway, Kennington Park Road, Camberwell New Road, Brixton Road and Mitcham Lane.

Emergency Routes.

Waterloo Road, Borough Road, Lancaster Street, St. George's Road, Lambeth Palace Road, Albert Embankment, Harleyford Road, Oval, Harleyford Street, Lambeth Road.

Of the three prototype Felthams, 2167 alone remained in London after 1936. Here it passes Telford Avenue in the closing months of 1939.

used in Central London, and it didn't have a plough-carrier. It went away by night, we never knew where it went. *(2)*

Twenty one-sixty seven was a funny little arrangement. Nobody liked it. The controller was different, in a box, and if anything went wrong you had to take the panel off first, but you didn't know what to look for, it was a completely different type of controller. It didn't last long after the War, though, because I believe they turned it over and scrapped it in Purley Depot.

They reckoned Telford Avenue was the only depot on the South-side that they could get them in, but when they put the Feltham on our traverser they found that the buffers were just catching the iron stanchions. So what they did was to put up new iron stanchions a little bit back from the others and pulled the old ones down.

Other depots were jealous of us, mind you, you could sit down, you had an air-brake and a magnetic-brake if you wanted it for an emerg-

2. It was bought and operated by Sunderland Corporation and is now awaiting restoration at the Crich Tramway Museum. A production Feltham forms part of the LT Collection.

ency. At first passengers used to stand behind the Driver watching, as if they were gazing in a shop window. There was only one thing that annoyed me, and that was if you had a crowd on, people used to stand behind the door holding onto it, because every time the tram swayed they jogged you. Several times I've had to turn round to people, in a very polite manner, and ask them to keep their hands off the door please. The seat was on the back of the door, and as you put the seat down a rod went down into a socket in the floor to stop the door opening.

The controls were so much easier than a Standard, too. On the Standard you used to have to jump on your sand-pedals, but on the Felthams there was a thumb-lever on the air-brake to release sand, although there was still a sand-pedal on the floor in case you needed it. If you wanted a double quantity of sand you used the thumb-lever and the pedal at the same time. They were faster than ordinary trams, because as well as eight notches — four series and four parallel — they had a booster notch, which you brought in by pushing down on the controller handle. It was useful if you wanted to pass something, because it added about five miles-an-hour to your speed. They did away with it in

For almost thirty years Telford Avenue operated Service 16/18 with Standard E/1 trams; Car 1240 leaves John Carpenter Street in August 1933, **above**. *Three years later,* **below**, *this view towards the back of Telford Avenue Depot shows that the two stanchions beyond the traverser have already been repositioned in preparation for the arrival of the Felthams.*

the end because they said it was interfering with wirelesses in the Croydon area. We were annoyed about that. People in Croydon called them the 'big trams'. They did away with the back stop-light as well, and the front air-door, because they were supposed to be illegal or unsafe.

On the Felthams there was a little red handle at each end, and if you felt queer or the conductor saw you leaning over the controller — something had gone wrong — you just pulled that handle down and that threw every particle of air onto your brake-blocks and stopped your tram. It would probably blow your breakers too. I never did try it.

If the rail was a bit greasy, dead leaves, wet leaves, you used to sand either on the air-brake handle or the right hand foot pedal, or both at the same time if you wanted a double quantity. The left hand pedal on a Feltham was your bell, and there was another one for the lifeguard, either tripping it or resetting it. We had a button up in the roof of the cab so that you could shut your bell off and the one at the other end would ring. It was used if you wanted your mate in a hurry.

A Feltham cab. The controller (left) and the line switch cupboard on the platform (right) are open. The dial registers brake air-pressure. The large wheel, the top of which can be seen on the right, was the hand-brake.

I should say you could get forty-five to fifty miles-an-hour out of a Feltham, although we didn't have a speedometer on them, so you had to judge your speed. *(3)* I came in one night on the last tram, leaving Purley after twelve o'clock. o'clock. We had the road to ourselves, and they say a good donkey knows his own way home. I had the old booster notch on coming up Brighton Road and I was moving, when I saw a car in the nearside mirror, so I let that booster notch up and planted a bit of air to slow it down. When I pulled up at the compulsory stop at the Swan and Sugarloaf the car pulled up alongside of me and a chap said — I thought it was the police but it wasn't — 'Do you know how fast you were going ?' I told him about thirty I suppose. 'Forty-eight miles-an-hour,' he said, 'I only paced you out of curiosity.' I wondered how the trolley stopped on the wire, although it was a straight road coming up from Purley.

Sometimes if you put up a tidy speed, especially if you had an empty tram and it was swaying — I always preferred a full tram myself — that would very often throw your pole off. We were supposed to make out a report every time the pole came off the wire, but we didn't. The only time we bothered usually was if the trolley-head came off, because they were so made, where the trolley-head fitted over the top of the pole, that if your pole came off and hit a cross wire, that would knock the head off to save pulling the wires down. If that did happen, the head didn't fall right off, it hung down at the end of a short length of rope, a safety precaution to stop it falling on anyone. If you were lucky enough to have a car with two poles, you could just tie that one down and bring your other pole round and carry on. You had to take it steady, hoping to God the head didn't dangle down and go through the window at the top. Of course, you had to make out a report then, and you had to go and see the guv'nor, but of course we never knew why the pole had come off, did we ?

All the Felthams went into Telford when they came over to the South-side, except for those that went into Brixton Hill — and they came under Telford. One foreman looked after both depots, but all the repairs were done in Telford. A list in the Depots showed which Depot to run into, but if you had a Standard it always went into Telford. It said on your timeboard if you

3. London trams were never fitted with speedometers, although strict speed limits, which varied from place to place and were often legally enforceable, were applied to them from the 19th Century.

had to run into Brixton Hill Depot, the old trailer shed that was, and you got ten minutes walking time for walking back to Telford, otherwise, if there was nothing on your board, you ran it straight down into Telford. Telford was all conduit inside, even the traverser was conduit, but Brixton Hill had the wires up inside and there was a change pit right outside.

There weren't enough Felthams to give a full service on the 16's and 18's, there was a mixed service with Standards in between. They were slower than the Felthams; with a Feltham you could leave a Standard miles behind. They could really shift. Felthams never went through the Tunnel. I think they'd be too long a wheel-base for the curves.

Brixton Hill Depot, **above,** *was simply a storage shed controlled from Telford Avenue. It was generally used for part-day cars, and was the only LCCT Depot without a traverser. In the entrance are catch-points and a change-pit, for there are overhead wires inside. In October 1936 it housed only Snowbroom 022 and one Standard tram. (022 is at present being returned to its original condition as Car 106). Felthams 2097 and 2125 stand at the head of the ramp in Telford Avenue on 8th May 1938,* **below.** *In the left background stands the LCCT experimental tram, Bluebird.*

We had three nighters running out of Telford and another three came out of Clapham. Between us we ran a figure-of-eight route from Tooting to the Embankment on both roads. Ours left Telford at about midnight, half past midnight and one o'clock, ran up to Kennington, then up over Westminster Bridge and back down Blackfriars Road to Kennington. From there we went straight down through Brixton to Streatham Library and round to Tooting. There was no stand-time at Tooting — officially, that is, although we usually managed to snatch a minute or two there — but instead of turning round you carried on round the corner into the High Street and up through Balham to Kennington again. Then it was the opposite way round London — up over Blackfriars and back down past County Hall, back to Kennington, but instead of going left, this time you carried straight on down through Clapham, round through Tooting to Streatham and so on.

Between us we ran a thirty-minute service all the way round, on both roads, but at Kennington both the up cars arrived at the same time, with the down cars coming a minute or two later, so you could change from one to the other to save a bit of time. It was all very cleverly worked out. We used to stop on either side of the triangle in the middle of the road junction.

Nighters were always a senior man's job. They gave you a regular week, because they didn't run on a Saturday night at all, and they were only a six-hour job with no break. A very soft job, although you'd be carrying loads all night long. I didn't get on regularly until the buses came, but I spent my last five years on the 287 which replaced the trams. I took over my brother's night job when he packed up, because I was the next senior Driver. But living locally and because I'd been on the job a few years, I used to get asked to go on the nighter quite often if someone went sick or anything like that. Sometimes I'd stay on it for a week or two. I remember one Christmas I was on the nighter — the regular Driver was off sick, he was always going sick, I don't know how he afforded it because we didn't get paid for it in those days. Coming up through Southcroft Road on the last trip the Conductor came through and gave me a handful of notes. Fifteen pounds each we had, and a bottle of whisky, I was rich. They were Christmas boxes from the regulars. 'Don't say anything to the regular Driver,' the Conductor told me, and of course I didn't. He would have died of shock if he'd known, but he never did.

Feltham 2138 working a night-turn at Tooting Broadway in September 1938. The white-coated lounger is probably the night trolleybus driver.

In August 1936 an E/1 operates as a nighter at Waterloo Bridge, **above.** *It carries the specially worded side route-board for night-cars, yet numbers itself as a rush-hour 4A (which route was at that time identical to the Streatham/Clapham night service). Night-cars were not officially numbered until 1946, when the Streatham/Clapham service was numbered '1'. Feltham 2110 stands at Blackfriars on 20th November 1950,* **below.**

A Holloway Depot Snowbroom at work in Pemberton Gardens, 30th March 1952.

Every depot had one or two snow-brooms. Clapham had two, Norwood had one and Telford had two, but if you had two you didn't necessarily use them both unless it was bad. They were like a small single-deck tram, donkeys years old, with no seats or anything in them. At one time they'd been double-deckers, but the tops had been taken off them and the bodies were raised up from the track to make room for the brooms. Of course, they never had vestibules on them, not even when all the passenger cars had them fitted. Underneath each platform was a revolving broom, and whichever direction you were working you lowered the broom at the front and raised it at the back end. The broom swept the snow out on the nearside. Inside the saloon we kept tools, bags of sand, ropes, freezing salt and God above knows what.

Whenever it snowed during the night, if I was on early turn I'd go up early on my own and report to Telford, or else they'd send someone down to get me out of bed, because I was one of the snow crews. It wasn't the sort of job you could put any old Tom, Dick or Harry on. Every depot had its own snow crews, and they covered their regular jobs with spare men. I remember one night I came home about eleven-thirty, it was snowing a little bit, but I had a wash and a bit of bread and cheese and a cup of tea for my supper, and I was just going to get into bed when someone knocked at the front door. I opened the front room window, it was someone from the Depot. 'Come on,' he said, 'get your clobber on, we want you to take the snow-broom out.' It was snowing like blazes, whacking great flakes. I had to get dressed and go back up again.

We used to take out bags of salt and, unofficially, perhaps a lump of rope and some paraffin. We had to keep the moving parts of points from getting so packed out with frozen snow that they jammed or wouldn't close properly. We'd soak the length of rope in paraffin and lay it in the track and light it to melt the ice first. Then we'd brush it all out with a point-brush and leave plenty of salt on it to keep it free of ice. The most important thing was to keep crossovers and single-track points clear. We covered from Kennington down to Norbury and round to Tooting, and used to more or less please ourselves where we went. Sometimes you had a Conductor on the snow-broom which was quite good, because it was often an all-night job. You might do, say, Brixton to Kennington or, if you were out all night, the whole route down as far as Tooting and Norbury — the old Croydon Corporation took over there — but there wasn't much to worry about on the wire. If we had two brooms out all night we'd work it between ourselves, but we had to keep in mind what time the nighter came through, and the first morning cars, but provided we kept out of his way we were alright. We'd do the single tracks first, because that helped the nighter, so that meant Streatham Library and Mitcham Lane by the Fire Station. We would go down to Southcroft

Road and wait there until the nighter came through from London, we'd know what time, then back to Mitcham Lane, do the first set of points, pull over for the nighter from Tooting, and then do the points at the other end. I don't remember holding a nighter up once.

I used to like the snow-broom. It was cold, but you'd get stuck into the work and very soon get warmed up. There was an all-night coffee stall at Tooting Broadway and another at Brixton Church, so you could always get a cup of coffee. We used to love it. I'd say to my mate sometimes, 'Do you want to have a go at the handles?' and I'd go inside the saloon for a bit of a warm up. We'd usually take sandwiches and a flask of tea. We did round London as well. You might be up at Kennington and meet another snow-broom, from Clapham say, and you'd have a few words and decide that perhaps he'd go up Kennington Road and round Westminster, and we'd go the other way round, up through the Elephant, sweeping the Blackfriars track. We could see what had been done and what needed doing, and we made sure that all the tracks were clear and the service kept going. There were no night Inspectors on the road, they knew we'd do the job, and we did.

We used to pack up the snow-broom about six in the morning, because by that time the service cars were running, but if the snow was very very heavy you'd get a day-crew on as well. If that happened they didn't worry about the trams keeping time. If you were going down the Brixton Road and there was a heavy fall of snow and you were sweeping down there, well you couldn't push it along as fast as a service car could go, so they had to trail behind you while you kept going. You had to keep the tracks clear. It made the service cars late all the time, but nobody took any notice of that.

A snowbroom operating on the Embankment early in January 1951. Non-passenger cars were never fitted with windscreens.

In the winter of 1947 trams were breaking down in hordes. They'd got snowed up under the cow-catcher *(4)* as they went along and forced it down onto the track until the tram couldn't move, and there was no chance of lifting the tray either. The snow was one solid block of ice on it. I was snowed up under the broom once like that, and all you could do was to try and knock it out with a pinch bar or point lever.

It wasn't only snow that could hold the service up, we used to get shocking fog as well, pea-soupers. The hardest part in the fog was on the single-track, because they used to send men out on what we called 'fogging', fog-duty. They'd keep a couple of trams in and borrow the crews for fogging, and how we used to work, say my Conductor and I, he'd go one end of the single and I'd be this end. If he had a tram coming up, we could hear it even though he couldn't see it, he would stop that tram just before the single and give me one whistle. If I had no trams on my side waiting to come down I'd give him two whistles, that gave him the all-clear. Then, while his tram was coming through on the single, I'd stop mine, then I'd give him one whistle and he'd give me two whistles if his end was clear. We used to get messed up sometimes. It was a rotten job, especially early in the morning because people started complaining because we were blowing our whistles and waking them up. But we tried our best to keep the trams running.

They used to do a lot of track maintenance work during the day, and they'd be at it all day long in different parts. You might be going along the road and there they'd be, with the road up. Perhaps the ganger would hold you up, 'Won't keep you many minutes.' Then they'd take a length of rail out and put a new bit in in front of you, one bolt on each end to hold it, then, 'Alright, driver, take it very steady.' You could feel it rattling as you went over, and of course you did take it steady, you were the man on the front.

Then, of a night-time, the grinder used to come out, and he knew exactly where to go. Where they'd put a new length of rail in, he'd grind the joints down. The grinder was an old tram, a single-decker, like the stores-van but not quite so big, with a powerful great emery wheel

4. Another name for the lifeguard tray.

Conduit track at Trinity Road in the early 1920's; the work is probably connected with the underground railway extension. Note the original 'short' conduit yokes.

underneath it, worked by electricity. There was more than one of them, but the South-side grinder used to run out of Clapham. It had a regular Driver on it, that wasn't anybody's job, it was a specialist's job.

When they were putting a new junction in, it would be several days work; the actual points themselves would be put in by night-time, but it would be all dug out during the day ready for the night men to come in. The Night Inspector might tell you that they were working single-track at such-and-such a place, and while they took out one rail and put one bit of the crossover in, you ran round on the other rail. You got your orders before you went out on the nighter, and you knew just where to change over from one track to the other. Say, if you were at Kennington, you could turn over there, because you knew you wouldn't meet anybody coming down from the Elephant, you knew all their times, then you'd go up on the wrong track. The night men used to like it. It was nearly all Irish who did the night work, big powerful old Irishmen. The old foreman, I can see him now, real Irish, ear-rings he used to have.

Special gangs used to go out all night cleaning the conduit. They used to have like a six or seven-foot pole, with a big half-moon blade on the bottom. That would go down the slot, then they would turn it, and keep raking the muck along the conduit towards the sump-holes. The pole was part of their night equipment. The gang used to shift about, might be up at Telford tonight, say, and up at New Cross tomorrow, but whatever depot they worked out of, they'd collect their gear from it and might only clean say, Telford to Water Lane one night, Telford to Streatham Library another. The whole South-side was all cut up, so that everything got done every so many nights. Then, every so often, the old sucker as we used to call it — it was a motor job — used to come round and clear all the sumps out, suck all the dirt and tram-tickets out, all the old muck that got pushed down there.

Trainee-paviors at work in the late 1940's; tram operators were obliged to maintain the whole roadway between points eighteen inches outside their tracks.

Welding and grinding track-joints by night in the early 1930's. By now portable apparatus — powered from the conduit — has replaced the rail-grinding trams. **Below**, *pointwork is also being renewed.*

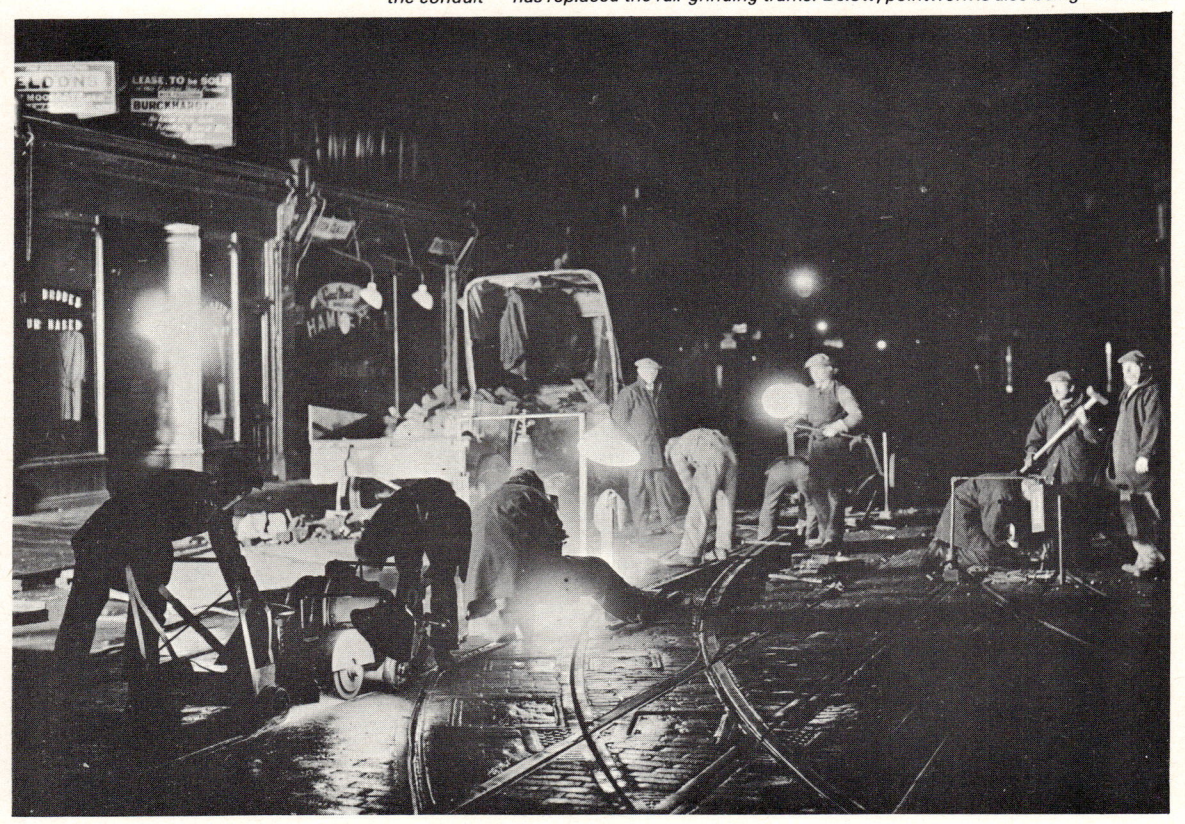

Cleaning out the conduit at Vauxhall in 1939, **above**; *during the War much track maintenance work was of necessity done by daylight. A short distance away,* **below**, *the points at Stockwell are being brushed out.*

We had Number One in Telford when the North-side trolleybuses came in. The LCC was going to build a fleet like it, but they only did the one and then old Ashfield went and bought the lot. Lots of Drivers were scared of it, wouldn't touch it, because it was something different, you had to know the dodge of driving it. Then they booked it up to me, and I went into the office and they asked me what I thought about it. 'It's alright,' I said, 'I can't find any fault with it and I've driven it several times.' They used to call it the Bluebird.

It wasn't on service all day, only a peak-hour car, Norbury Extra's usually. They did try to put it into all-day service and several drivers had a go at it, but they were holding the service up. Before the War the inside staff used to ask what I was on next week, and if I was on Norbury Extra's — they were spreadovers — they would bung the Bluebird on me and I'd do a few trips with it in the morning and another two or three in the evening. It had a different air-brake, the action was quite different to a Feltham and it wanted a lot of getting used to. On the Felthams the air-brake went to the right and you were gradually picking up air, but on the Bluebird — where the brake handle was on top of your controller — you had a lever which you pulled towards you. Fellows used to snatch it, trying to put full air on, but it wouldn't take it. What you had to do was to take it in gently, picking your air up very gently, and then the brakes were as good as gold.

I remember one night I had to run it into Telford with a weak air-brake. I was feeding it, but it wasn't satisfactory. Mind you, you could use your magnetic-brake if you wanted to, although they didn't want you to do that, but on this particular night I had to. I told the foreman — old Holyhead was his name — there was an air-leak on it, but he said there wasn't, they'd had a leak reported before but they could never find one. We both went down under the pit and I followed the air-pipe until I found a little bend. I held my lighter up to the air-pipe and it blew the flame out, there was the leak. I suppose they put a new elbow in, but it was as good as gold after that.

It was a beauty, the Bluebird, a pleasure to drive it, I always called it my baby. It was really comfortable — the passengers loved it and when I had it on Norbury Extra's they used to wait for it on the Embankment — and if you let it out it was really fast. For some reason they wouldn't allow standing passengers on it, so the Conductors liked it too. After the War it didn't come out very often, although there was one Driver-instructor, old Alf Perry, who used to drive it on tours, but I think he was a bit afraid of it. On the last day of the trams at Telford I took the Bluebird out with a special party and they said it was the finest ride they'd ever had on it.

Bluebird —Car number 'one' in the LCCT and LT fleet — was an experimental tram of radical design built at the LCCT Central Repair Depot in 1931/32. Here it stands outside Telford Avenue Depot in July 1949.

Bluebird was a great improvement on previous LCCT designs; it was claimed to be better than the Combine's Feltham, probably justly, for it was a more practical design. Until 1937 Bluebird operated from Holloway Depot in the distinctive blue and ivory livery which inspired its nick-name. It was then repainted in LT red and transferred to Telford Avenue Depot in April 1938, but was used infrequently thereafter. Here it is seen reversing at Norbury, around 1948, and again at Lambeth Town Hall in 1951, where Jimmy Cagney offers a wry comment. Later in 1951 it was sold, with the Felthams, to Leeds Corporation. Bluebird is now at the Crich Tramway Museum awaiting restoration.

Although it was replacing trams with trolleybuses in the 1930's, LT did not neglect its remaining trams. In January 1935, Standard car 1038 was extensively 'rehabilitated' at the CRD. It was the first of around 150 trams to be similarly treated during the two following years.

Most of the more useful improvements were internal, for the upper saloon seats were upholstered and the appearance of various fittings was modernised.

The standard rehabilitation process included fitting a blind for the service numbers at each end of the tram, although this benefit was not conferred on 1038; Car 1769, seen in May 1938, shows a rare display. Although the depth of the indicator display on these cars was increased to show three lines of route information, during the Second World War many of them were masked off to show the usual two-line display.

Car 1236, with a non-standard stencil indicator, squeezes past T 86 outside Telford Avenue Depot in 1937, **above**. Pullman Court is being built in the background, and Thos. Tilling's buses are still in competition. In 1938, **below**, Feltham 2067 cannot pass T 251 during clearance tests in Croydon High Street. Behind the camera, the track remained single until it was lifted in 1951.

102

Looking up the ramp at Telford Avenue in 1947. Halfway up are catch-points and levers, to prevent runaway cars reaching the main road.

Up beside Telford Avenue Depot there used to be Saint Anne's Home, a sort of Workhouse, and every Sunday they used to let the inmates out, and you'd see the old fellows walking along picking fag-ends up out of the gutter. They used to come into the entrance of the Depot and ask the sweepers if they had any fag-ends, because the sweepers would collect them up when they swept them off the trams and gave them to the old boys. They'd open them up and either put them in their pipes or roll cigarettes with them.

Then they knocked Saint Anne's Home down and built Pullman Court — a block of flats — where it had stood, and they had to pull down a big tree that used to be outside the Depot. All round the tree there was a low brick wall that we used to sit on when we were waiting to take-on. We hadn't got anywhere to sit, so we sat on the wall of Pullman Court, but someone complained about that — it must have looked bad seeing men in uniform sitting there — and an order came out that we weren't to sit on the wall. Instead they put forms out on the pavement for us to sit on.

7

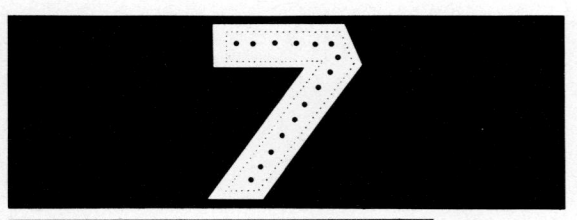

1939 to 1945

WARTIME

The 1914 War had been rather chaotic for the LCCT, for many of its staff had volunteered for Kitchener's Army, or had been conscripted from 1916. Things were better organised this time, for although conscription began in 1939, there already existed a schedule of reserved occupations which exempted certain ages and grades of transport worker from conscription. Later in the War, authority was even required to change jobs. As the War progressed, women increasingly took over the jobs of men, on trams (but never driving) and in the depots and CRD.

The trolleybus conversion programme ceased in May 1940, when about 140 trams were replaced by trolleybuses at Bow and Poplar, after which there was only a maximum of 815 trams scheduled to operate in London. It is a curious fact that, at the end of the War there was only a maximum of 734 cars in service, or 10% fewer than in 1941. It would therefore seem that no real attempt was made to increase tram mileage to directly replace bus mileage, nor was there any increase in the number of trams in service to allow for reduced speeds in the blackout. Most of the reduction in tram operation came in one year, 1941. The reason cannot be war-damaged trams, for LT still had a hoard of spare cars in 1945, nor can it lie in reduced traffics, for 23% more passengers were carried in both 1943 and 1945 than in 1941 (admittedly a low year).

There were several perplexing features of LT's tram and trolleybus policy during the War, but there is no doubt that most tramwaymen showed both courage and endurance, particularly in the Blitz. Inevitably, much maintenance of both tracks and vehicles was neglected, and by 1945 London's trams were in a rather sorry condition.

Everyone knows about the blackout, street lamps were left unlit, interior lights dimmed and headlamps masked, and there was a general twenty-mile-an-hour speed limit, but we drove right through it without any trouble, although it wasn't too easy until you got used to it. A trained tram-driver always knew where he was because the wheels would tell him. The wheels were music to us, they talked to us in our language. We got to know every rail-joint, every bit of special work and every section break. On curves the wheels made a different noise, a sort of humming, and going over a dead-hatchway or a crossover the lights would go out and then come up again, and you'd think Angell Road or Christ-Church or wherever it might happen to be. You could see in the blackout almost as well as you could in the daytime.

Holborn Station in the Kingsway Subway in June 1944. Car 1969 with signs of reduced lighting and restrained capitalism around it. A pre-war view is shown for comparison.

On the overhead, the trolley-wheel would talk to us and tell us exactly where we were. You could hear that wheel going under every ear, and if the wires were a bit lower or a bit higher than usual you heard a different sound. Under the railway arch at Norbury Station — it was only a four-mile-an-hour under there — you could hear that wheel making a long drawn out sound as much as to say, 'I'm coming down to get under the bridge,' and you'd slow down. It was practically talking to us. You would know when you were under the bridge because the wheel made no noise at all, but as soon as you were out the other side the wire began to lift and you'd hear that wheel whistling and you'd open up again. Then a little further on you'd hear the wheel going under a section insulator skate, where it was dead, the lights would flicker and you'd know you were passing such and such a feeder pillar. Even in a thick fog in the blackout you would never get lost.

Some funny things used to happen in the blackout. I was going up Brixton Hill one night and pulled up behind a stationary car at New Park Road. But the brake chain caught and I just couldn't stop in time and went very gently into the back of the car. I just touched him enough for my bumper to put a slight dent in his boot. Quick as a flash I jumped down and told the driver that he ought to keep his foot on the foot-brake if his hand-brake wasn't working properly, because he'd rolled back into my tram. He was lucky that my tram wasn't damaged. He believed me too! You had to think quickly at times like that. Mind you, there were very few cars around during the War and not as many buses as usual, so often we had the road to ourselves.

The only thing in the blackout that used to annoy me was people at stops who shone torches straight at you, because a sudden bright light in the blackout would take your sight away for a few seconds. Generally people shone them down on the ground and that was quite enough to see them by. We knew where the stops were anyway. Early one morning, going up past Kennington Cross, this happened to me, big powerful torch it was, right in my eyes he shone it, so I opened the side window — you could do that on the Felthams — and as we went by I held my hand out and sent his torch flying. I just gave him a mouthful of soldier's language and didn't stop for him. He wasn't there the next morning. It was just lack of thought.

We got used to the bombing too. Directly the sirens started we had to stop and direct passengers to the nearest shelter — we were all issued with a list of them — but I don't remember people often getting off. I always kept going, and they preferred that as well.

One Sunday night we were going through Blackfriars Road on the 18's — we had a Feltham — and it was as quiet as could be, not a single passenger on. My Conductor, Alf Mole, was standing behind my door smoking and I'm having a good old smoke too, but when we turned off Blackfriars Bridge we picked up a load at John Carpenter Street, then a few more at Waterloo Bridge, and by the time we reached Westminster we had a load on. I could tell we were overloaded, because I could feel the motor casings grinding on the cobbles, and I told Alf not to pick up any more.

We gradually got through to Kennington when bang went the sirens, so I stopped the tram and turned round. 'Ladies and Gentlemen,' I said, 'the sirens are going. Anyone who wants to go down the shelter, there's one just up the road,' I forget now exactly where it was. That was orders, we had to do that. One old boy standing near me asked me if I was going down the shelter. 'I am not,' I said, 'I'm going to fight my way home.' 'Good,' he said, 'the Driver's going on, the Driver's going on,' he tells everyone, he was ever so excited, just like a little schoolboy. Nobody got off, so we tootled on down Brixton Road, dropping them off, dropping them off. When I stopped at the bottom of Brixton Hill the old chap asked me if he could get out of the front door. He wasn't supposed to in the blackout, but the tram was still full and he couldn't get through to the back, so I opened the air-door and let him off the front. Just as he's getting off he puts a pound note in my hand and says, 'There you are, Driver, this is for a drink, and thank you for fetching me home.' When we were reversing at the end of that journey I told Alf and gave him ten bob, but he told me that the old chap had run round the back and given him a pound as well. They used to be pleased to get home. You see, the service used to get a bit irregular at times. Routes would be short-turned or diverted around bomb damage, and the situation would change almost from day to day.

To give an example, a bomb fell on the corner of Christchurch Road and set a gas main alight. For a while we worked single line between Upper

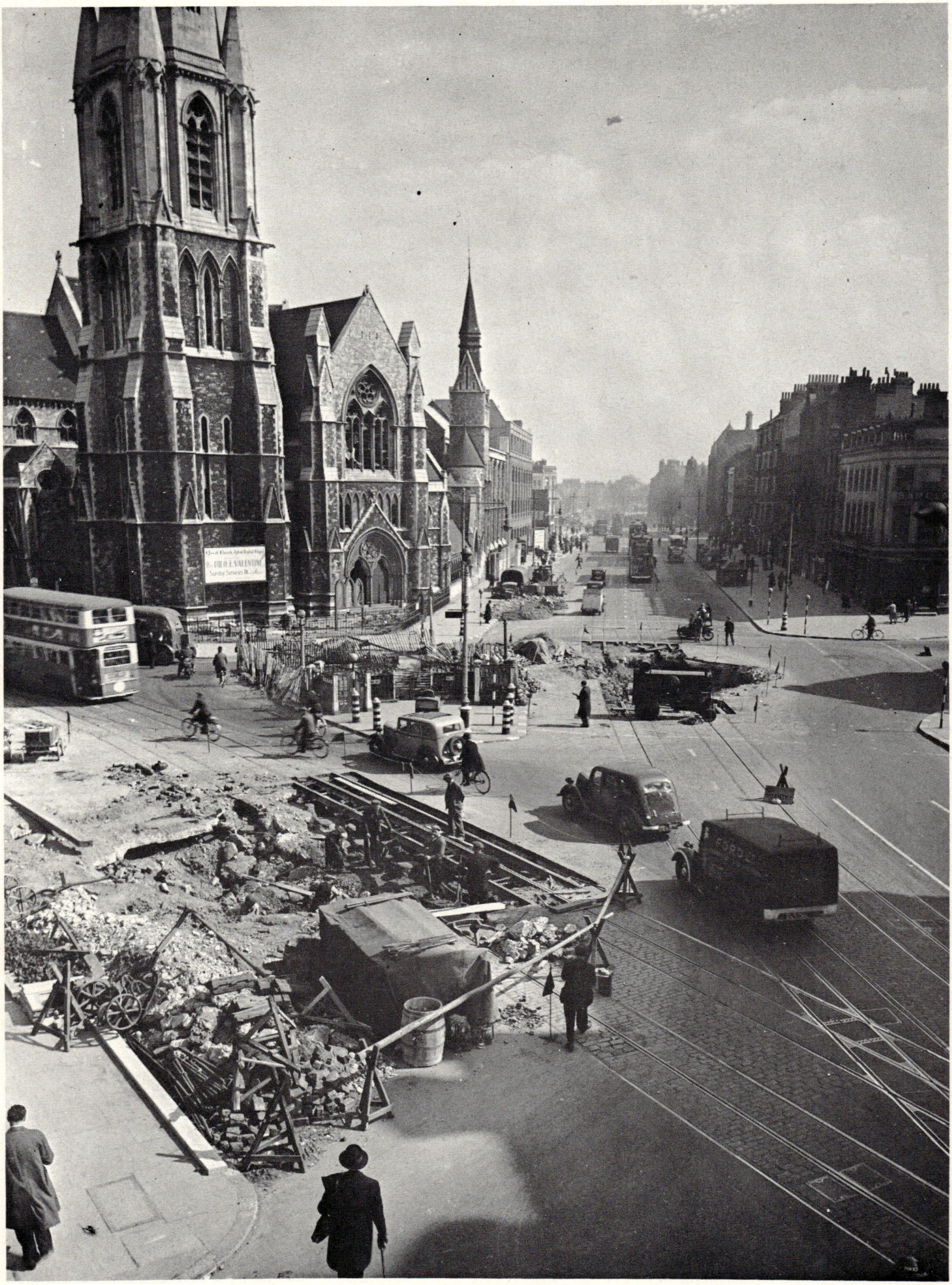

Tulse Hill, past Brixton Hill Depot to Telford Avenue, but then a temporary single track was laid round the crater, and that lasted several weeks. Two Drivers, Alden and Gresney, looked after each end, passing cars through in convoys if it was busy. The last car each way carried a bit of wood which the Driver gave to the Inspector at each end. This method of working was quite common in breakdowns, but it could easily hold the service up at busy times.

The trams got into a shocking state. They didn't get painted. Windows got blown out and trams were running round with the windows boarded up — they couldn't get the glass you see — sometimes for weeks. The buses were the same.

When he started blowing the tram-track out we used to have to find our own way home. Sometimes you might be two or three hours late back into the Depot. No one took any notice of timekeeping in the blackout, we used to let it right out and away we went. As long as the trams were running, that was all they worried about. I don't know how we kept going, but we did.

One night I came in from Purley, just managed to scrape through a fire at a rubber works at Thornton Heath, and when we got up to Telford Avenue young Reg Barham stopped me. He was the Regulator, and he asked how much more I had to do. All round London, I told him, and back down to Thornton Heath Pond. 'Don't go round London tonight,' he said. 'he's dropping them up there like pills, but you can go down as far as Brixton Station if you like, there might be a few want to come up here.'

But the points at Brixton Station would only half open, and as I didn't want to risk getting stuck on the crossing we went round the corner into Stockwell Road, came back over the crossing by the Astoria, and stopped at the traffic lights which were showing red. Over on the other side of the road, where Barclay's Bank used to be, was a copper with his cape on and old Peg-leg, the Pointsman, who pulled the points for the 34's — he had a wooden leg — so I shouted across to them to get under cover because there was a chandelier of flares coming down. I said to my Conductor — it was Alf

The last great German night raid on London was on May 10th/11th 1941, and it wrought considerable damage to the South London tramways. Christ Church, Lambeth, **left**, *on 16th May.*

Services on Brixton Hill were affected for several weeks after a bomb fell at the end of Christchurch Road in January 1941; Feltham 2096, **below**, *is given the 'token' which allows it to proceed south over a specially laid section of single track past the crater. 2096 wears an early design of the blackout mask which was fitted to all tram head-lamps in 1939.*

107

Mole, he was always behind my door in a raid, said it was so that we could go together — I said, 'I'm not stopping here with that red light, copper or no copper,' so I got round into Brixton Road, the copper never said anything, shut the juice off, and down it came. It didn't half roar, I can hear it now. Right where I'd just left, it dropped.

When I got up to Telford Avenue I told Reg Barham that the points at Brixton Station were jammed up and that we'd gone round the corner to the Astoria, and he said, 'You couldn't have done, there's just been a thousand-pound bomb outside the Astoria.' He'd just had a 'phone message. Then he looked at the back of the tram. It was just as though you'd gone up with a big axe and sliced that end right off, but fortunately it hadn't broken any contacts. All the paint at the back end had just disappeared. Then Alf said to me,'Now you know why I stand behind your door.' All the glass was broken, and the vestibule was all bent. It was the blast that had done it. Reg Barham said to me, 'You'd better put that one away, you're not going down the Pond tonight.'

When I came home they were all down in the shelter and they'd heard the bomb. I told my daughter Betty who was working at Quin and Axtens *(1)* at the time, 'There's not much good in your going to work in the morning.'

Another time, towards the end of the blitz, I was on the Victoria road, number 8, driving a Feltham. Reg Barham was on again at Telford as we came round from Southcroft Road. 'Unless you get anyone on don't go through to Victoria, it's hardly necessary, come back at the Bridgefoot,' he told me. Of course, I had to pick up a bloke so I had to work through. Coming back down Vauxhall Bridge Road we picked up a few people, over the Bridge and round into South Lambeth Road. Just past the Express Dairy a bloke came running up and waved me down. He told me I couldn't get through because a bomb had just dropped on the corner of Victoria Mansions and there was rubble all over the tram tracks.

1.   Quin & Axtens was a departmental store at the junction of Brixton and Stockwell Roads.

Stockwell Road at Brixton Road, 22nd May 1941. The bomb which caused this damage was probably the one which Stan Collins just avoided.

So Alf and I walked down to have a look at this, but before we even got there we could see this big heap of bricks across the tracks. Just at that moment another bomb fell in Higgs and Hills and the Sunnybank Laundry caught fire. I had the breeze up, I don't mind telling you. 'Come on,' I said to Alf, 'if he sees these fires he'll come back and bomb the hell out of us.' I decided that the best thing was to cut round through Perry Street and go back through Nine Elms. The way he was dropping them I wanted to keep away from Central London. We got through into Parry Street and under the bridge and there were three trams blocking our way. There wasn't a soul about, our passengers had all hopped it, the three Drivers had gone down the shelter under the Southern Railway Club, and I couldn't move the other trams because our Feltham controller keys wouldn't fit Standard cars, and they'd taken all their keys with them.

So I took the hand-brakes off them all, told Alf to stand on the back of the front tram where I could see him, and pushed them all round into Wandsworth Road. Alf put the hand-brake on the back car as hard as he could — I checked it after, because he was only a Conductor — but there was no chance of the tram running back. Then Alf pulled the points over and we turned right into Nine Elms Lane.

Just past the Dog's Home there's a railway bridge, and I thought, 'Oh hell, we're never going to get under there.' You see, the Feltham was a little bit higher than a Standard, and it had a big base on its trolleys. Very slowly we eased underneath and I could hear the base of the trolleys scraping the bridge, but we cleared that and carried on up, past the Latchmere to the Princes' Head.

Old Jock Cornwell was up there, a big fat Regulator he was, and he says, 'What the so-and-so are you doing up here?' I told him I was trying to get back to Telford as best I could. 'These Felthams have never been up this road yet,' he says, and I told him that there was one had come up here now and what was he going to do about it? I told him I was going up Falcon Road and up over Lavender Hill. I wasn't staying out there all night, not with him dropping them like that, I wanted to get back to Telford.

We left old Jock Cornwell swearing at us, and went round into Falcon Road, all twists and bends. I was a bit worried about the bridge at Clapham Junction but I knew trolleybuses went under there, so I thought we'd be alright, and we were. When you get to the end of Falcon Road you go left onto Lavender Hill and there's a bit of a slope up. I'm praying to myself, and I said to old Alf, 'Get on the back and get ready to knock that breaker back in if it goes, because I don't want to run back.'

Anyway, we got round onto Lavender Hill and down as far as Cedars Road, and there's a very ighty-flighty cocky Inspector in the doorway of the baker's. 'What are you doing round here?' he says, and I told him I was trying to work my way back to Telford if I could. 'You can't go up Cedars Road,' he says, 'go straight down to Vauxhall and round that way.' 'Don't be daft,' I said, 'see all those flames, that's Vauxhall, we've just come from there, he's brought a load of buildings down in South Lambeth Road, and I'm not going back for you or any blue pencil.' 'You'll never get round this bend,' he said, pointing at the curve round into Cedars Road. I said, 'I'm going to have a go, I'm driving this tram, not you.' They couldn't drive them anway.

So I took it very steady. I'd got the wind up, little butterflies in my stomach, and very gently we came round the curve. I'm leaning out of the near-side cab window working the controller with my right hand and the kerb's coming nearer and nearer as the front end swings round — a Feltham is much longer than a Standard and you had to watch that overhang — and as I came round the pilot gate just touched the kerb and then we were on the straight.

We took it very gently up Cedars Road in case the switches blew out, and onto the level. I said to old Alf, 'That's it, we're in the clear now.' But half way along Long Road we came up behind a string of trams, about ten of them, right up to Clapham, so we were stuck. There was nothing we could do, we couldn't go back, we'd have to see it out. I could have cried.

All the way from Vauxhall the tram had been empty, I was out of service, but I had given a copper a lift part of the way up through Nine Elms. I was really choked to think that we'd come all that way and then we were stuck. Anyway, we walked along this line of trams but couldn't see any Drivers or Conductors until we came to the café at the Plough which was open all night. By then it was getting on for two o'clock, and we stuck there until the all-clear went about five that morning, and God above knows where the Drivers turned up from, but they all came up and away went the trams.

We drove up as far as the Plough, and Regulator Hunt was on early turn. He asked where we'd come from and I had to explain it all to him. Now I knew I couldn't get up Stockwell Road, because they'd been working single-line the day before, and anything could have happened during the night, so I reversed at the Plough and went down on the up track as far as Nightingale Lane — there was nothing coming up that time in the morning — and went round the loop the wrong way round — I told Alf to hang onto that lever — which brought us onto the down track. Then I changed ends again and we carried on through Tooting down to Streatham until we got to Telford and I had to explain it all again.

The Depot Inspector told me that Felthams had never been round that district at all before, they weren't supposed to stray off the Purley route under any circumstances. I said, 'Well they have now, this one has.' He said, 'You'll be on the carpet in the morning, up in front of Bill Witty the Superintendent.' I told him, 'I've got my tram back home, that's all I'm worried about.' (2)

It was six-thirty when I got home and then I went straight round to my sister. Her husband

---

2. It has proved impossible to discover the date of this diverting episode.

worked at Higgs and Hills, but he'd gone to work already and I told her he'd be home presently. He was ! Then I went to bed and a couple of hours later the sirens went off again, so that was that. My wife had gone to work, so I went out to try and scrounge a bit of dinner for us both, and I believe that was the day I couldn't get a damned thing and we ended up having one fried egg between us for dinner. I was back on duty again at four o'clock and both Alf and I were told that we couldn't book up any overtime for the previous night. Charlie Scrivens, the Union Secretary, got it for us in the end. The next night there wasn't even a single alert, I couldn't believe it.

Two or three weeks later I was talking to Bill Witty, the Superintendent, nice old fellow he was, and he congratulated me, wanted to know how I'd done it. I told him I was worried about that turn into Cedars Road, but nothing would have made me go back to Vauxhall, not even him, I told him.

Coming down Brixton Road one night, Alf told me to stop the tram and we watched a plane caught in the search-lights above us. 'He's been chasing us from Kennington,' said Alf, 'come on, let's get out of it.' We hadn't got far up, nearly to Telford Avenue, when we heard one come down on that little church at the bottom of Brixton Hill, right opposite the Prison Avenue.

This Feltham was an early victim of the London blitz. Most of the damage is caused by blast. Brixton Hill Depot, 1st November 1940.

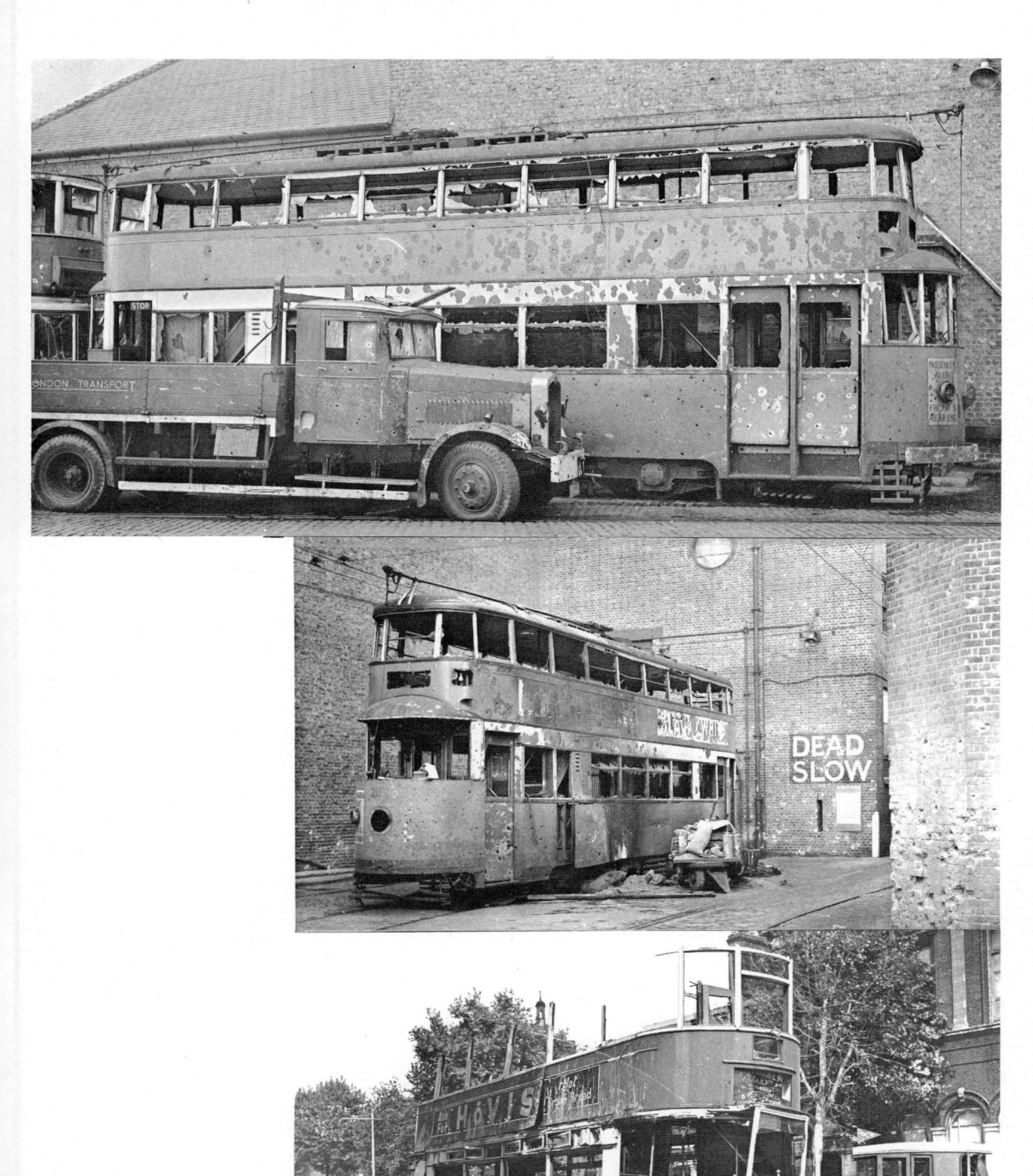

The aftermath of a raid on the Central Repair Depot at Charlton, 23rd October 1940. Both these Felthams were repaired, as was Car 1385, **right**, overturned and badly damaged in an air-raid on Kennington in 1940. 1385 had been rehabilitated at Charlton in 1936.

111

Another night a bomb fell near us, in Kings Avenue, so I went out and phoned up our Control and they put me through to the bus people, and I warned them that the 137 bus wouldn't be able to get through in the morning. I never even got a thank-you for that, or my tuppence back.

During the War we had a one-day token strike at Telford because unbeknown to the passengers our brakes weren't working properly. Our hearts were in our mouths when we were driving, the shoes were worn so thin that we had trouble stopping them regardless of pressure. Many of the shoes were wearing into wafers, even on the magnets. If the passengers had known what they were riding on they wouldn't have got on them. We never knew whether we'd stop when we wanted to, especially the Felthams. Even with the magnetic-brakes, with the blocks worn so thin, you were losing half your braking power. It was decided overnight. Charlie Scrivens was the Secretary — he's dead and gone, he used to be my brother's conductor — and we complained to him. We had a meeting about it. The Depot Foreman said there was nothing he could do because he hadn't got any replacement shoes, they hadn't got the steel. So Charlie told him, we'll have to take the law into our hands, we'll have a token strike.

So we had pamphlets printed to tell the public what the strike was all about, that the trams weren't safe for them to ride on, and then came out for a day. We threatened to come out for longer if nothing happened, but we won. Within days the Ministry of Supply released some more steel and it was delivered to Charlton. Charlton got its furnaces going and the shoes and brake blocks came in galore.

There weren't any other serious disputes, except for the strike for Saturday afternoon money after the War, but I was an Instructor then.

I remember once another Secretary at Telford found two duties in the new schedules that didn't comply — this was just after the war — so he called a general meeting and said there would be no trams after midnight and no nighters that night. Nothing would run until we had that duty rectified. I stood up and told him that I wasn't coming out and I'd be up at twenty to four the next morning, no unofficial strike for me. Everyone cheered and said they'd back me up and it faded out.

When we had a dispute just concerning Telford, Clapham used to turn its cars back at

Damage to Tracks, Enemy Action   2663

In order that tram services may be restored as soon as possible after damage by enemy action it may be necessary in some cases for trams to run over skeleton (unpaved) track; during the black-out a red lamp will be placed at each end of such open track and, before a tram can proceed, the Conductor must remove the red lamps and, after the passage of the tram, replace the lamps in position on the track.

Bombing between September 1940 and May 1941 disrupted tram services all over South London; diverted and shortened services were common. Effra Road, a fortnight after the raid on 19th April 1941; the generator is powered from the overhead wire. Trams could still operate to West Norwood, via Coldharbour Lane.

the Manor at Streatham, and Thornton Heath only came up as far as Norbury. These were the divisions between the depots. But these sort of strikes were rotten for working people, because they relied on the transport.

I was in the London Transport Home Guard. *(3)* When it was your turn you used to be on guard outside Telford Avenue there, behind the old railings that used to be there they built a guardroom for us. Then we used to patrol through the depot, if there was a raid on we were supposed to have a mooch through the depot, but there were workmen up there, all-night workers, if anything happened, we knew everything was alright.

Then sometimes we'd have to do a patrol down the road, up Christchurch Road, and round Daysbrook Road — round the back of the sub-station — just two of us might go for a walk up there at two o'clock in the morning if we got a bit fed up. You just had a look round. We used to get three bob subsistence money, take a sandwich or something in your pocket.

I remember one night someone came to the Guard-room door and said they could see a chink of light showing up in Pullman Court, so I went up there to sort it out with one of our drivers. We knocked at the door, a foreign bloke answered, we tried to explain what was wrong, and eventually my mate went through and fixed the blackout for him. There were bottles of whisky, bottles of gin and bottles of God knows what in his flat, and he offered us a drink. 'Oh no,' said my mate, 'not while we're on duty,' and we went. When we got outside he pulled a bottle of whisky out of his pocket, 'They won't miss this one,' he said. We had a good old drink-up that night!

The Depot at Telford was never hit, but one Sunday morning one dropped right at the top at Telford Avenue in the middle of the road. It broke some of our windows.

3. Tram and trolleybus men formed two of LT's original six — later seven — Home Guard battalions in 1940. All had an honourable record, and 30,000 LT staff passed through them before they were stood down in December 1944.

After the War came the official Victory Celebrations, on 10th June 1946; crowds immobilise trams at Westminster, and the street lights are on again. After this War the clippie on the platform of the 56 (left) will be allowed to remain in her job.

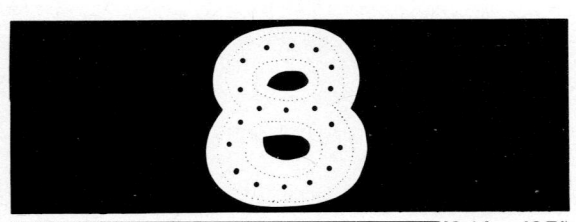

8
1946 to 1951
DRIVING INSTRUCTOR

After the War came the first undeniable signs that LT was treating its trams as a sort of poor relation; by now the need for replacements was all too apparent, and at a time when supplies were limited it was perhaps inevitable that the trams should continue virtually on a minimum-maintenance basis. Mr. Thomas, by then LT's General Manager, retired in 1946, and in the same year it was announced that London's remaining trams would be replaced by diesel buses.

In 1948 there was created a new post in LT, Operating Manager (Central Road Services), and the job went to Mr. J.B. Burnell, an LGOC man who had hitherto been Operating Manager (Central Buses). Those who worked on the trams at that time suggest that it was in these early post-war years that their organisation and procedures were first really interfered with. By 1950, when the bus and tram (and trolleybus) administrations were formally merged, it is fair to say that most key positions were in the hands of men trained in the LGOC tradition, and most of the remaining distinctive features of the Belvedere Road attitude to public transport were soon discarded.

This is not to disparage Mr. Burnell and his busmen. In any undertaking formed by amalgamation there will be internal competition, and there was a certain rivalry in LT between the bus and tram administrations, for each thought their own methods best. It is also most unlikely that bus crews could have been induced to accept the more flexible conditions under which tramwaymen had always worked, however beneficial these were to travelling London.

London Road,
at the Elephant & Castle,
in 1946.

When the War ended, London Transport started recruiting again, the troops were coming back from Germany, and in 1946 they decided to make up one more Instructor at each depot, so I had to go to the Clapham Motor School — my brother was already there — and became an Instructor. I was still attached to Telford Avenue, though I had to train men from other depots.

Of course everything was quite different then compared to after the first one. There was no real unemployment, in fact a lot of the clippies stopped on the job, and new men didn't stay as long on the job as they had done in the 1930's for example. I remember one young fellow up at Telford, he'd been on a few weeks, talking to me one day, he said he was packing the job in. I said, 'Why, the job's alright isn't it ?' He said, 'It's not so much the job, I like my weekends off, I like to go out, I like to go down to the coast.' So I said, 'To get down to the coast you've either got to go by coach or train and someone's got to drive you down there, but you don't want to drive anybody else.' He didn't like me for that but it's quite true. After the War they could pick and choose their jobs. Let's face it, there was better money to be had doing other things by then, and a tram-driver, or a bus-driver come to that, didn't have the status that he'd had before the War. The job was beginning to go down the drain.

It was a good job, regular nine-to-five middle turn, every Sunday off, with an hour off for lunch and a bit in a coffee shop here and there, or perhaps in a depot. We were always ready for a cup of tea. We got, I think it was five-bob a day extra for instructing. I carried on as a full-time Instructor up till January 1951 because, although I passed out as a bus-driver in 1950, they still took on new men as tram-drivers to keep the service going while the regular tram men learnt buses. They trained us in batches over the weeks leading up to the changeover.

Every new entrant started off at the Motor School, even if you came from as far away as Abbey Wood. When you went into the Motor School as a new entrant they took you into the School Room where there was a single-deck tram with all the windows out, chopped down the middle and mounted on rollers to show how the wheels worked. It was all connected to the juice, the controller worked just like any ordinary one except that the tram didn't actually move. There would be lectures. then we'd give them a bit of controller practice. There used to be twelve — I think, it might have been ten — controllers lined up on a stage where we used to lecture them.

Then we'd take them round Clapham Depot, say you might have half-a-dozen with you, you'd explain the function of the controllers, show them how the juice came up through the plough, the bus-bars and the plough-leads into the controllers, and show them how the fingers inside the controller on the drum functioned. Then you explained the hand-brake and the idea of the little clutch at the bottom which we always called the dog, and the rest of the braking system, how when you shut the power off and came round onto the brake notches you were generating your own juice to bring those electro-magnets down onto the rails with terrific power. And we explained sand operation, why you used it, how it helps on a greasy rail, and why you don't wind the hand-brake up until the car is almost at a standstill in case you skidded, by which time the magnets will have lifted, and then hold the car stationary on the hand-brake. We showed them the pits, the traverser and had a general look round the Depot. This first part of the instruction usually lasted around two or three days, although if you had a good bunch you could get through it in less time.

After that we'd take them out on the road in a Special Car, just an ordinary tram, one that happened to be in the Depot at the time. This part of the training took place from whichever depot they were going to work from. We went all over the place, especially over the routes they were going to work, but we were teaching them to drive, they learnt their actual routes later on a passenger car with an experienced Driver. They'd probably be on a Special Car for three or four days, and at the end of the day we filled in a progress sheet for each man, and Mr. Wallis — he was in charge of the Motor School — would decide when to send them out on the next stage, on passenger with a regular Driver, just as I did when I started in 1923.

I used to fix up with the CDI at Telford Avenue who the men would go out with to learn the various routes and stopping places. We made sure they went out with well-trained Drivers. The trainee did the driving, with the regular man watching and explaining everything to him, and believe you me, you could have the wind put up you at times.

Then, after a week of this trainee-driving we'd take them back in the School and give them a final going over ready for passing-out day. Mr.

Wallis used to take them out and test them and we weren't allowed to talk to them on the test, we just had to be there, ready to take over in case anything went wrong.

They just had to drive the tram along to Mr. Wallis' instructions and he would watch to see that they knew how to handle the tram and had a good road sense. Then he'd pick a quiet stretch of road, Southcroft Road, say or Downham Way, and coming down the grade he would quietly reverse the controller at the opposite end. This cut the magnetic-braking out. Then he'd give them a bell to stop, and the driver would find he'd got no magnet, so he was on his hand-brake straight away if he knew what he was about. We used to warn them that this would happen, although we weren't supposed to, so they were ready for it. If the car isn't slowing when you reach your second or third brake notch, we told them, go quickly to the top to test the magnets, and then put the hand-brake on.

Clapham's car 1675 on training duties at Victoria in 1950, **left.** *The car is drawn up to the rail ends; this is probably connected with the tea-stall that stood here for many years. 'L' plates were not necessary on trams, but seem to have been commonly used after the War. Manor House terminus in May 1948,* **below,** *Trolleybus 862 passes Norwood's car 1949. After 1940 this was the northernmost point reached by London's trams.*

Mr. Wallis was a good bloke, though. He'd only do something like that if it was all clear behind and in front, and he'd give me the wink beforehand. He was ready on the back platform to put the controller key back, so there was no danger. Another little trick was to lean out of the back when you were on the wire and pull the trolley-pole down just to see how quickly the driver reacted. But you had to be quick tram-driving, all sorts of things could happen on the road, so it was as well to be ready for them. We had very, very few failures, and if he failed a man one day Mr. Wallis wouldn't say, 'You're no good,' but, 'Mr. Collins or Mr. Sharman or whoever it was, take him out on his own and knock it into him.' He was a nice old bloke. While we were passing-out he'd even buy us all a cup of tea if we were up at Grove Park terminus or somewhere where there was a canteen.

We kept to the South-side. The only time we went over on the North-side was with Norwood men and a Norwood tram, generally to show trained men the Subway service. *(1)* All Norwood Drivers started off on the South-side routes, the 48 and 78 and later on the 10's, but after they'd been on the job for six months or two years — I forget which — they were passed out for the Subway service, the 33's, which went right up to Manor House. I'd take a bunch of them up, put one bloke on the handles, he'd know his way to Waterloo Bridge, and just sat back inside till we got there. Then I took over.

If they hadn't been through the Tunnel before they used to get the wind up sometimes, especially leaving Holborn Station going north. You had to leave the Station smartly directly the light went out, and get the power onto top notch going down the short, sharp dip just outside the Station, to give yourself a good run up the ramp that led up into Theobalds Road. There was always a policeman at the top directing traffic, and if he was an experienced man he would keep an eye open and give trams the right-of-way coming out of the Tunnel. But nine times out of ten you'd come up to find the copper with his arm up and that meant stopping just on the top of the slope before you'd reached the level. If you gave it too much power re-starting you could easily blow your switches and roll back, too little power and you'd roll back anyway. On any hill like that, the Conductor always had to be on the back platform ready to smack that switch back as soon as the Driver had shut off power, and to use the hand-brake and sand if it was needed. You'd never know which set of switches would blow out, it could be the back, or it could be the front. When we were training we'd always tell them not to build up on the controller too quickly and, when the switch blew out with a bang, they'd jump out of their skins and look up to see what had happened. That was part of our fun.

There were signals at the north end of the Tunnel to stop trams leaving Theobalds Road or Holborn while there was another tram on the slope, just in case one did run away. Mind you, it was bad driving to blow a switch.

Going through the Tunnel passengers had to get on and off at the Driver's end — the platforms were between the tracks — and you were supposed to have the chain across both platforms. At each station the Driver had to switch his controller key off before unhooking the chain just in case anyone touched it.

Generally speaking all new entrants had the same training, but if there were any Drivers for Telford Avenue, me and my brother — we were the two Instructors for Telford — would take them out on training after they'd come out of the School. Probably in the morning we'd take them out on a Standard, and in the afternoon on a Feltham, or we might take them out on a Feltham for the whole day. It was harder to train a Driver on a Feltham than a Standard, because when we found a man was getting on well on a Standard we could stand right back against the door and just watch him as he was going along, but with a Feltham the two of you had to cramp yourselves in the cab together, there was none of this Instructor sitting behind in the saloon like you have on buses. At one end you had to sit on the change-over box, and as they were air-braked you had to have your left hand ready in case you saw a spot of danger coming along, or if he wasn't using his brake properly you had to get hold of his hand and use the air-brake yourself. Sometimes in the summer it used to get so warm sitting there that I've nearly gone to sleep. But I will say this, the majority of fellows soon fell into it, and then when they passed out they'd often moan if they didn't get onto a Feltham.

A Driver in training had to know a lot. As well as driving, he had to know the inside of the controller, which fingers to isolate if a motor burnt out or the controller was faulty. If you had

---

1. The three Kingsway Subway services were all that remained of the North-side tramways after the conversion programme was suspended in 1940. The 31 continued operating until 1950, the 33 and 35 until April 1952.

In 1930 the Kingsway Subway was rebuilt for double-deck trams. Two days before the official re-opening on 14th January 1931, E/3 Car 1924 starts a test run from Bloomsbury, **right**. The north ramp of the Subway in January 1937, **right lower**. The Embankment entrance to the Subway was resited in 1937 and incorporated in the new Waterloo Bridge. There was always an official on duty at both ends. Around 1933, **left**, he acts as a flagman to hold up motor traffic; in 1947, **below**, he is less zealous. The Driver of Car 182 has lodged his hat behind the protective bars on the lower saloon bulkhead window.

35
Player's
Navy Cut
SPECIAL CAR
1924
CHOCOLATES
CUT PRICES

35
WALTHAM

a burning plough you had to get to a hatchway as quickly as you could, get it up and your tram over it, and change your plough over.

We used to take the trainees to the loop at Nightingale Lane to teach them how to change the plough, because there was a dead-hatchway on it. Two keys, kept in the tool-box on the tram, fitted in the hatchway and opened it out either side of the slot-rail. Then we'd let the tram coast over the hatchway, open the hatches in the tram — they were in the middle of the lower saloon floor — and then teach them how to pull the bus-bars up, take the plough out and re-plough it. Then they'd all have a go. If there were, say, six trainees on we'd have a shilling sweep and the quickest took the six bob. We kept an old pair of overalls to put over their uniforms and I'd time them, but sometimes they forgot to put the leads back on. It used to be a bit of a laugh, and it kept them interested.

We had to take them out on the wire, show them the change-pit routine and how to put a trolley-pole up. It was harder to train men when you got them on the wire, because of losing your pole. You'd get the individualist who'd say to themselves. 'I'll show them what I can do,' and you had to watch them. Then, when you got down to the end of Norwood Road at Herne Hill, where the 33's turned into Dulwich Road and the 48's went the other way, under the bridge into Milkwood Road, there was a junction and you had to be very careful not to get your pole off. Because if your pole came off and got up between where the skates were, you had a hell of a job to get it down. Then again, what used to be more dangerous on that road was down at Brockwell Park, where the trams ran a foot from the kerb, because you had to watch out for people stepping off the kerb. It was the same on Blackfriars and Westminster Bridges.

There were four of us went for bus driver training, I forget the exact date, some time in 1950. I did eighteen hours actual training on the bus before I passed out, that was three weeks in the School.

We had one of the old LGOC men, Jack Smith, [2] to train us. He'd been on the job

---

2. Jack he was, but not Smith. This is the only name which has been altered throughout the text, but it seemed fair to do so.

Congestion on Westminster Bridge in 1947.

donkey's years. I was about the only one he kept nagging, funnily enough. I was a lemon, as you might say, new to it, never touched a steering wheel in my life, and I was just turned fifty. He kept on saying, 'You won't be no bloody good, you won't pass-out,' and I said, 'I don't care whether I pass-out or not, there's still trams at Camberwell and Norwood, I can still drive one of them.' I didn't tell him I was an Instructor. It was nothing to do with him, and when I went on his bus I had to take my blue Instructor's badge down and put a Driver's badge up. The others knew I was an Instructor, two of them were my former pupils, but they didn't say anything.

One Friday night we pulled in at Telford and he said, 'Well, that'll do for today, lads. I'll see you up here in the morning.' I said, 'I shan't be up here in the morning, I'm going to Chiswick.' 'Look,' he said, 'it's no good you going to Chiswick without a word from me.' Well, that did it. I was going to make a complaint, the way he kept swearing and such, I couldn't swallow that. As an Instructor I never, never swore at any of my pupils. If they did anything wrong I'd show them again, I'd still show them. But he kept on. He wanted to know what I was going to Chiswick for. 'Look,' I said, 'there's a phone-box over there. I can phone Chiswick so-and-so, and I can go over and see Mr. Wallis or Mr. Wakelin any time I like.' Reg Wakelin used to be a tram-driver at Telford before he went on buses. 'Do you know them?' he said. 'Then don't be a fool, you be back here tomorrow morning.' I thought I'd give the old bugger one more chance, so I turned up the next day.

Now he always picked on me to drive first, I was always the first in the saddle, I don't know why. 'Well,' he said, 'you can go first this morning, I don't care where you go, anywhere.' 'Look,' I said, 'We'll go to Victoria, in the canteen, and have a cup of tea, but sit still and let me get on with it. I'll be alright, just keep your bloody trap shut.' We set off, down Brixton Hill, round Stockwell Road, South Lambeth Road, as easy as that, into the garage. 'Did I do alright?' I said. 'I didn't think you had it in you.' We only did half a day on Saturday, then Monday morning came.

'You're passing-out today lads,' he said. 'They might,' I said, 'but I won't, you told me I'd never pass out.' I was first in again, and off we went, down through Streatham Hill, Southcroft Road, Garratt Lane, until we got to Putney Bridge Road where we used to change the old plough, then I got down and one of the others took over. When we got to Chiswick old Jack Smith said, 'Well, we might as well do a bit of reversing.' I used to hate that, leaning out, I was always afraid of falling out. So I did one reverse and knocked the pole down for a start. Then Mr Wakelin came over. He had me up first, so I had to go into the saddle.

He asked me how I was, shook hands with me, and old Jack Smith, I don't know what happened to him, he just wilted, he looked like nothing on earth. 'You're passing-out today,' said Mr Wakelin. 'I'm not,' I said, 'the guv'nor said I shall never pass-out, so I'm not a bit worried, am I? I can still drive trams.' 'Anyway,' he said, 'we can still have a go at it, we'll go down to

Almost 2000 tram-drivers were re-trained for buses between 1950 and 1952; every one of them went on the skid patch at Chiswick, where STL 1267 performs in August 1950.

Wandsworth and have a cup of tea.' There was only one thing I was hoping for, I was hoping there was no traffic coming along when I got to the gates as you come out of Chiswick. Luck was with me, we came out of Chiswick, along the High Road, down, round, up over Hammersmith Broadway, easy as you like. Then I came up behind a trolleybus going down Fulham Palace Road and I thought to myself, 'Shall I follow him, or shall I go round? No,' I thought, 'here I go.' Right, change down, hand out and away, I left the old trolleybus behind. When we got to Jews Row Mr Wakelin asked me for my provisional licence, bang-bang, that was that. 'Am I alright, then?' 'Of course,' he said, 'you can go up this afternoon and get your full licence.' So I passed-out, I'm a bus-driver now as well as a tram-driver.

Mr Wakelin told me to report back in the Motor School the next day, so I went back to Clapham in the morning, and I had to go over to New Cross to pick up a tram and four new boys. We came out of New Cross Depot, up to the traffic lights, and I stopped. Then a bus pulled up on the nearside, and who should be on it but Jack Smith. He looked over at me and I just pointed to my hat, with its blue Instructor's badge on it. He had ten fits. I think he died soon afterwards. Then, a little while afterwards I happened to have some learners on, and he pulled into Telford with his bus.

Now bus-men always believed themselves to be a cut above tram-men, and he'd always said any bloody fool could drive a tram, so I said to him, 'Why don't you come for a ride on my tram, Jack, see what you think of it, I'll show you how easy it is.' Well, he didn't really want to, but off we went down to Mitcham Lane, and I showed him the handles and he had a go. Instead of notching up gradually, he put four on straight away, the tram jumped and that put the wind up him straight away. So I put my hand on top of his on the controller handle, 'Take it up to top notch,' I said, and we were away, down Southcroft Road hell for bloody leather, the old tram was bouncing and rolling, lovely straight road it was along there. When we got to Amen Corner I thought he'd had enough, so we turned back and I said to Jack, 'Do you think it's easy now?' 'No,' he said, 'I've had enough.' But I hadn't finished with him yet, I gave him a good run back down Southcroft Road, round that bend — you knew just how fast you could take those bends — and up Mitcham Lane. I put the wind up him good and proper.

When the contractors began converting Clapham Depot into a bus garage, the Training School shut and we went down to the CRD at Charlton. We had an empty old office down there, what had been the old canteen. We had our own trams down there, we took them down from Clapham, left them there at night and would go backwards and forwards passenger. It was a long day, though, an hour and a half to

New Cross Depot was bombed during the War; compare this view with that on page 15. Outside the depot, crews wait to change over and the Pointsman stands in his shelter. The Driver of Car 1227 adjusts his destination blind. On the lamp-post has appeared a new tram stop flag, although the trams will be replaced in three years time; this was common in South London at the time. March 1949.

Car 1826 stands outside the CRD after the Motor School had moved there from Clapham, **left**.

Mitcham Lane, by the single track at Thrale Road, **right**.

Charlton in the morning and an hour and a half back, but we were paid travelling time for it.

After I passed out as a bus driver I carried on instructing until January 1951, when they put the first lot of buses into Telford.

I only once had a go at a trolleybus, unofficially, while I was instructing. We'd been out on a training run and pulled into Jews Row for a cup of tea, when I happened to bump into an old tram-driver I knew who was on the trolleybuses. Everyone at Wandsworth was trained for trolleybuses. I sent the lads on ahead to the canteen and then drove the trolley almost down as far as the Inspector, at the bottom of Jews Row, but I didn't think much of it. You just did with your feet what you do with your hands on a tram, but they were the fastest thing on the road.

By that time, of course, we knew at Telford that we'd be going over to buses in a year or two. The plan had been to give us trolleys, but the War had stopped all that, it was the bombing that finished them off really. Up at the top of Wandsworth High Street by York Way there was a whole network of trolleybus wires. One night he dropped a load of bombs and a huge great premises there caught alight. Up came the firemen, but they were cooked, they couldn't get their ladders up because of the trolleybus wires. They got up there in the end, but I heard that several people lost their lives in the fire who might have been saved had it not been for those wires. There were a lot of complaints, and I do believe that had something to do with the abolition of trolleybuses.

Just about the time the War started, though, they marked all the numbers for the new trolleybus poles up on the wall right through from Kennington and up Brixton Hill, but the War broke out and stopped it. We weren't worried about trolleybuses.

Inside Wandsworth (Jews Row) Depot, September 1949. The shed is already being rebuilt for the buses that replaced these trams and trolleybuses on 1st October 1950. Temporary overhead wires are already in place to allow the tram conduits and pits to be filled in.

Cedars Road, where it met Lavender Hill, in 1950. Cars 1395 and 194 swing round the notorious bend. Until 1937, Service 32 had continued straight across this junction into Queenstown Road.

A sight of Streatham's tram services in their last years. Looking clockwise: Feltham 2074 at Lambeth Palace on the revised 22/24 service; Norwood Depot's 1966 at Southwark Bridge on an unscheduled short-working; Clapham's 1837 turning at Savoy Street on an early 22/24 in 1950; Rehabilitated car 996 outside Telford Avenue in December 1950. (996 is a Norwood car, on loan from New Cross at the time: it has a metal stencil number in place of a number blind.)

9

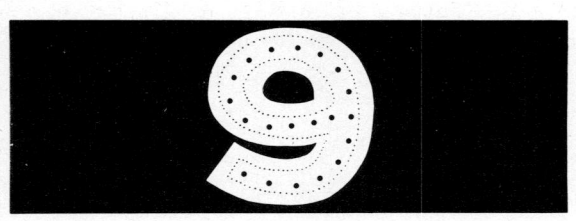

1951

LAST TRAM TO TELFORD AVENUE

The conversion of London's remaining tram services began at Wandsworth and Clapham Depots at the end of Saturday 30th September. The process was a complex one, and the organisation was more sophisticated than it had been before the War. At roughly three-monthly intervals a group of tram services ceased to exist after the close of traffic on Saturday night, and on the following day, new and revised bus routes operated in their place. At each of the eight conversion stages around 100 trams were taken off the road, and a similar number of buses took their places. Conversion trams were frequently re-allocated to the remaining depots, for it was generally the older cars which were scrapped first.

The re-building programme was hindered by certain sporadic and acute shortages of particular materials, in addition to the general limit on supplies. A sudden shortage of cement, for example, caused the tram-replacement garage at Thornton Heath to be designed as a steel-frame construction, whilst the design of Stockwell Bus Garage — which in part replaced Norwood Tram Depot — reflected a later (and perhaps fortunate) shortage of steel.

Hand-in-hand with this relatively simple replacement of vehicles and timetables, went a more complicated depot re-building and staff re-training programme. Seven of the tram depots were rebuilt while they continued to operate. Before the trams were withdrawn, inspection pits were dug and fuel tanks sited; in some cases it was necessary to erect temporary overhead wires to replace conduits which had been filled in. There was at this time a general scheme of garage re-building, for not only did the existing bus fleet need new premises, but many bus garages had to be altered to accommodate the new RT bus.

Tram-drivers were taken off service in batches for re-training as bus-drivers, and this required the short-term training of additional tram-drivers to cover their absence. Other staff also required re-training or transfer to non-tramway duties.

Once a conversion had taken place, there still remained much re-building at each new garage, and in several cases replacement buses operated from temporary open sites (including one beside Norwood Tram Depot). There was also the question of track-lifting. It is a compliment to London Transport's organisational ability that this complicated conversion programme passed off without any interruption to services.

At Telford Avenue, re-building began towards the end of 1949, although the preliminaries had already touched the depot. In June 1949, the all-day frequency of Services 16/18 was reduced, as it was also on Services 2/4 and 6. In July 1949, Telford took over the whole of Services 8/20 and part of 22/24 from Clapham Depot, together with a part of the Thornton Heath allocation on Services 16/18. At the same time, 19 of the 21 trams required for Service 10, plus two rush-hour Extra's on the Purley service, were sent to Norwood Depot. Thus the combined Telford operations from July 1949 required 97 trams (plus spares), whereas they had before required 93.

It now becomes necessary to distinguish between Telford Avenue and Brixton Hill Depots, for Brixton Hill — which it was intended to close — had spare accommodation, whilst space was required in Telford Avenue for its re-builders. In stages, Brixton Hill took an increased number of rush-hour cars from Telford Avenue. By the time that the first group of Streatham services was converted to buses — in January 1951 — Brixton Hill was running virtually all the rush-hour Extra's, whilst Telford Avenue — which was operating a maximum of 51 trams — was almost empty throughout the working day. After the January conversion, when the only tram service that remained in Streatham was the 16/18, Brixton Hill became almost a proper running-shed, for it provided 11 all-day cars on the Purley route, and up to 22 rush-hour Extra's, and it put out cars on seven days in the week. For the last three months that Telford Avenue remained a tram depot, it ran only 10 of the 39 all day cars on the 16/18 and none of the rush-hour Extra's, while Norwood transferred its 19 additional trams from the now-converted Service 10 to the 16/18's.

At the beginning of 1951 I was top of the safety first list at Telford — I had 34 consecutive awards when I finished — and on the Friday before the Saturday when the last tram ran out of Telford our guv'nor called me in and told me that he has a special job for me the next day. I had to take the Bluebird to Highbury, pick up a special party of Light Railway enthusiastics and take them where they wanted to go. So at nine o'clock on the Saturday morning I left Telford and ran empty till I picked them up at Islington Green. Then we went up to the foot of Highgate Hill, they wanted to take photographs, back down to Bloomsbury, through the Tunnel, and into Aldwych Station. They wanted to take some more photographs, so I told them to be quick — they were all photographs this lot — then out onto the Embankment and over Westminster Bridge into the Addington Street siding. Then a quick run through to Purley terminus with them all standing behind my door watching. By that time it was about one o'clock and they wanted a cup of tea. I thought I'd have to go back to Purley Depot, but they invited me to come and have some tea and sandwiches with them in Lyons, so I left the tram on the end of the tracks with the poles down until we'd finished.

Then we went back up to Telford, turning off up the Thornton Heath line on the way, put Bluebird away and took out a Feltham. Off we went again, up to Southwark Bridge, back to the Elephant, up to County Hall and along the Albert Embankment to Vauxhall. Now the old 22's and 24's had already gone three months before, and the tee-rail was a bit rusty and dirty. I was a bit scared in case the juice went off and I was stuck there on my own, but although smoke and sparks and filth were coming up out of the slot causing quite a commotion, we got through alright. We turned at Vauxhall, up to Victoria and back round through Brixton, Mitcham Lane, Tooting Broadway and I don't know where. It was about six o'clock when I put it away, but I enjoyed it. They had a collection for me, fifteen pounds, and five pounds for the Conductor. They enjoyed it, they had the windows open and were singing on top.

7th APRIL 1951

Bluebird at Highgate terminus and in the Kingsway Subway, **overleaf**, while touring with tramway enthusiasts on its last day in service in London. The second part of the day's tour was undertaken in a Feltham — this was also their last day on London's streets — and here 2079 is seen at Southwark Bridge terminus. Tram service 10 had already been replaced by bus 95 in January 1951. Stan Collins stands on the right.

FOR TRAMS
VICTORIA EMBANKMENT
TO
CHARING CROSS
WESTMINSTER
BRIXTON 33
HERNE HILL 33
WEST NORWOOD 33
ELEPHANT & CASTLE 35
NEW CROSS 35
FOREST HILL 33
EXTRA
SPECIAL
ALDWYCH
OUT

Then the CDI told me he had another job for me, to drive the last tram in from Norbury that night. It was the first I knew about it. Come back around ten o'clock he said, so I nipped off home for a couple of hours, had a bite to eat, a wash and brush-up, and then did the last trip. My wife was very excited, and the family all came out to watch it come back.

On a normal Saturday night, the last Service 16 car left Thornton Heath Pond at 11.56 p.m., passed Norbury at 12.4 a.m. and arrived at Telford Avenue at 12.15 a.m. But on the night of Saturday 7th April 1951, a Special car, hired by Streatham Ratepayers Association, left Norbury at 12.10 a.m. for a farewell ceremony outside the Streatham Astoria. (That cinema put on a special late film for those wishing to see the last tram arrive; in those days all cinemas were normally closed by 10.45 p.m.)

Because all Telford Avenue's trams were required for service elsewhere, an older car from another depot was provided for this last run.

I took the tram down to Norbury where clippies decorated it, strung it up with balloons and chalked on it, and one of the old spots down at Norbury, Hoppy Utting, got on the front. He had been an Inspector, but when he retired he was a plain-clothes spot who used to go out trying to catch Conductors on the fiddle or passengers not paying. A cripple he was, we used to call him the Galloping Major. 'I'm starting this tram,' he said, so I asked him where his licence was. I was joking, of course. He ran over the crossover and onto the straight, but motors were already beginning to pile up behind us hooting, so I took over. I had 'SPECIAL' up.

The tram was well crowded with people who had bought special tickets and I couldn't tear it up the hill to Streatham Common. Just past the Greyhound I stopped to let the resistances cool down. I had an extra sack of sand with me and a can of water, and I spread the sand out over the platform and damped it with the water, to help cool the resistances. That was an old tramwayman's dodge. I knew what would happen.

We got to the Astoria and there were crowds milling around all over the place. We were supposed to pick up Alderman Carr, because he was going to drive the tram back to Telford himself under my guidance. To tell you the truth I don't know if he did get on. My instructions were that he would drive under my guidance, but I can assure you that he never touched it. I wouldn't have let him drive it because the resistances were running so warm by then. I was the only one that could coax it along, there were so many people about. All I could do was to creep along very carefully at a snails pace, on — off, 'Get out of the way,' on — off, 'oi, hop it,' holding my breath all the way to Telford. At Streatham Hill Station I had to stop to let the resistances cool off again, because I daren't go over four notches — half power — because of the crowds, hundreds of them there were.

At Norbury, before leaving on the last run to Telford Avenue. Beside Stan Collins stands his Conductor, Bert Edwards, and behind him — on the platform — eighty-years-old Mr. George Utting waits to take car 947 over the crossover. 947 has been withdrawn from New Cross Depot for scrapping.

129

THE LAST 'SPECIAL'

The Streatham Times reported thus: 'The density of the crowds was such that the car could not travel at more than a snail's pace at any time along the route ... Certainly no tram ever had such attention ... The turning out of the passengers from the tram at Telford Depot marked the end of the official journey — and the end of an era. From the Depot the tram — now empty — made its way to the 'tramatorium' in Charlton where it will be broken up and burned.'
Stan Collins and the Deputy Mayor of Wandsworth, outside Telford Avenue depot, **centre**.

Feltham 2086 enters the Penhall Road scrapyard in 1950, **opposite**. Ninety Felthams and Bluebird were stored here before being taken by road to Leeds, where the Corporation was still operating Felthams until its last tram ran in 1959.

It took us an hour from Norbury to Telford Avenue, and by the time I got there there wasn't much of the tram left. All the removeable stuff went, even the point lever and the gong pedal had gone, and I don't know why the resistances hadn't burnt out. Outside the Depot my wife got up on the front and gave me a kiss, then I had to throw all the people off, pick up my Conductor and take the tram down to Charlton to be turned over and scrapped.

We took it up to Kennington, and turned it at Magee Street crossover, and went down through Camberwell. We stopped short the other side of New Cross for ten minutes — all the trams had gone by that time — and we had a cup of tea and a sausage sandwich from the all-night coffee stall. The coffee-stall keeper asked what a tram was doing there at that time of night — the New Cross routes were still running, but of course there were no nighters on a Saturday night — and I told him it was the last tram from Streatham on its way to the scrapyard. 'Thank Christ for that,' he said, 'have this one on me.' He was glad to see the back of the trams.

It was about 2.30 when we got to Penhall Road, and by that time there were a few other trams behind us, from Purley Depot I think. We had a bus laid on to take us back, and on the way the Driver pulled into New Cross Depot for a cup of tea. 'Are you blokes in a hurry?' he said, 'I don't want to go home yet, because this is all double time to me,' so we stopped in the canteen for a bit. It was six o'clock by the time I got home. The following week I picked up the biggest wage packet I ever had.

I was very sad when I drove that last tram. I was choked really to think that was the last time we'd see the old trams again. They had such pleasant memories for me, from a kid upwards as you might say. I never drove a tram again.

There were no longer any trams in Streatham or Clapham after Telford Avenue was fully converted to bus operation in April 1951, although trams from Norwood Depot continued operating through Brixton and Kennington until 6th April 1952. The last London trams ran in service on 5th July 1952.

10
BUS DRIVER & RETIREMENT

When they converted Telford Avenue Depot, they parked the first buses out in the open in an old field behind the Streatham Hill Theatre, where the Gas Building is now, but soon half the new garage was completed. We didn't have as many trams then, anyway, even before the first buses came, because our number 10's had gone to Norwood and that left them space to get on with the new garage. It was very strange when we went to get that first bus out, off that mud, because we hadn't had a lot of experience in learning to drive. The old wheels were spinning and the bus wouldn't hardly move. Then somebody had a brainwave and sent away for a load of big branches and twigs and slung them down, and that's how they used to get out.

I took my first bus out on the Sunday morning, 7th January 1951, after the first trams went. On the Saturday night I'd said to my missus, 'I'd better get up early in the morning and go up and have a look round, because I'm taking a bus out.' She told me to go steady, but I told her not to worry, I'd be alright. I had to be up there at five-twenty because I was the third bus out of the garage, on the 95's. When I climbed up into that cab I thought, it's not the same. I remember looking at the steering-wheel and the hand-brake, and I looked in the nearside mirror and everything seemed miles away. I was scared being off the lines, and the sweat was pouring off me by the time I got to Tooting Broadway on the first trip, and I was booked for being five minutes late. Then up to Cannon Street, and I started feeling my feet a bit.

When we got back to Tooting after doing that first journey I drank four cups of tea straight off, and then I was still thirsty. There was a bus Inspector there on the first day, watching us, and he came across, all smiles, and asked what I thought about bus driving. 'Rotten,' I said, 'I don't like it. Give me my old tram back.' 'Don't worry, boy,' he said, 'you'll come round to it.' And I did. I remember I used to think at first

Purley Depot's car 385, built for Croydon Corporation in 1928, passes Telford Avenue Depot shortly before Services 16/18 ceased operating in April 1951. The 'new' depot (left) is already demolished.

that I'd never pass that bloke down the road without hitting him, but of course I never did.

Going round by Saint George's Church on that first journey, I didn't quite leave myself enough room to get round and the back wheel came over the kerb, but fortunately there was no lamp-post there or anything. It taught me a useful lesson, I realised I had to take a wider sweep, so after that I visualised tram-lines in my own mind and followed them round until I got used to it. But after about a fortnight I forgot all about trams. One thing I can say is that I never hit the kerb with the front wheels once, but it was all so strange really, not being out in the middle of the road any more. With it being January I was worried in case we had snow, but we managed to get through to the Spring without any rough weather.

We did four journeys in all on that first day, and I finished just in time to sneak a quick pint before they shut down at two o'clock. When I got home, I'd no sooner got in the door when young Bet shouted out, 'Stop worrying, Mum, he's home.' First thing the missus asked me was how many lamp-posts I'd knocked down. Fine greeting!

After two or three weeks I got used to it, though, although one of the hardest parts was that windscreen wiper, we'd never had them on the trams, backwards and forwards, I found my eyes following it. And the fog used to worry me, you never worried in fog with a tram, you always knew where you were with a tram, the tram wheels were music to us, they used to talk to us.

Behind the Romanesque facade of Telford Avenue Depot, Brixton bus garage is being put together, **right**. *Bus RT 3264,* **below**, *stands outside the freshly completed building.*

Fog used to annoy me, because you've only got to lose a bend in the road, and before you know where you are you're over on the other side of the road. I've had the wind put up me more than once. It was alright in a tram because you knew where you were all the time, the wheels used to tell us. You couldn't tear it along, and you'd have loads of cars following you, they knew they were quite safe following your lights.

I had a puncture once in Kennington Road, during the day, up by Fitzalan Street. Now I knew there wasn't a café until we got past Kennington Cross, but I chucked my passengers off onto the one behind and went very gently along, because when they took the wheel off they could see if you'd been running on a flat tyre, the tube would be cut to pieces. I just drizzled it along until we got to the coffee shop. That was an unwritten rule for a busman, he always broke down near a café.

In 1959 Stan Collin's elder brother retired, and Stan took his place on the night-bus rota at Brixton Garage. He spent his last five years with LT driving one of Brixton's three night-bus turns on Route 287, which at that time exactly followed the tram night-route. All these night-turns were of just under five hours, without relief, for six nights a week. (Night buses never ran on Saturday night.)

In the winter of 1962 I was driving the night bus, and we had a load of snow that lasted for several weeks, the roads were frozen. Each time I pulled out of a stop the bus was skidding round and I was in a bit of a pickle. Although we'd been on the skid-patch at Chiswick, that was more or less to cover them, it wasn't much use in practice, but I mastered it in the end. Fog was different. One particular night I'd gone up to town clear as a bell, then down to Clapham and down came a thick fog, you could hardly see. So I hugged the kerb with my spot-light on as best I could, but once you lose the kerb, at a junction, say, you've lost yourself until you get back and find it. We crept slowly, right round through Tooting, and got round onto Streatham Hill and the fog lifted. There was no fog at all down at Brixton, and I was about an hour late. By the time we got up to Charing Cross there were all these printers waiting. 'Where the so-and-so hell have you been, where's the fog,' they said, they didn't believe me. In the meantime the fog had shifted round to Kennington, and I stopped in the Brixton Road and went round and said to them, 'There's the fog, this is what its been like all night up this part.' You can appreciate it, I suppose, if you've been standing for an hour waiting in the cold, where's the bloody bus and such, but what they don't understand is there's usually a reason for it. I put it away at Telford Avenue, I was glad that night was over.

I'd always told my wife that the day I was sixty-five I was packing up driving, so I retired in 1964. There were no pensions in those days, all I got was a gratuity of £674. I had to go up to

Bus 109 shared the Embankment with trams until 1952. RT 4003 vainly attempts to show its flexibility at Hungerford Bridge in April 1952.

Camberwell and saw some-one up there who congratulated me and asked me to stop on, but I said no. He tried as hard as he could, he said that when they lost us old folk they couldn't replace us. I told him, 'I've enjoyed every minute of my job, but I've had enough of it.' 'Forty-one years,' he said, 'that's a good record.' You'll never get a bus driver in times to come who can say he did forty-one years. *(1)*

Being a lazy man, I put my night bus away on the Saturday morning, had Sunday off, then started at the Tate Gallery on security on the Monday. I packed that up when I was seventy, and in 1973 I saw an advert for a part-time canteen cleaner at Brixton Garage, but I had to pack that up after a few weeks, when I was queer. I used to look out of the window sometimes and remember the time when I'd seen that garage absolutely empty, or with only two or three buses standing in it, but now it was half packed with buses in there, that's how short the staff was.

I've never been up there since, there's none of the old ones up there now. There might be one or two that came on after the War, when I was instructing, but I don't bother. You feel out of place. It's not the job I knew. Their ways of working are different, they don't seem to work amicably like we used to. For instance, when I was bus driving, if you were my leader and I saw you'd got a heavy road on, I'd shoot round you to pick up the next load when you stopped to pick up, we'd do one and one and one, but they won't do it today. You see them going down Brixton Hill five and six trailing. One bloke pulls up and all the others pull up behind him, and he's doing all the work. I used to hear them up in the garage, 'You follow Old Collins, he'll clear the road for you.' Sometimes I've shot round a bloke to help him out, and then he's stayed behind me and my mate's caught it. The job's gone to pot, they haven't got any idea now. When I started, back in the LCC days, you had to do your job and you did it, a hundred per cent.

I've had some happy times. I've had some good experiences on the trams and some bad ones as well. If we had trams now I'd go back driving tomorrow if I could, even if they didn't have glass fronts on ! Happiest days of my life were when I was tram-driving. Yes, when I look back I've enjoyed my life.

---

1. The Central Bus South Divisional Office was above Camberwell Bus Garage. In 1964 LT was exceedingly short of staff.

APPENDIX ONE

SOME NOTES ON THE DEVELOPMENT OF TRAM SERVICES IN STREATHAM AND CLAPHAM.

The basic pattern of tram services in London was already well-established in the late nineteenth century, and although most individual services were extended as the system was extended into the suburbs, the pattern remained generally stable until 1950. Therefore, although LCC tram services were not allocated numbers until 1912, throughout these appendices, where there is an obvious continuity of route, I refer to horse, cable and early electric services by the numbers allocated to their equivalents in 1912.

In this first appendix is given a short account of how tram services developed in Streatham and Clapham, followed by certain extracted information. On pages 138 and 139 are charts of the services operating at four random dates for which good information is available, presented so as to distinguish between 'all-day' and additional rush-hour services. On pages 140 to 145 are given full details of services operating in 1905 and 1940. The information for 1940 is directly reproduced from the LT Tram Allocation Book dated 8th May 1940. Each section of each service scheduled to operate has its own entry for each day, with the varying service frequencies expressed in 'Trams per hour'; the table on page 141 will convert 'Trams per hour' into the interval between one car and the next. The information for 1905 comes from the LCC Tramways Department Accounts for the year ended 31st March 1905, and is re-presented in a form similar to that for 1940.

The size and population of London was fast growing in the late 1800's, and metropolitan man was learning that he had to devote an increasing amount of time to simply moving himself from one place to another. For a few people — the superior classes, some called them — this mattered little, for their incomes did not generally depend on how usefully they allocated their time, and they had lately taken to establishing their homes by choice on the fringes of London. Between the fringes and the centre — in Brixton and Kennington, for example — dwelt the clerks, tradespeople and skilled artisans, an ill-defined and expanding class, typified by Mr Pooter and those who share his diary; it was mainly for them that road public transport developed in London. It was for them, too, that plenty of relatively cheap rented housing was being built in the suburbs, on land not required for the expansion of trade, for industry tended to remain where it had always been, on and near the River Thames.

Within and around the centre of London, where all these people had once lived, remained the working man, for he generally lived within walking distance of his work-place. The unskilled (and often casually employed) worker could rarely afford the luxury of a suburban terraced house, and he frequently had to be at work — or out looking for it — at times when the limited rail and tram workmen's services then provided were of little use to him. The working man and his family all too often suffered an unhealthy and over-crowded existence, as the number of homes in Central London was being steadily reduced by those who well knew that land bearing offices or manufactories was more profitable than land being merely dwelt upon.

It was to profit from this new demand for movement that there was opened in 1870 a horse tramway from the Lambeth side of Westminster Bridge to Kennington, and from there to Brixton Station and the 'Swan' at Stockwell. (Permission was sought for a linking line along Stockwell Road — possibly to operate circular services — but was not then given). In 1871, both lines were extended, to the foot of Brixton Hill and to the 'Plough' at Clapham. By 1875, further lines had been opened, north of Kennington, giving direct access to Blackfriars Bridge and the Borough, but then the London Tramways Company — owners of these and other lines, mainly to the east of the Elephant & Castle — stopped expanding; the first tramway boom was over, and it was plain that trams would not be allowed across the River into the lucrative central areas of London. For the next five years, the Company followed a policy of adapting its services to the demand, and it stopped making profits. It also levied a uniform fare of two-pence, (later three-pence), but after 1880 fares were reduced and services became more frequent. Agressive marketing and intensive production enabled the Company to increase its annual receipts without adding to its route-mileage.

The misery of the many, whose grinding poverty trapped them in the central areas of London, worsened in the 1880's. Lambeth was one of the most over-crowded districts. The Chairman of the LT Company recognised, but failed to understand the situation when he claimed that his trams had 'relieved London of an immense number of poor people by carrying them out to the suburbs'. (He also stated, quite incorrectly, that trams were to the poor what railways were to the rich; perceptions of poverty have always varied with the viewpoint of the perceiver.)

There was, as yet, no central authority able to regulate the un-planned way in which London was developing. Since 1855, the government of London (except the City) had been shared between local vestries, an indirectly-elected Metropolitan Board of Works (MBW) and a collection of appointed Boards and Commissions. Anyone who wanted to operate trams on the public highway could do so only by obtaining an Act of Parliament, and without the MBW's consent it was almost impossible for such an Act to be passed. Tramway Acts contained one common clause: twenty-one years after they were passed, the local authority was entitled to compulsorily buy the section of line authorised. (Turnpike Trusts had been authorised by similar Acts, but most Trusts had found it easy to retain control of their investments; the compulsory purchase clause in tramway Acts was almost certainly an attempt to avoid a repetition of the blatant profiteering and neglect of many such Trusts.)

A majority of the councillors elected to the new LCC were reforming Radicals who became known as the 'Progressives', but though their philosophy was strong, their plans were weak. In 1891 there was published 'The London Programme', some of the collected thoughts — though not all were original — of Sidney Webb, a Fabian dreamer and later LCC councillor. Sidney's manifesto became the Progressive catechism for the next decade or more. The gospel ran broadly thus : municipal housing would be built in the suburbs, and frequent services of free municipal trams — cleansed with municipal water and powered by municipal electricity — would run throughout the day along streets furnished with municipal gas-lamps, telephone booths and parks. Thereby, and with shorter working hours, would the dignity of man be raised. Few of the Progressives were socialists — an average of only six at any one time were

Fabians — and several went on to become Liberal MP's. Rather they were an idealistic Radical-Liberal Group, quite prepared to pursue collective ownership of necessary public services, but equally concerned that private ownership should flourish elsewhere. This political background is essential to an understanding of why the LCC tramways developed as they did, for only two of the Progressive aims came near to being realized: housing and tramways, inextricably linked in theory but rarely so in practice.

In the same year that the LCC first met, the London Tramways Company extended its Clapham line to Tooting, and a year later sought a second, short extension to this line, together with the projection of the Water Lane services to Telford Avenue. By now, however, the LCC had taken over the MBW's function as highway authority, and the price of its agreement was the provision of two daily 'artisan's cars' at fares even lower than those already in force, even though the LT Company already offered the cheapest fares in London. In 1892, the Brixton Hill cable-tramway was opened, and such was its success that the LT Company shortly afterwards introduced half-penny single fares on all its lines in South London. By now, three elements of what were later to become standard LCCT operating policy were established: cheap fares, frequent services and special early cars and fares for workmen. A fourth element was added in 1894, when the LCC insisted that an hours-of-work clause be a condition of the extension of the cable line to Streatham.

Regulation of tram services in this indirect way was not enough for the Progressives. The first length of twenty-one year-old track had matured in North London in 1891, but an unhappy combination of circumstances forced the Progressives to accept an arrangement whereby the LCC bought the whole North London tram system and then leased it back to the original owners in 1896. The first lengths of eligible track in South London lay around the Elephant & Castle, but instead of buying them in 1895, the Progressives waited until the bulk of the LT Company's system became purchaseable in 1898. After unsuccessfully seeking a lease-back arrangement, the Company agreed to sell to the LCC all its lines, premises and equipment. On 1st January 1899, the ecstatic Progressives became owners and operators of their first network of tramways, about one-sixth of the lines in London. At the time of the take-over, the Company employed almost 2000 staff, of whom around 25 were 'officers' and around 30 were women; most remained with the LCC, and inevitably many Company practices continued within what was now the London County Council Tramways Department. For the next 34 years, the LCCT was directly responsible to the Highways Committee of the Council.

Service improvements — notably the provision of certain all-night and additional early morning cars — followed, and from 1st January 1901 workmen were allowed to travel any distance before eight o'clock for one penny, with return allowed at the same fare later in the day. Fares generally were reduced by extending the lengths of stages, and conditions for staff were much improved. These measures cut the profitability of the lines, but the Progressives saw this as a form of profit redistribution. By 1902, 45% of LCCT passengers were being carried at half-penny fares, with a further 42% paying one penny, and although the maximum single fare remained at three-pence — as it had been in Company days — the Chairman of the LCC Highways Committee predicted that it would not be long before fares were standardised at one penny and a half-penny. The millenium was nearer then than ever it would be.

The penny maximum fare never came; more important, neither did many of the extensions of its tracks into new districts which the LCC sought from 1900 onwards, for by then the new London Boroughs had the power to veto new track construction, and they frequently used it. An Act of 1900, however, authorised the LCC to electrify all its existing tracks, and in 1901 it was decided to thus rebuild the Tooting line, 'experimentally', using the underground conduit system. Quite why the Highways Committee opted for the conduit — at roughly twice the installation cost of the overhead which was in use almost everywhere else in Britain — will probably never be known. The Progressives desperately believed that London deserved the best, and conduits offered certain visual advantages, particularly at a time when new telephone standards and wires were offending the sensitive metropolitan eye. Conduits also had practical advantages when overhead power or telephone cables broke, and they were said to avoid the damage to underground gas and water pipes which it was alleged could be caused by electrolysis. It was also believed — quite wrongly, as it turned out — that conduit maintenance costs would be cheaper than those of any other system. It is likely that the idea of a conduit containing electricity was attractive to those officers who were used to the efficiency of conduits containing cables, and it may well be that the idealism of the Progressives was rather taken advantage of by those whose interest in the conduit system was less public-spirited.

Reconstruction of the Tooting lines began in the Spring of 1902, and eventually, on 15th May 1903, after a curious opening ceremony at which a gentleman from the Board of Trade praised the undoubted advantages of the conduit, and a gentleman from Buckingham Palace spoke of his interest in the working classes, the first electric LCCT services began operating. Within a year, electric cars were also climbing Brixton Hill to Streatham.

It was not chance that led the first electric car to Tooting, for beside the terminus, on land bought in 1900, the LCC began in 1903 to build what was then its biggest planned concentration of houses, the Totterdown Fields Estate. When it was finished, in 1911, over 8000 souls dwelt there. This estate, with two others at Norbury and Tottenham, were the nearest the LCC came to achieving Sidney Webb's ideals until the 1930's; certainly they proved the theory that Corporation housing could be provided in the suburbs at a rent which, if added to a week's tram or rail workmen's fares was less than the cost of equivalent housing in the central London area. But it must not be overlooked that Working Class Dwellings were being built by the LCC in many parts of London from the 1890's, and they were often on or near tram routes. Shortly after electric cars came to Streatham in 1904, for example, there was completed an estate of 113 tenements — Briscoe Buildings — on Brixton Hill.

In 1907 the Progressives lost control of the LCC. They had sought to do little more for London than was being achieved in many provincial cities, but their idealism too often led to silly mistakes and lost opportunities. Nevertheless, while they were in power there was developed a policy which was to remain in the tramway planner's subconscious until after the Second World War. From the time that electric lines were opened, trams ran at frequent intervals on all services within the LCC — and from 1933, LT — area, from early morning until midnight or later, with all-night cars on several routes and cheap workmen's fares available on all cars before eight o'clock in the morning.

(continued on page 144)

1879
44 or 46 seat horse cars

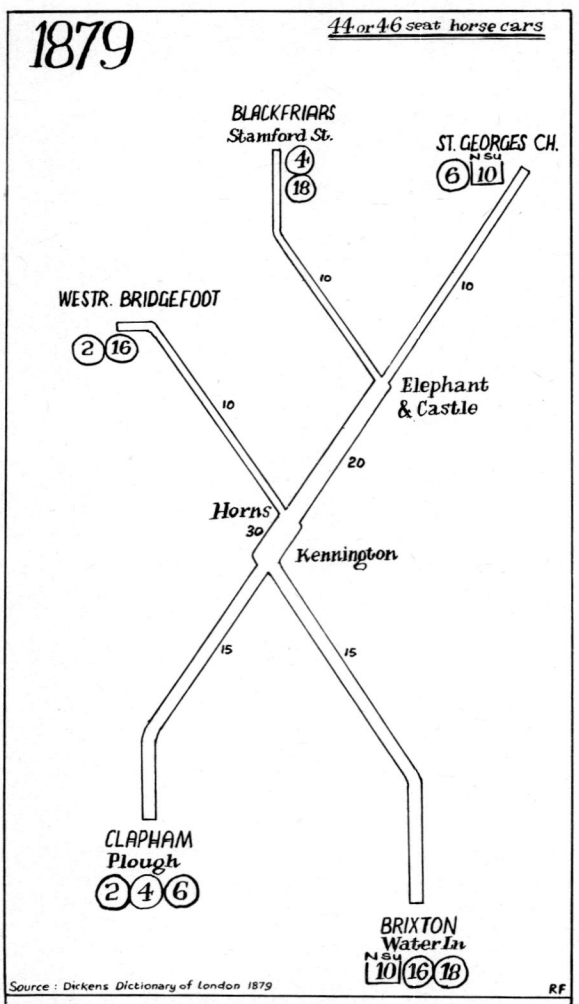

BLACKFRIARS Stamford St. ④ ⑱
ST. GEORGES CH. N SU ⑥ ⑩
WESTR. BRIDGEFOOT ② ⑯
Elephant & Castle
Horns 30
Kennington
CLAPHAM Plough ② ④ ⑥
BRIXTON Water Ln N SU ⑩ ⑯ ⑱

Source: Dickens Dictionary of London 1879   RF

Services operated every 12 minutes between 8.0am approx (from outer terminii) and 11.30pm approx (from London), except that Services 6 & 10 operated from 7.20am from the Borough and finished at 10.10pm from Brixton, 10.15pm from Clapham. Sunday services began one hour later.

DEVELOPMENT OF TRAM SERVICES IN STREATHAM & CLAPHAM

The thickness of each line indicates the frequency of service thereon on weekdays; the white section shews 'midday' services and the shaded section shews the additional service operated in rush-hours. The scale is as follows; measured in cars per hour.

(Beside each section of road the frequencies are shewn thus: midday service/full peak service)

NOTES: Services were not numbered before 1913, but as the basic pattern of services altered little over the years, the numbers allocated in 1913 are also used on the earlier maps. Additional services, not from Clapham or Streatham, are not shewn on Brixton & Stockwell Rds.

1894
44 or 46 seat horse cars

④ ⑱ BLACKFRIARS Stamford St.   13⅓/26⅔
㉚ WATERLOO STN 6⅔/20
BOROUGH St Geo's Ch.
WESTR. BRIDGEFOOT ② ⑯   20/46⅔
'Horns'   13⅓/40
Elephant & Castle
26⅔/53⅓   6⅔/6⅔
BOWLES RD OLD KENT RD Ld. Wellington ⑩
40/93⅓
Kennington

NOTE
Cable-hauled cars ran between Kennington & Streatham; all other services were horse-drawn.

HORSE CAR SERVICE, NOT CONNECTED AT BRIXTON OR STOCKWELL

20/60   20/33⅓
Brixton
STREATHAM Telf'd Ave.
⑩ (YELLOW CARS)
⑯ (RED CARS)
⑱ (DARK BLUE CARS)

LWR TOOTING Totterdown St.
② (DARK RED CARS)
④ (DARK GREEN CARS)
㉚ (RED CARS)

Source: L.C.C. Report on Locomotion 1895   RF

Selected Service Information

	FIRST CARS		LAST CARS		AV. SPEED	RUNNING TIME
	UP	DOWN	UP	DOWN		
Ser. 10	7.0 am	6.57 am	10.45 pm	11.20 pm	5.7 mph	65 mins
" 16	7.2 am	7.52 am	11.8 pm	11.45 pm	6.0 mph	40 mins
" 18	7.3 am	7.45 am	10.55 pm	11.45 pm	6.0 mph	50 mins

Additional Workmens Cars

Ser 2: 6.0am from Tooting; 5.55am from Westminster.
" 4: 5.55am from Tooting.
" 16: 5.55am from Streatham (horse throughout).
" 16: 5.30pm from Streatham.

(ALL ONE CAR PER TRIP)

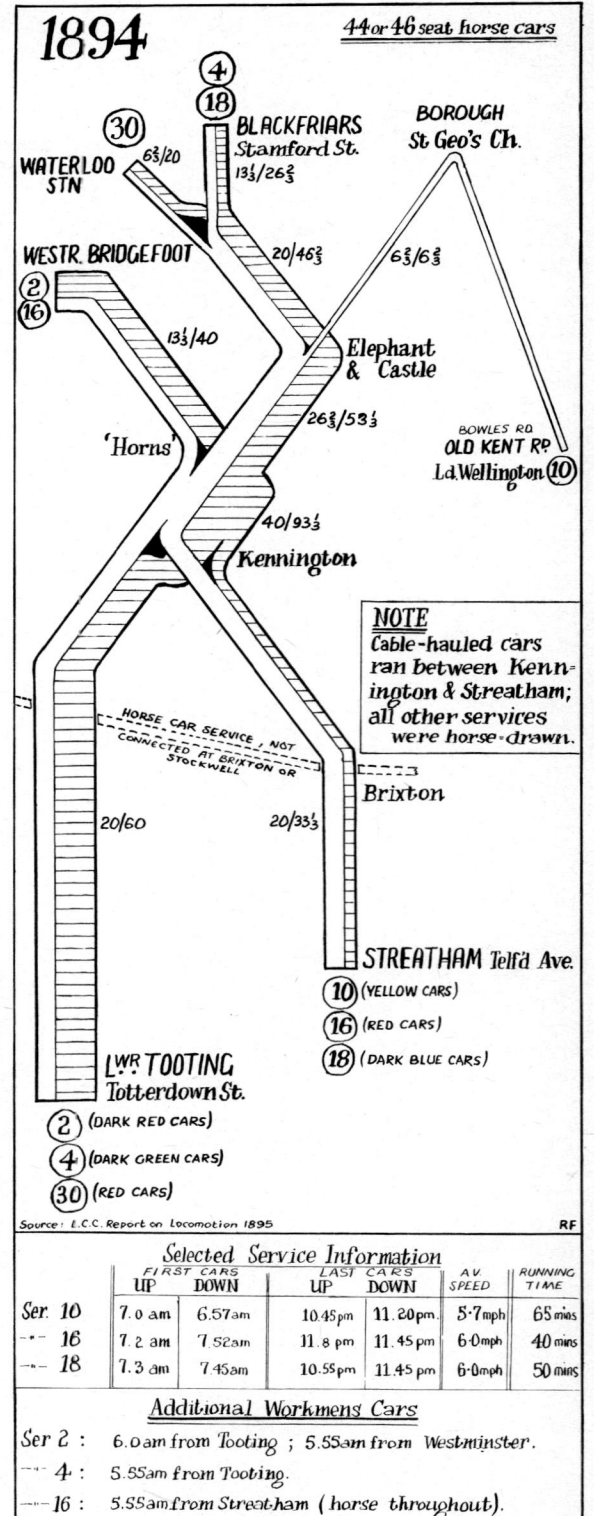

1905

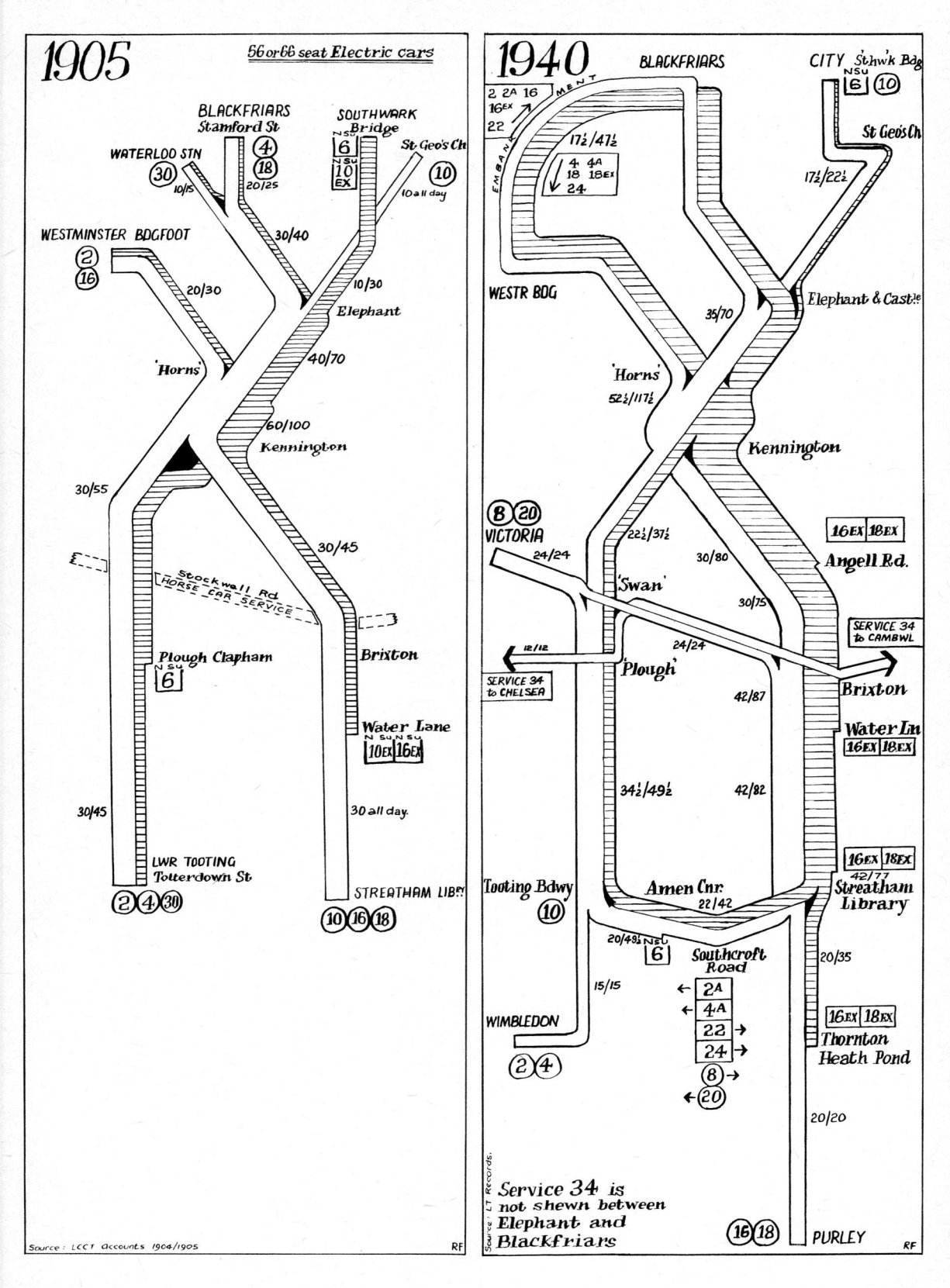

56 or 66 seat Electric cars

- WATERLOO STN — (30)
- BLACKFRIARS Stamford St — (4) (18)
- SOUTHWARK Bridge — NSU (6) NSU 10 EX
- St Geo's Ch — (10) 10 all day
- WESTMINSTER BDG FOOT — (2) (16)
- 10/15, 20/25
- 20/30, 30/40, 10/30
- 'Horns'
- Elephant 40/70
- Kennington 60/100
- 30/55, 30/45
- Stockwell Rd HORSE-CAR SERVICE
- Plough Clapham NSU (6)
- Brixton
- Water Lane NSU NSU 10EX 16EX
- 30 all day
- 30/45
- LWR TOOTING Totterdown St
- STREATHAM LIBY
- (2)(4)(30)   (10)(16)(18)

Source: LCCT Accounts 1904/1905   RF

1940

- BLACKFRIARS — 2 2A 16 16EX 22
- CITY Sthw'k Bdg — NSU (6)(10)
- St Geo's Ch
- EMBANKMENT
- 17½/47½ ↓ 4 4A 18 18EX 24
- WESTR BDG
- 17½/22½
- 35/70
- Elephant & Castle
- 'Horns' 52½/117½
- Kennington
- (8)(20) VICTORIA
- 24/24
- 22½/37½
- 30/80
- 16EX 18EX Angell Rd.
- 'Swan'
- 30/75
- ← 12/12 SERVICE 34 to CHELSEA
- 24/24 'Plough'
- SERVICE 34 to CAMBWL →
- Brixton
- Water Ln 16EX 18EX
- 42/87
- 34½/49½   42/82
- 16EX 18EX 42/77 Streatham Library
- Amen Cnr. 22/42
- Tooting Bdwy (10)
- 20/48½ NSU (6) Southcroft Road
- 20/35
- 15/15
- ← 2A
- ← 4A
- 22 →
- 24 →
- (8) →
- ← (20)
- WIMBLEDON (2)(4)
- 16EX 18EX Thornton Heath Pond
- 20/20
- (16)(18) PURLEY

Service 34 is not shewn between Elephant and Blackfriars

Source: LT Records   RF

139

LONDON COUNTY COUNCIL TRAMWAYS
Services operating in Streatham and Clapham, 31st March 1905
(see next page for explanatory notes)

No.	Route	Day	Trams per hour am pk	Trams per hour m day	Trams per hour pm pk	Trams per hour pm nor	Trams per hour eve	Depot	No of Trams peak	No of Trams Total	Remarks	First trams to London (As 'Route' column.)	Last trams from London ('Route' reversed.)
2	Tooting (Totterdown Street) & Westminster Bridge	M-F	15*	10	15	15	10	Clapham	22		* 20 minute service from 4.23am till 5.1am from Tooting on each route, then 7½ cph until 7.56am from Tooting.		12.28am
4	Tooting (Totterdown Street) & Blackfriars Bridge		15*	10	15	15	10		23				12.28am
30	Tooting (Totterdown Street) & Waterloo Station.		15*	10	15	15	10		22	67	+ 9 extra cars at very busiest times.		12.28am
2	Tooting (Totterdown Street) & Westminster Bridge.	Sat	15*	10	15	15	10	Clapham	22				12.28am (1.7am to Plough)
4	Tooting (Totterdown Street) & Blackfriars Bridge.		15*	10	15	15	10		23				12.28am (1.12am to Plough)
30	Tooting (Totterdown Street) & Waterloo Station		15*	10	15	15	10		22	67	+ 9 extra cars at very busiest times.		12.28am (1,17am to Plough)
2	Tooting (Totterdown Street) & Westminster Bridge	Sun	-	6⅔	-	10	10	Clapham	15			Early Service: Cars at 8.30am, 9am and 9.30am from Bridges and W'loo.	12.7am
4	Tooting (Totterdown Street) & Blackfriars Bridge.		-	6⅔	-	10	10		16				12.12am
30	Tooting (Totterdown Street) & Waterloo Station.		-	6⅔	-	10	10		15	46			12.10am
6	'Plough' Clapham & Southwark Bridge.	M-F	10	-	10	10	-	Clapham	10	10	No service at Sthwk; 10.2am-4.9pm.	6.38am	9.57pm
6	'Plough' Clapham & Southwark Bridge.	Sat	10	-	10	10	-	Clapham	10	10	No service at Sthwk; 10.38am-12.33pm	6.38am	6.27pm
6	Sunday service discontinued												
10	Streatham Library & St. George's Church	M-F	10	10	10	10	8	Clapham	13			5.0am, then every twenty minutes till 6.28am.	10.59pm
10Ex	Water Lane (Brixton) & Southwark Bridge.		10*	-	10	-	-		10	23	* till 8.24am at Water Ln.	6.59am 3.30pm	9.53am at Water Ln.
10	Streatham Library & St. George's Church	Sat	10	10	10	10	8	Clapham	13				10.50pm.
10Ex	Water Lane (Brixton) & Southwark Bridge		10	-	10*	-	-		10	23	* till 5.2pm Water Ln.	As Mon-Fri.	9.53am at Water Ln.
10	Streatham Library & St. George's Church.	Sun	-	6⅔	-	10	6⅔	Clapham	13	13		Early service: Cars at 9am, 9.30am and 10 am.	10.39pm
10Ex	Sunday service suspended												
16	Streatham Library & Westminster Bridge.	M-F	10	10	10	10	8	Clapham	13			5.0am, then every twenty minutes till 6.28am	12.32am
16Ex	Water Lane (Brixton) & Westminster Bridge.		5	-	5*	-	-		4		* till 8.12am at Water Ln.	7.11am 3.54pm	9.47am at Water Ln.
18	Streatham Library & Blackfriars Bridge.		10	10	10	10	8		14	31			12.31am
16	Streatham Library & Westminster Bridge	Sat	10	10	10	10	8	Clapham	13			5.0am, then every twenty minutes until 6.28am	12.30am
16Ex	Water Lane (Brixton) & Westminster Bridge		5	-	5*	-	-		4		* till 4.58pm at Water Ln.	7.11am 3.54pm	9.47am at Water Ln.
18	Streatham Library & Blackfriars Bridge.		10	10	10	10	8		14	31			12.20am
16	Streatham Library & Westminster Bridge	Sun	-	6⅔	-	10	6⅔	Clapham	13			Early service: Cars at 9am, 9.30am, and 10am from both Bridges.	12.3am
16Ex	Sunday service suspended												
18	Streatham Library & Blackfriars Bridge.		-	6⅔	-	10	6⅔		14	27			12.12am.

	ALL NIGHT TRAMS (except Saturday night)										
	'Plough' Clapham & Westminster Bridge.	Every 28 minutes					Clapham	2		12.15am-4.27am from 'Plough'	Water Ln - Blckfrs and 'Plough' - Westr night cars are timed to connect at Kennington Gate in both directions.
	'Plough' Clapham & Blackfriars Bridge.	Every 28 minutes					Clapham	2		12.19am-4.13am from 'Plough'	
	Water Lane (Brixton) & Blackfriars Bridge	Every 28 minutes					Clapham	2	6	1.10am-4.55am from Water Ln.	Workmen's fares are available on all cars leaving any terminus after 1.30am.

140

NOTES REGARDING 1905 OPERATIONS (previous page)

1. Service numbers were not used in 1905. Those shewn were allocated in 1912.
2. The times of the subdivisions of 'Trams per hour' column should be understood as follows. Note the variations from day to day, and that the times are approximations. They give some indications of the sort of turns which were being worked.

	am pk	m day	pm pk	pm nor	eve
Monday-Friday	7-9.30am	9.30am-4pm	4pm-8pm	8-9.30pm	9.30pm to last car
Saturday	7-9.30am	9.30am-Noon	Noon-6pm	6-9.30pm	9.30pm to last car
Sunday	-	10am-Noon	-	Noon-9pm	9pm to last car

3. 'At the very busiest times' on Weekdays there were 140 cars in service; at slack times there were 86 on the road. On Sundays there were 86 cars in service after mid-day.
(From 1906 to 1910 the LCC claimed an average service speed for electric cars of 8½mph. Where actual running-times are not known, they have been estimated with reasonable accuracy by dividing the length of the route by this average speed. Layover is calculated at a minimum of one minute at each end of the route - for the LCC was never over-generous with layover - and no allowance is made for cars working alternately on different routes, although such 'joint compilation' of services was likely.
4. According to the Chief Officer's Report for 1904/5 the converted cable-car Depot at Streatham was not yet re-opened on 31st March 1905. Therefore it has been assumed that all these services operated from Clapham Depot, which could accommodate 174 cars at this time. Some may have operated from Marius Road Depot, but this temporary car-shed was used at least in part for storing withdrawn horse-cars.
5. On 31st March 1905 the LCC owned 401 electric trams, the whole of Classes A B C and D and the 1900 experimental car. The average number of trams in daily use - including those used on the New Cross lines - is estimated at 310, or 78% of the fleet.

LONDON TRANSPORT TRAMS
Services operating in Streatham and Clapham, May 8th 1940

The times of the sub-divisions of 'Trams per hour' should be understood as follows :

	am pk	m day	pm pk	pm nor	eve
Monday-Friday	7am-9am	9am-4pm	4-7pm	-	7pm-finish
Saturday	7am-9am	9am-Noon	Noon-2pm	2pm-7pm	7pm-finish
Sunday	-	Start-Noon	-	Noon-7pm	7pm-finish

'Trams per hour' conversion table

Trams per hour :	15	12	10	8	7½	7	6⅔	6	5½	5	3½	3	2
Minutes between cars :	4	5	6	7½	8	8½	9	10	11	12	17	20	30

Route No.	Route.	Day.	Trams per hour. am pk	m day	pm pk	pm nor	eve	Time Sched No.	Duty Sched No.	Allocation. Depot.	No. of Trams. am	pm	Total No. of Trams. am	pm
2	Wimbledon & Victoria Embankment (via Westminster Bridge)	M-F.	7½	7½	7½	—	7½	2774	4175	Clapham	29	30	29	30
4	Wimbledon & Victoria Embankment (via Blackfriars Bridge)		7½	7½	7½	—	7½							
2	Wimbledon & Victoria Embankment (via Westminster Bridge)	Sat.	7½	7½	7½	7½	5	2779	4173	Clapham	28	29	28	29
4	Wimbledon & Victoria Embankment (via Blackfriars Bridge)		7½	7½	7½	7½	5							
2	Wimbledon & Victoria Embankment (via Westminster Bridge)	Sun.	—	10	—	10	6	2780	4172	Clapham	34	35	34	35
4	Wimbledon & Victoria Embankment (via Blackfriars Bridge)		—	10	—	10	6							

| Route No. | Route. | Day. | Trams per hour | | | | | Time Sched No. | Duty Sched No. | Allocation. | | Total No. of Trams. | |
			am pk.	m day	pm pk.	pm nor.	eve			Depot.	No. of Trams.		
											am | pm	am | pm	
2a	Streatham Library & Victoria Embankment (via Clapham & Westminster Bridge)	M–F.	7½	–	7½	–	–	1641	4166 4175	Brixton Clapham	— | 6 44 | 42	44 | 48	
4a	Streatham Library & Victoria Embankment (via Clapham & Blackfriars Bridge)		7½	–	7½	–	–						
22	Tooting Broadway & Victoria Embankment (via Streatham & Westminster Bridge)		7½	–	7½	–	–						
24	Tooting Broadway & Victoria Embankment (via Streatham & Blackfriars Bridge)		7½	–	7½	–	–						
2a	Streatham Library & Victoria Embankment (via Clapham & Westminster Bridge)	Sat.	7½	–	7½	–	–	1355	4171 4173	Brixton Clapham	11 | 15 33 | 33	44 | 48	
4a	Streatham Library & Victoria Embankment (via Clapham & Blackfriars Bridge)		7½	–	7½	–	–						
22	Tooting Broadway & Victoria Embankment (via Streatham & Westminster Bridge)		7½	–	7½	–	–						
24	Tooting Broadway & Victoria Embankment (via Streatham & Blackfriars Bridge)		7½	–	7½	–	–						
6	Tooting (Amen Corner) & City (Southwark)	M–F.	7½	7½	7	–	7	2781	4175	Clapham	11 | 11	11 | 11	
6	Tooting (Amen Corner) & City (Southwark)	Sat.	7½	7½	7½	–	–	2783	4173	Clapham	11 | 14	11 | 14	
6	Wimbledon & City (Southwark)		–	–	–	7½	6						
8	Victoria Stn. & Victoria Stn. (via Clapham & Streatham)	M–F.	12	12	12	–	7½	2771	4166 4175	Brixton Clapham	— | 2 18 | 20	31 | 33	
20	Victoria Stn. & Victoria Stn. (via Streatham & Clapham)		12	12	12	–	7½		4166	Streatham	13 | 11		
8	Victoria Stn. & Victoria Stn. (via Clapham & Streatham)	Sat.	12	12	12	12	12	2775	4173 4171	Clapham Streatham	20 | 22 11 | 11	31 | 33	
20	Victoria Stn. & Victoria Stn. (via Streatham & Clapham)		12	12	12	12	12						
8	Victoria Stn. & Victoria Stn. (via Clapham & Streatham)	Sun.	–	6	–	7½	7½	2776	4172 4178	Clapham Streatham	7 | 9 8 | 10	15 | 19	
20	Victoria Stn. & Victoria Stn. (via Streatham & Clapham)		–	6	–	7½	7½						

Route No.	Route.	Day.	Trams per hour.					Time Sched No.	Duty Sched No.	Allocation.		Total No. of Trams.	
			am pk.	m day	pm pk.	pm nor.	eve			Depot.	No. of Trams.		
											am | pm	am | pm	
10	Tooting Broadway & City (Southwark)	M–F.	15	10	15	–	7½	2772	4166 4166	Brixton Streatham	8 8 17 19	25 27	
10	Tooting Broadway & City (Southwark)	Sat.	15	10	15	–	–	2773	4171 4171	Brixton Streatham	6 7 19 19	25 26	
10	Tooting Broadway & St. Georges Church (Borough)		–	–	–	12	10						
10	Tooting Broadway & City (Southwark)	Sun.	–	6	–	6	6	2782	4178	Streatham	9 9	9 9	
12	Wandsworth High St. & London Bridge (Borough)	M–F.	12	10	12	–	7½	2893	4268 } 4267 }	Wandsworth	16 17	16 17	
12	Wandsworth High St. & London Bridge (Borough)	Sat.	10	10	10	10	10	2872	4277 } 4278 }	Wandsworth	14 14	14 14	
12	Wandsworth High St. & London Bridge (Borough)	Sun.	–	6	–	7½	7½	2879	4273	Wandsworth	8 10	8 10	
16	Purley & Victoria Embankment (via Westminster Bridge)	M–F.	10	10	10	–	7½	2770	4166 4166	Brixton Streatham	– 1 29 30		
18	Purley & Victoria Embankment (via Blackfriars Bridge)		10	10	10	–	7½		4158	Thornton Hth.	21 21	50 52	
16 Ex	Thornton Heath Pond or Telford Avenue or Water Lane or Angel Road and Victoria Embankment (via Westminster Bridge)	M–F.	15	–	–	–	–	1941	4166 4166	Brixton Streatham	32 23 5 4	37 27	
18 Ex	Thornton Heath Pond or Telford Avenue or Water Lane or Angel Road and Victoria Embankment (via Blackfriars Bridge)		15	–	–	–	–						
16/18 Ex	Norbury & Victoria Embankment (via Westminster or Blackfriars Bridges)		–	3	–	–	–						
18 Ex	Thornton Heath Pond & Victoria Embankment (via Blackfriars Bridge)		–	–	10	–	–						
16 Ex	Thornton Heath Pond & Victoria Embankment (via Westminster) Bridge)		–	–	5½	–	–						
16	Purley & Victoria Embankment (via Westminster Bridge)	Sat.	10	10	10	10	10	2777	4171	Streatham	30 32		
18	Purley & Victoria Embankment (via Blackfriars Bridge)		10	10	10	10	10		4161	Thornton Hth.	20 20	50 52	
16 Ex	Norbury & Victoria Embankment (via Westminster Bridge)	Sat.	7	5	5½	–	–	1365	4171	Brixton	22 17		
	Telford Avenue & Victoria Embankment (via Westminster Bridge)		3½	–	–	–			4171	Streatham	4 –	26 17	
18 Ex	Norbury & Victoria Embankment (via Blackfriars Bridge)		7	5	5½	–	–						
	Telford Avenue & Victoria Embankment (via Blackfriars Bridge)		3½	–	–	–							
16	Purley & Victoria Embankment (via Westminster Bridge)	Sun.	–	6	–	7½	7½	2778	4178	Streatham	13 21		
18	Purley & Victoria Embankment (via Blackfriars Bridge)		–	6	–	7½	7½		4180	Thornton Hth.	16 16	29 37	

| Route No. | Route. | Day. | Trams per hour. | | | | | Time Sched No. | Duty Sched No. | Allocation. | | Total No. of Trams. | |
| | | | am pk. | m day | pm pk. | pm nor. | eve | | | Depot. | No. of Trams. | | |
											am	pm	am	pm
34	Chelsea (Kings Road) & Blackfriars	M–F.	12	6	12	–	6	2785	4168	Clapham	28	29	28	29
34	Chelsea (Kings Road) & Camberwell Green		–	6	–	–	6							
34	Camberwell Green & Blackfriars		6	–	6	–	–							
34	Chelsea (Kings Road) & Blackfriars	Sat.	12	12	7½	7½	6	2784	4179	Clapham	27	26	27	26
34	Chelsea (Kings Road) & Camberwell Green		–	–	7½	7½	6							
34	Camberwell Green & Blackfriars		3	–	3	–	–							
34	Chelsea (Kings Road) & Blackfriars	Sun.	–	6	–	6¾	5	2804	4170	Clapham	11	21	11	21
34	Chelsea (Kings Road) & Camberwell Green		–	–	–	6¾	5							

ALL NIGHT TRAMS.

(Saturday Night Excepted)

Route	Depot.	Trams per hour.	No. of Trams.
Streatham Library & Victoria Embankment … … … Via Balham, Clapham, Blackfriars, Westminster.	Clapham	2	3
Tooting Broadway & Victoria Embankment … … … Via Streatham, Brixton, Kennington, Westminster, Blackfriars.	Streatham	2	3

(continued from page 137)

In 1905 there was a tram every two minutes throughout the day between Streatham and London, with extra cars from Water Lane in rush hours. 'At the very busiest times', trams headed north from the Plough Clapham with an average interval of only 65 seconds — less than 300 yards — between them. Here, at last, was the 'people's carriage', the Progressive legacy to working-class London; a quality and quantity of service at cheap fares. Where LCC trams ran, they provided what was surely the most intensive and convenient service to be found anywhere in Britain. This policy did not help the LCCT to balance its books, particularly in the 1920's, when its trams competed during the day with buses which provided neither early services nor workmen's fares. And even though the chronically poor could still not afford to live in the suburbs in the 1930's, they could at least take the occasional cheap trip at weekends to Bostall Woods or Purley.

The policy endured. By 1940 the theoretical interval between rush-hour cars on Brixton Hill was down to forty seconds, and of the 290 trams which hourly crossed Westminster and Blackfriars Bridges onto the Embankment in the morning rush-hour, one-third came direct from Streatham or Clapham. During rush-hours almost every suburb on the LCCT system had a direct service to two or three London terminals, for not only were more cars operated in rush-hours, many of them followed special routes.

The extracted information should not be read too literally, for there were at times certain differences between what was scheduled to operate and what did operate. LCCT trams were efficiently supervised 'on the road', and this practice continued after 1933. Inspectors and Regulators would short-turn or extend cars to cover irregularities in a service, and even diverted trams from one service to another to cope with delays or unpredicted queues.

Nor do simple comparisons tell the whole story, for there is here no information on competing bus or rail services, important after 1920. Look at the reversed importance of the Clapham Road and Brixton Hill services by 1940 to understand something of the effect of connecting the Northern Line with the West End and extending it south from Clapham in 1926.

Full details of the extensions and alterations made to LCC services after 1903 are given in maps in Appendix Two. Right up to the end of trams in Streatham and Clapham, in 1950 and 1951, services along the two main roads continued (with the exception of Service 34) an almost independent operation within the LCC and LT network, following the basic route pattern laid down by the London Tramways Company in the late nineteenth century. In 1977, buses still leave Wimbledon and Purley, to run via Clapham or Streatham to Kennington, over Westminster Bridge, along the Embankment and back over Blackfriars Bridge. But they do so less frequently than did the trams, and workmen's tickets are no longer sold.

TRAM ROUTES

P.M. times are in heavy figures

2 / 4 — WIMBLEDON STN. – VICTORIA EMBANKMENT
Via South Wimbledon, Merton, Tooting, Balham, Clapham, Kennington, (2) Westminster Bridge, (4) Blackfriars Bridge

Time 54 mins. Service 4 mins.

WEEKDAYS		SAT.			SUNDAY	
First	Last	First	Last		First	Last
4 54	11 43	4 53	12 11	Wimbledon to Embankment	7 39	11 40
4 54	**12 0**	4 53	12 11	Wimbledon to Clapham	7 39	**12 3**
4 46	**11 6**	4 52	**11 17**	Embt. (Savoy St.) to Wimbledon	6 46	**11 8**
4 46	**12 30**	4 52	**1 25**	Emb'km't (Savoy St.) to Merton	4 48	**12 17**
4 46	**12 30**	4 52	**1 39**	Emb'km't (Savoy St.) to Tooting	4 48	**12 17**
4 15	**12 40**	4 19	**1 10**	Clapham to Embankment	4 23	**12 32**
4 26	**11 30**	4 26	**11 42**	Clapham to Wimbledon	7 9	**11 35**
3 49	**12 54**	3 49	**2 30**	Clapham to Merton	5 12	**12 44**
4 5	**12 26**	4 5	**12 55**	Merton to Embankment	5 29	**12 17**

2A / 4A — STREATHAM LIBRARY – VICTORIA EMBANKMENT
Via Mitcham Lane, Southcroft Road, Tooting, Balham, Clapham, Kennington, (2a) Westminster Bridge, (4a) Blackfriars Bridge

Time 54 mins. Service 4–5 mins.

WEEKDAYS (Peak Hours only)			Saturday	
	First	Last	First	Last
Streatham Library to Embankment	7 31	6 12	7 13	**1 30**
Embankment to Streatham Library	7 47	6 58	7 45	**2 26**

6 — TOOTING Amen Corner – CITY Southwark
Via Balham, Clapham Common, Stockwell, Kennington, Elephant, Southwark Bridge

Time 43 mins. Service 8–12 mins.

WEEKDAYS ONLY			
	First	Last	Sat.
Amen Corner to City (Southwark)	5 15	**11 9**	**4 16**
Amen Corner to Clapham	5 15	**12 21**	**4 49**
City (Southwark) to Amen Corner	5 56	**11 41**	**3 33**
City (Southwark) to Clapham	5 56	**11 52**	**12 31***
City (Southwark) to Wimbledon	—	**3 40**	**10 43**
Wimbledon to City (Southwark)	—	**4 13**	**11 42**†

(After 3.30 p.m. on Saturdays, this Route is diverted at Tooting Broadway to Wimbledon)
*To or from St. George's Church only.

8 / 20 — TOOTING BROADWAY – VICTORIA STN.
(8) Via Southcroft Rd., Mitcham Lane, Streatham, Brixton, Stockwell Rd., South Lambeth Rd., Vauxhall Bridge, returning via Vauxhall Bridge, South Lambeth Rd., Clapham, Balham, (20) To Victoria via Clapham, returning via Streatham

Time 34 mins. via Clapham, 44 mins. via Streatham. Service 5–8 mins. each route.

WEEKDAYS		SAT.			SUNDAY	
First	Last				First	Last
5 19	**11 44**	**11 49**	Tooting to Victoria Station*		7 42	**11 47**
6 24	**11 17**	**11 27**	Tooting to Victoria Station†		7 44	**11 21**
5 53	**12 16**	**12 15**	Victoria Station to Tooting*		7 14	**12 8**
6 48	**11 40**	**12 8**	Victoria Station to Tooting†		8 19	**11 59**

* Via Clapham. † Via Streatham.

10 — TOOTING BROADWAY – CITY Southwark
Via Southcroft Road, Streatham, Brixton, Kennington, Elephant, Southwark Bridge

Time 48 mins. Service 5–10 mins.

WEEKDAYS				SUNDAY	
First	Last	Sat.		First	Last
4 52	**11 28***	**11 49***	Tooting B'way to City (S'wark)	6 59	**11 14**
4 52	**12 58**	**1 24**	Tooting B'way to Streatham Lib.	6 59	**12 46**
4 6	**11 42***	**12 3***	Streatham Lib. to City (S'wark)	7 12	**11 27**
4 41	**12 14***	**12 37***	City (S'wark) to Tooting B'way	6 21 / 7 25 }	**12 3**

* To or from St. George's Church only.
After 3 p.m. on Saturdays, service operates to St. George's Church only, and times of first and last cars are to or from this point.

16 / 18 — PURLEY – VICTORIA EMBANKMENT
Via Croydon, Norbury, Streatham, Brixton, Kennington, (16) Westminster Bridge, (18) Elephant, Blackfriars Bridge

Time 71 mins. Service 3–5 mins.

WEEKDAYS		SAT.		SUNDAY	
First	Last			First	Last
5 56	**11 46**	**11 51**	Purley to Embankment	7 35	**11 49**
4 6	**12 53**	**12 48**	Norbury to Embankment	7 25	**12 18**
4 46	**10 32**	**10 34**	Emb't. (Savoy St.) to Purley	7 5*	**12 4**
4 46	**12 44**	**12 45**	Emb'nt. (Savoy St.) to Norbury	7 5*	**12 14**
4 46	**1 36**	**1 32**	Emb'nt. (Savoy St.) to Streatham Lib.	5 47	**12 14**
4 41	**11 51**	**11 56**	Red Deer to Embankment	7 9	**11 53**
4 46	**11 52**	**12 16**	Embankment to Red Deer	7 5*	**11 34**

* From Blackfriars

22 / 24 — TOOTING BROADWAY – VICTORIA EMBANKMENT
Via Southcroft Road, Streatham, Brixton, Kennington, (22) Westminster Bridge, (24) Elephant, Blackfriars Bridge

Time 47 mins. Service 4 mins.

WEEKDAYS (Peak Hours only)			
	First	Last	Sat.
Tooting Broadway to Embankment	6 59	6 7	**1 30**
Embankment to Tooting Broadway	7 29	**7 11**	**2 24**

34 — CHELSEA Kings Road – BLACKFRIARS*
Via Battersea Bridge, Falcon Road, Clapham Junction, Lavender Hill, Clapham Common, Stockwell Road, Brixton, Coldharbour Lane, Camberwell, Elephant, Blackfriars Bridge

* Alternate Cars operate to Camberwell Green only during certain hours

Time 58 mins. Service 5–8 mins.

WEEKDAYS		SAT.			SUNDAY	
First	Last				First	Last
5 8	**11 13**	**11 10**	Chelsea to Embankment		8 47	**10 55**
5 8	**12 38**	**12 34**	Chelsea to Camberwell Green		8 47	**12 1**
5 41	**11 30**	**11 35**	Embankment to Chelsea		8 45	**11 30**
4 28	**12 34**	**12 30**	Camberwell Grn. to Clapham Junc.		7 24	**12 23**
5 8	**12 49**	**12 44**	Clapham Junc. to Camberwell Grn.		8 16	**12 58**

EXTRACTS FROM THE LT TRAM MAP DATED 1940, No.1.

As the time schedules then operating were introduced well before September 1939, it seems that there was at this time no special allowance made for operation in the blackout.

The running of each of the six all-night trams can be traced throughout the night. The first three columns for each service show the first trips of each car from Telford Avenue or Clapham Depots. All cars ran alternate journeys on both services, operating a figure-of-eight route, with three minutes layover at either Savoy Street Strand or Blackfriars. So, at the Tooting Broadway timings simply transfer to the same times on the other service. Note that five of the cars continue as part of the day service. Note also the connections at Kennington, the centre of the figure-of-eight.

ALL-NIGHT TRAMS
(Saturday Nights excepted)

SOUTHCROFT ROAD – VICTORIA EMBANKMENT Circle
Via Tooting Broadway, Balham, Clapham, Elephant & Castle, Blackfriars, Westminster, Kennington

Southcroft Road	..				1 16	1 46	2 16	2 46	3 16	3 46	4 16	4 46
Tooting Broadway					1 23	1 53	2 23	2 53	3 23	3 53	4 23	4 53
Clapham	..		12 6	12 36	1 6	1 36	2 6	2 36	3 6	3 36	4 6	4 36	5 6
Kennington			12 16	12 46	1 16	1 46	2 16	2 46	3 16	3 46	4 16	4 46	5 16
Elephant & Castle			12 22	12 52	1 22	1 52	2 22	2 52	3 22	3 52	4 22	4 52	5 22
Victoria / Embankment { B'friars, Savoy St.		12 30	1 0	1 30	2 0	2 30	3 0	3 30	4 0	4 30	5 0	5 30
		12 33	1 3	1 33	2 3	2 33	3 3	3 33	4 3	4 33	5 3	5 33
Kennington			12 50	1 20	1 50	2 20	2 50	3 20	3 50	4 20	4 50	5 20	
Clapham			12 59	1 29	1 59	2 29	2 59	3 29	3 59	4 29	4 59	5 29	5 59
Tooting Broadway			1 13	1 43	2 13	2 43	3 13	3 43	4 13	4 43		5 43	6 13
Southcroft Road			1 20	1 50	2 20	2 50	3 20	3 50	4 20	4 50		5 50	6 20

TOOTING BROADWAY – VICTORIA EMBANKMENT Circle
Via Streatham, Brixton, Kennington, Westminster, Blackfriars, Elephant & Castle

Tooting Broadway	..				1 13	1 43	2 13	2 43	3 13	3 43	4 13	4 43
Streatham Library					1 26	1 56	2 26	2 56	3 26	3 56	4 26	4 56
Kennington	..	12*16	12*46	1*16	1 46	2 16	2 46	3 16	3 46	4 16	4 46	5 16
Victoria / Embankment { Savoy St. B'friars		12 30	1 0	1 30	2 0	2 30	3 0	3 30	4 0	4 30	5 0	5 30
		12 35	1 5	1 35	2 5	2 35	3 5	3 35	4 5	4 35	5 5	5 35
Elephant & Castle		12 43	1 13	1 43	2 13	2 43	3 13	3 43	4 13	4 43	5 13	5 43
Kennington			12 50	1 20	1 50	2 20	2 50	3 20	3 50	4 20	4 50	5 20	5 50
Streatham Library			1 9	1 39	2 9	2 39	3 9	3 39	4 9	4 39	5 9	5 39	6 9
Tooting Broadway	..		1 23	1 53	2 23	2 53	3 23	3 53	4 23	4 53	5 23	5 53	6 23

* Depart Telford Avenue 17 minutes Earlier

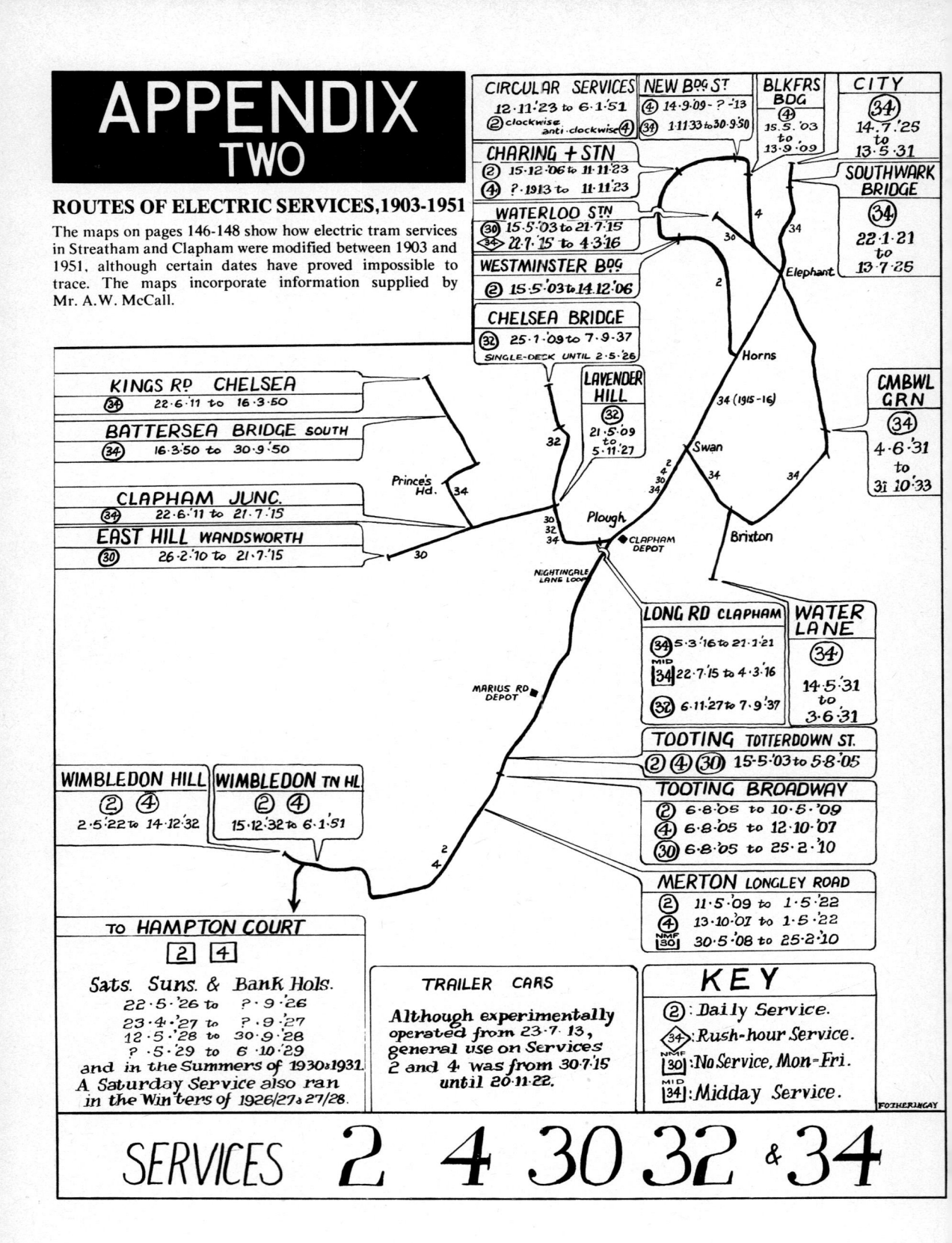

APPENDIX TWO

ROUTES OF ELECTRIC SERVICES, 1903-1951

The maps on pages 146-148 show how electric tram services in Streatham and Clapham were modified between 1903 and 1951, although certain dates have proved impossible to trace. The maps incorporate information supplied by Mr. A.W. McCall.

CIRCULAR SERVICES
② 12.11.23 to 6.1.51
② clockwise anti-clockwise ④

NEW BDG ST
④ 14.9.09 - ? .13
34 1.11.33 to 30.9.50

BLKFRS BDG
④ 15.5.'03 to 13.9.09

CITY
34 14.7.'25 to 13.5.31

CHARING + STN
② 15.12.'06 to 11.11.'23
④ ?.1913 to 11.11.'23

SOUTHWARK BRIDGE
34 22.1.21 to 13.7.25

WATERLOO STN
30 15.5.'03 to 21.7.15
34 22.7.15 to 4.3.16

WESTMINSTER BDG
② 15.5.'03 to 14.12.'06

CHELSEA BRIDGE
32 25.1.09 to 7.9.37
SINGLE-DECK UNTIL 2.5.'26

LAVENDER HILL
32 21.5.09 to 5.11.27

CMBWL GRN
34 4.6.31 to 31.10.33

KINGS RD CHELSEA
34 22.6.11 to 16.3.50

BATTERSEA BRIDGE SOUTH
34 16.3.50 to 30.9.50

CLAPHAM JUNC.
34 22.6.11 to 21.7.15

EAST HILL WANDSWORTH
30 26.2.10 to 21.7.15

LONG RD CLAPHAM
34 5.3.'16 to 21.1.21
MID 34 22.7.15 to 4.3.16
32 6.11.27 to 7.9.37

WATER LANE
34 14.5.31 to 3.6.31

TOOTING TOTTERDOWN ST.
② ④ 30 15.5.'03 to 5.8.05

TOOTING BROADWAY
② 6.8.05 to 10.5.'09
④ 6.8.05 to 12.10.'07
30 6.8.05 to 25.2.'10

WIMBLEDON HILL
② ④ 2.5.'22 to 14.12.32

WIMBLEDON TN HL
② ④ 15.12.32 to 6.1.51

MERTON LONGLEY ROAD
② 11.5.'09 to 1.5.'22
④ 13.10.'07 to 1.5.'22
NMF 30 30.5.'08 to 25.2.'10

TO HAMPTON COURT
2 4
Sats. Suns. & Bank Hols.
22.5.'26 to ?.9.'26
23.4.'27 to ?.9.'27
12.5.'28 to 30.9.'28
?.5.'29 to 6.10.'29
and in the Summers of 1930 & 1931.
A Saturday Service also ran in the Winters of 1926/27 & 27/28.

TRAILER CARS
Although experimentally operated from 23.7.13, general use on Services 2 and 4 was from 30.7.15 until 20.11.22.

KEY
② : Daily Service.
34 : Rush-hour Service.
NMF 30 : No Service, Mon-Fri.
MID 34 : Midday Service.

FOTHERINGAY

SERVICES 2 4 30 32 & 34

KEY

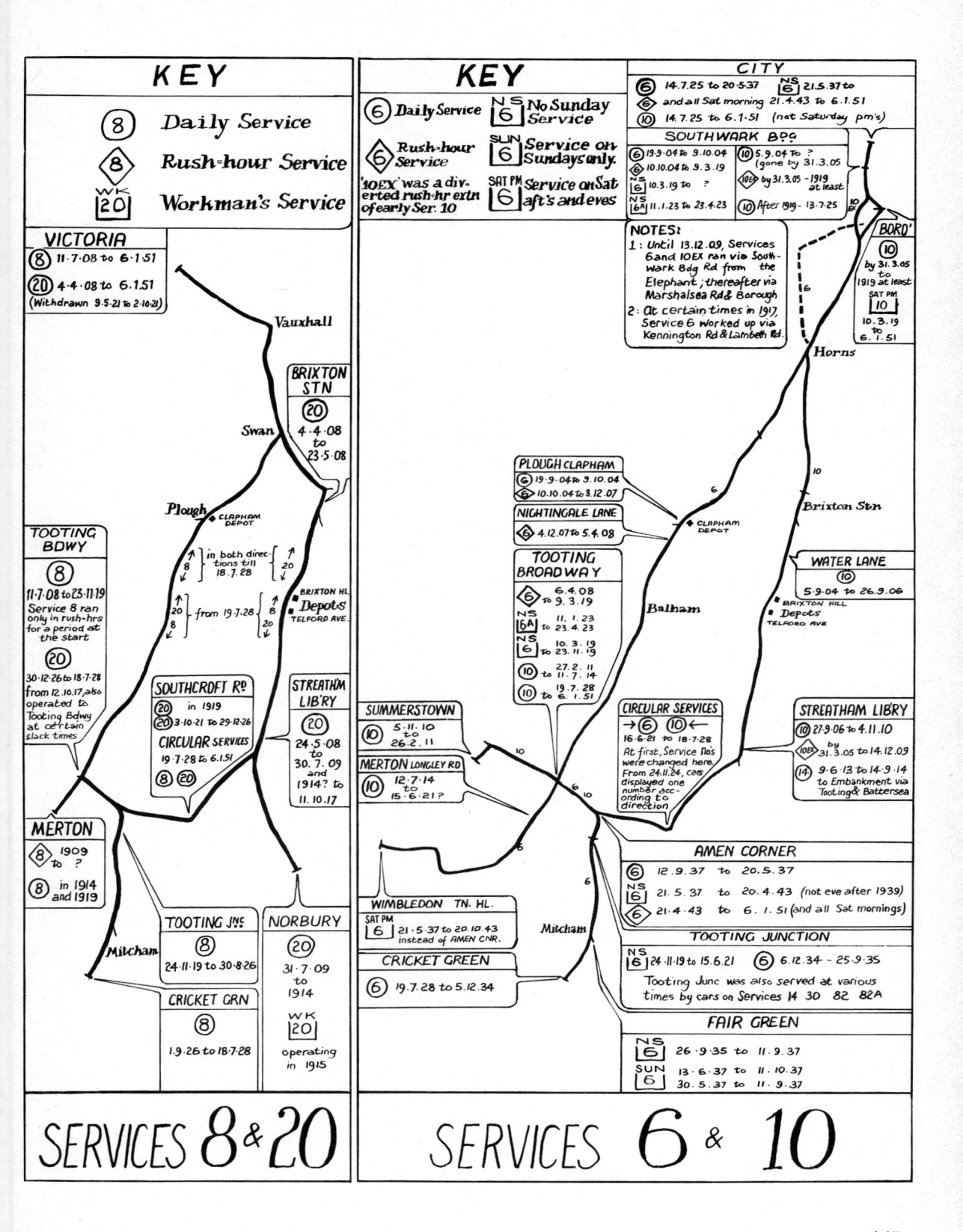

- (8) Daily Service
- ◇8 Rush-hour Service
- ◇WK 20 Workman's Service

KEY

- ⑥ Daily Service
- ◇⑥ Rush-hour Service
- NS ⑥ No Sunday Service
- SUN ⑥ Service on Sundays only
- SAT PM ⑥ Service on Sat aft's and eves

'10EX' was a diverted rush-hr extn of early Ser. 10

VICTORIA
- (8) 11.7.08 to 6.1.51
- (20) 4.4.08 to 6.1.51
- (Withdrawn 9.5.21 to 2.10.21)

CITY
- ⑥ 14.7.25 to 20.5.37
- NS ⑥ 21.5.37 to and all Sat morning 21.4.43 to 6.1.51
- ⑩ 14.7.25 to 6.1.51 (not Saturday pm's)

SOUTHWARK BDG
- ⑥ 19.9.04 to 9.10.04
- ⑥ 10.10.04 to 9.3.19
- NS ⑥ 10.3.19 to ?
- NS 6A 11.1.23 to 23.4.23
- ⑩ 5.9.04 to ? (gone by 31.3.05)
- 10EX by 31.3.05 - 1919 at least
- ⑩ After 1919 - 13.7.25

NOTES:
1: Until 13.12.09, Services 6 and 10EX ran via Southwark Bdg Rd from the Elephant; thereafter via Marshalsea Rd & Borough
2: At certain times in 1917, Service 6 worked up via Kennington Rd & Lambeth Rd.

BORO'
- ⑩ by 31.3.05 to 1919 at least
- SAT PM ⑩ 10.3.19 to 6.1.51

Vauxhall

BRIXTON STN
- (20) 4.4.08 to 23.5.08

Swan

Plough • CLAPHAM DEPOT

in both directions till 18.7.28
from 19.7.28

BRIXTON HL Depots TELFORD AVE.

PLOUGH CLAPHAM
- ⑥ 19.9.04 to 9.10.04
- ◇⑥ 10.10.04 to 3.12.07

NIGHTINGALE LANE
- ◇⑥ 4.12.07 to 5.4.08

TOOTING BROADWAY
- ⑥ 6.4.08 to 9.3.19
- NS 6A 11.1.23 to 23.4.23
- NS ⑥ 10.3.19 to 23.11.19
- ⑩ 27.2.11 to 11.7.14
- ⑩ 19.7.28 to 6.1.51

• CLAPHAM DEPOT

Balham

TOOTING BDWY
- (8) 11.7.08 to 23.11.19 Service 8 ran only in rush-hrs for a period at the start
- (20) 30.12.26 to 18.7.28 from 12.10.17, also operated to Tooting Bdwy at certain slack times

SOUTHCROFT RD
- (20) in 1919
- (20) 3.10.21 to 29.12.26
- CIRCULAR SERVICES (8) (20) 19.7.28 to 6.1.51

STREATH'M LIB'RY
- (20) 24.5.08 to 30.7.09 and 1914? to 11.10.17

SUMMERSTOWN
- ⑩ 5.11.10 to 26.2.11

MERTON LONGLEY RD
- ⑩ 12.7.14 to 15.6.21?

CIRCULAR SERVICES
→ ⑥ ⑩ ←
16.6.21 to 18.7.28
At first, Service No's were changed here. From 24.11.24, cars displayed one number according to direction

WATER LANE
- ⑩ 5.9.04 to 26.9.06

BRIXTON HILL Depots TELFORD AVE

STREATHAM LIBRY
- ⑩ 27.9.06 to 4.11.10
- 10EX by 31.3.05 to 14.12.09
- ⑭ 9.6.13 to 14.9.14 to Embankment via Tooting & Battersea

MERTON
- (8) 1909 to ?
- (8) in 1914 and 1919

Mitcham

Mitcham

TOOTING JN?
- (8) 24.11.19 to 30.8.26

NORBURY
- (20) 31.7.09 to 1914
- WK 20 operating in 1915

WIMBLEDON TN. HL.
- SAT PM ⑥ 21.5.37 to 20.10.43 instead of AMEN CNR.

CRICKET GREEN
- ⑥ 19.7.28 to 5.12.34

AMEN CORNER
- ⑥ 12.9.37 to 20.5.37
- NS ⑥ 21.5.37 to 20.4.43 (not eve after 1939)
- ⑥ 21.4.43 to 6.1.51 (and all Sat mornings)

TOOTING JUNCTION
- NS ⑥ 24.11.19 to 15.6.21
- ⑥ 6.12.34 - 25.9.35

Tooting Junc was also served at various times by cars on Services 14 30 82 82A

FAIR GREEN
- NS ⑥ 26.9.35 to 11.9.37
- SUN ⑥ 13.6.37 to 11.10.37
- ⑥ 30.5.37 to 11.9.37

CRICKET GRN
- (8) 1.9.26 to 18.7.28

SERVICES 8 & 20

SERVICES 6 & 10

147

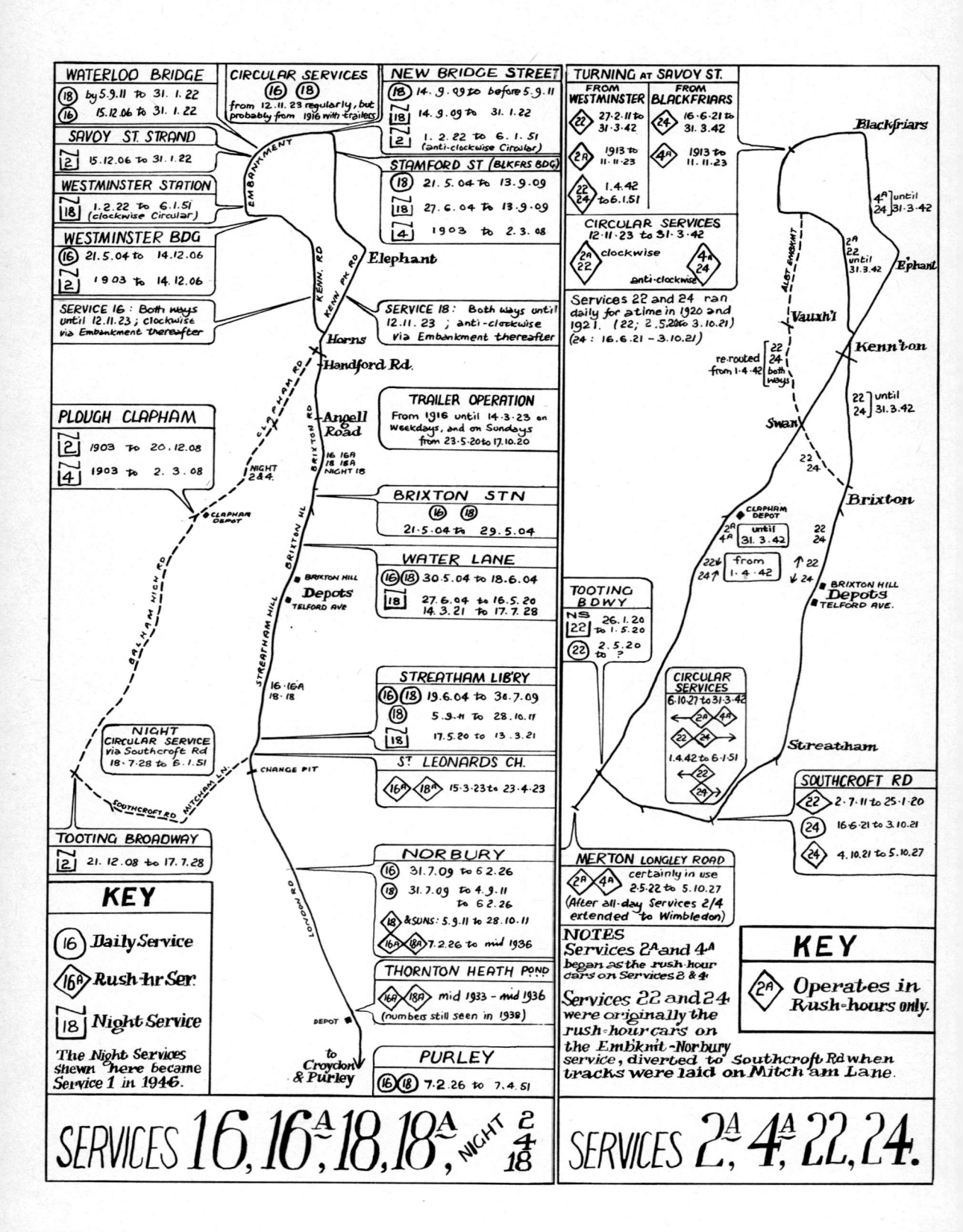

SERVICES 16, 16ᴬ, 18, 18ᴬ, NIGHT 2/4/18

WATERLOO BRIDGE
- ⑱ by 5.9.11 to 31.1.22
- ⑯ 15.12.06 to 31.1.22

SAVOY ST. STRAND
- ② 15.12.06 to 31.1.22

WESTMINSTER STATION
- ② 1.2.22 to 6.1.51
- ⑱ (clockwise Circular)

WESTMINSTER BDG
- ⑯ 21.5.04 to 14.12.06
- ② 1903 to 14.12.06

SERVICE 16: Both ways until 12.11.23; clockwise via Embankment thereafter

CIRCULAR SERVICES
⑯ ⑱ from 12.11.23 regularly, but probably from 1916 with trailers

NEW BRIDGE STREET
- ⑱ 14.9.09 to before 5.9.11
- ⑱ 14.9.09 to 31.1.22
- ② 1.2.22 to 6.1.51 (anti-clockwise Circular)

STAMFORD ST (BLKFRS BDG)
- ⑱ 21.5.04 to 13.9.09
- ⑱ 27.6.04 to 13.9.09
- ④ 1903 to 2.3.08

Elephant

SERVICE 18: Both ways until 12.11.23; anti-clockwise via Embankment thereafter

Horns
Handford Rd.
Angell Road

TRAILER OPERATION
From 1916 until 14.3.23 on weekdays, and on Sundays from 23.5.20 to 17.10.20

BRIXTON STN
- ⑯ ⑱ 21.5.04 to 29.5.04

WATER LANE
- ⑯ ⑱ 30.5.04 to 18.6.04
- ⑱ 27.6.04 to 16.5.20, 14.3.21 to 17.7.28

Brixton Hill Depots Telford Ave.

STREATHAM LIB'RY
- ⑯ ⑱ 19.6.04 to 30.7.09
- ⑱ 5.9.11 to 28.10.11
- ⑱ 17.5.20 to 13.3.21

ST LEONARDS CH.
- ⑯ᴬ ⑱ᴬ 15.3.23 to 23.4.23

NORBURY
- ⑯ 31.7.09 to 6.2.26
- ⑱ 31.7.09 to 4.9.11 to 6.2.26
- ⑱ & SUNS. 5.9.11 to 28.10.11
- ⑯ᴬ ⑱ᴬ 7.2.26 to mid 1936

THORNTON HEATH POND
- ⑯ᴬ ⑱ᴬ mid 1933 – mid 1936 (numbers still seen in 1938)

DEPOT
to Croydon & Purley

PURLEY
- ⑯ ⑱ 7.2.26 to 7.4.51

PLOUGH CLAPHAM
- ② 1903 to 20.12.08
- ④ 1903 to 2.3.08

CLAPHAM DEPOT
BALHAM HIGH RD
CLAPHAM RD
KENN. PK. RD
BRIXTON HILL
STREATHAM HILL
NIGHT 2/4/18
CHANGE PIT
MITCHAM LN
SOUTHCROFT RD.
LONDON RD

NIGHT CIRCULAR SERVICE via Southcroft Rd
⑱ 18.7.28 to 6.1.51

TOOTING BROADWAY
- ② 21.12.08 to 17.7.28

KEY
- ⑯ Daily Service
- ⑯ᴬ Rush-hr Ser.
- ⑱ Night Service

The Night Services shewn here became Service 1 in 1946.

SERVICES 2ᴬ, 4ᴬ, 22, 24

TURNING AT SAVOY ST.

FROM WESTMINSTER
- ㉒ 27.2.11 to 31.3.42
- ②ᴬ 1913 to 11.11.23
- ㉒ ㉔ 1.4.42 to 6.1.51

FROM BLACKFRIARS
- ㉔ 16.6.21 to 31.3.42
- ④ᴬ 1913 to 11.11.23

CIRCULAR SERVICES
12.11.23 to 31.3.42
- ②ᴬ ㉒ clockwise
- ④ᴬ ㉔ anti-clockwise

Services 22 and 24 ran daily for a time in 1920 and 1921. (22: 2.5.20 to 3.10.21) (24: 16.6.21 – 3.10.21)

re-routed from 1.4.42 ㉒ ㉔ both ways

Blackfriars
④ᴬ until 31.3.42
②ᴬ ㉒ until 31.3.42
E'phant
Vauxh'l
Kenn'ton
㉒ until 31.3.42 ㉔
Swan
㉒ ㉔
Brixton

CLAPHAM DEPOT
②ᴬ ④ᴬ until 31.3.42
㉒ ㉔
㉒ ㉔ from 1.4.42 ↑22 ↓24
Brixton Hill Depots Telford Ave.

TOOTING BDWY
- NS 26.1.20
- ㉒ to 1.5.20
- ㉒ 2.5.20 to ?

CIRCULAR SERVICES
6.10.27 to 31.3.42
②ᴬ ④ᴬ
㉒ ㉔
1.4.42 to 6.1.51
㉒ ㉔

Streatham

SOUTHCROFT RD
- ㉒ 2.7.11 to 25.1.20
- ㉔ 16.6.21 to 3.10.21
- ㉔ 4.10.21 to 5.10.27

MERTON LONGLEY ROAD
②ᴬ ④ᴬ certainly in use 2.5.22 to 5.10.27 (After all-day Services 2/4 extended to Wimbledon)

NOTES
Services 2ᴬ and 4ᴬ began as the rush-hour cars on Services 2 & 4.

Services 22 and 24 were originally the rush-hour cars on the Embkmt - Norbury service, diverted to Southcroft Rd when tracks were laid on Mitcham Lane.

KEY
- ②ᴬ Operates in Rush-hours only.

APPENDIX THREE

A SHORT HISTORY OF TRAM SERVICES 16 AND 18

Operationally, the story of tram services 16 and 18 can be divided into four distinct periods, covering the years from 1870 to 1951. (Arguably there was a fifth, for an idiosyncratic American entrepreneur — one George Francis Train — had operated a tram service along Kennington Road for almost a year in 1861 and 1862, but Train's eccentric activities had no connection with later tramway developments in London apart, perhaps, from encouraging a certain amount of opposition to the notion of vehicles running on rails laid in the public highway). The four periods were as follows:

1870-1892: Horse tram services from Westminster and Blackfriars Bridges (hereinafter 'the Bridges') to Brixton and Water Lane (1871).

1892-1904: Cable service from Kennington to Telford Avenue and Streatham Library (1896).

1904-1926: Electric operation throughout, with the Bridges linked via the Embankment (1906) and the service extended to Norbury (1909).

1926-1951: Service extended via Croydon to Purley.

Two points should be remembered. The Clapham Road and Brixton Road services were always closely related to each other, particularly before 1903 and again after the Southcroft Road Circular services began running in the 1920's, and there is thus a certain artificiality in looking only at services 16 and 18. Furthermore, they were always really two services — one to Westminster, the other to Blackfriars — although, from the 1920's, it was expedient to operate them as one, for the Embankment was used as a long turning loop, thereby avoiding the need for cars to reverse on one of the busiest sections of tram track in London.

1870-1892

Between May 1870 and August 1871 the Metropolitan Street Tramways Company began operating trams over four sections of its authorised lines from Westminster Bridge-foot to Brixton Water Lane. The opening dates were as follows:

a) Horns, Kennington to Brixton Station: 2nd May 1870.
b) Horns, Kennington to Christ-Church: 5th October 1870.
c) Christ-Church to Westminster Bridge: 23rd December 1870.
d) Brixton Station to Water Lane: 21st August 1871.

The service was operated by double-decked horse cars, and at first it made good profits. At the end of 1870 the Metropolitan Street Tramways Company merged with a second company to form the London Tramways Company, which in time became the second largest tramway operator in London.

In August 1871 the Company opened a line from the Elephant & Castle to a terminus in Blackfriars Road, to which it was possible for cars to run from Brixton via Westminster Bridge Road, for it was not until 1874 that tracks were laid up Kennington Park Road, from the Horns to the Elephant & Castle. In that same year a line was also opened from the Elephant to St. George's Church, and thus the basic network of tram services from Brixton Hill was completed.

By 1874 the Company had not opened lines for which it had approval in Water Lane. Effra Road and Coldharbour Lane, although the latter line was opened in 1883 by another company. In fact, the London Tramways Company opened no more lines until 1890, when its line from Kennington to Clapham was extended to Tooting.

The earliest date for which I have been able to obtain seemingly accurate information on services 16/18 has been 1879, and this is included in the charts in Appendix 1. It is enough here to note that all three services from Water Lane, to the Bridges and the Borough operated at twelve minute intervals from 8 a.m. (from Brixton) until approximately 11.30 p.m. (from London), thus giving a combined service in total from Brixton to Kennington of 4 minutes. According to the source of this information, there was no service before 8 a.m. — except to the Borough — nor were there any extra cars operated in rush-hours. These features of LT Company tram services in 1879, together with the fact that there is no mention of any workmen's fares at this time, suggest that the 'people's carriage' was patronised mainly by the skilled artisan classes and the lower middle classes. The absence of both early services and cheap fares would have prevented their being of much use to the really poor and mass needy of those days.

However, from about 1879 the policy of the London Tramways Company changed significantly, for its profits had fallen since 1875; at one point it was even paying dividends out of its capital. More cars entered service, tracks were doubled and repaired, extensions — including one over Westminster Bridge — were discussed, and fares lowered. One of the barriers to extension was Brixton Hill, considered too steep for efficient operation by horses at a time when the Company was spending twice as much on its horses as on its men, and after approval was given in 1889 to extend its line from Water Lane to Telford Avenue, it was decided to employ cable traction on this section rather than horses.

1892-1904

The London Tramways Company had first seriously cast its eyes in 1888 towards the expanding residential market developing beyond its Water Lane terminus, but had not persisted with that part of an authorising Bill, in return for which the Metropolitan Board of Works had endorsed the Company's application to extend its line south from Clapham to Tooting Bec Road. (The MBW frequently indulged in horse-trading of this sort with tramway operators).

A year later, the Company again went to Westminster with a Bill seeking to extend its lines to Telford Avenue, but by now the LCC had taken over the highway functions of the Metropolitan Board of Works and it gave its consent, conditional only upon the Company running two daily artisan's cars along the line. A year later, the Company sought approval for the use of mechanical power on both the new extension and the long, almost straight road to Kennington. This was not the first time that cable haulage had been proposed for London — in 1884 a cable tramway had been opened on Highgate Hill, but it was not wholly successful. In America, however, cable traction had been more profitable, and so it was also to prove on Brixton Hill, after the line opened in December 1892.

A new car-shed and Power House were built at Telford Avenue, and from the new terminus to Kennington there ran a continuous underground cable. At Kennington there was built a second, smaller depot. At first the Board of Trade would not allow the Company to connect passenger cars directly onto the cable, and 'gripper' cars were used as tractors until 1898.

Although the 2¾ mile long cable tramway was commercially successful — by 1895 it was claimed that the line was carrying one eighth of its total passengers and providing one seventh of all mileage operated on the Company's 24½ miles of line — it brought certain problems. Allegedly due to inexperienced gripmen, working expenses were high at first and there were accidents with the cable. (It is said that when the cable broke down, horses were brought along Acre Lane from the Company's Depot at Plough Clapham). The superior classes, who at that time considered Brixton Hill a rather superior place, cared little for the cable noises and frequently complained. Predictably, perhaps, the Streatham shopkeepers resented the fact that they now had to compete with the cheaper shops in Brixton, while at the other end of the line, congestion was caused at the point at which cars transferred from mechanical to horse power.

In 1895 the line was extended south once again, as the Company had always intended that it should, this time to Streatham Library. Between Telford Avenue and Streatham Library, the Company bought strips of front gardens for road widening and presented the local authority with certain 'fine wide stone footpaths' and newly paved sections of road. But although the Company wanted to extend its lines at least as far as Streatham Common, it was unable to agree with the local authority on the allocation of road-widening costs through the commercially developed centre of Streatham. In fairness to the Company — which was doubtless acutely aware of just how much it could afford to speculate against limited future profits, and had already accepted an LCC hours-of-labour clause as a condition of the extension being approved — some metropolitan local authorities did rather over-play their hands when bargaining with tramway companies around this time.

For the extension to Streatham Library a second cable was laid in, and for a few years, in a long pit in front of Telford Avenue Depot, the new and old cables moved beside each other, the gripper being first raised from one cable, then lowered onto the second. Between the main road and the depot was an auxiliary cable, to haul cars up the incline into the car shed. Concurrently with the extension a new type of car was introduced, with angled bulk-heads which both increased the effective width of the platforms and allowed two more seated passengers in each car. Whereas the Company had at one time contemplated that this extension should be a single line, it was built — as was the whole cable tramway — as a double track line.

Services on the new line continued to operate to the Bridges (16 and 18) and the Borough, although by 1892 the Borough service (10) had been extended down the Old Kent Road to Bowles Road, where the Company had a tram depot. Frequencies had been considerably improved when, in 1894, the LCC investigated road public transport services in London for a fascinating Report on Locomotion which appeared in 1895. In Appendix 1 is reproduced a chart of services, frequencies and times culled from this statistical gold-mine, although it must be pointed out that it is possibly inaccurate insofar as peak hour services are concerned, for it gives service intervals as follows: Service 10, every 9 minutes; Service 16, every 6, 9 or 12 minutes; Service 18, every 9 minutes. (On the three Tooting services — the horse operated 2, 4, and 30 — the report refers to each service operating at 6, 9 or 12 minute intervals 'according to pressure').

It is likely that, excellent though cable-traction was, the all-day frequencies on the Brixton Hill services after 1895 came near to the limit acceptable to the lines' four high-pressure compound steam engines (of which only one pair was normally in use at any one time), and thus few extra cars were operated in rush-hours. This limitation would not have applied on the Tooting roads. The one early morning workman's car operating from Streatham in 1895, at 5.55 a.m. to Westminster Bridge, was horsed over the whole journey, for it ran down Brixton Hill and there was little point in starting the cable before the full service operated from 7 o'clock.

Shortly before the LCC acquired the whole London Tramways Company network on 1st January 1899, the forty

Telford Avenue Depot, looking towards London, around 1898, after grippers had been fitted to Standard horse-cars.

gripper cars on the line, — there had been only thirty until 1895 — were replaced by adapted horse cars, and a process of attaching or removing the gripper apparatus at Kennington was evolved which slightly increased journey times. Services thereafter were improved, more workmen's cars were operated and a service of night-cars was introduced as far as Water Lane from 1900.

When it was decided to electrify the Tooting and New Cross lines, the LCC Highways Committee seems not to have been sure of what to do with the Streatham cable-road. Electrification was planned, but in late 1901 it was suggested that, because a horsed service would be required whilst track conversion work was in progress, this should wait until **sufficient surplus horses were available from other lines.** However, after horse-cars were withdrawn from the Tooting lines in May 1903, the LCCT promptly sold the 850 redundant horses. In 1900 and 1902 the LCCT sought powers to extend the line to Norbury, but in vain. If the powers had been granted how would the extension have been operated ? It is possible — because by 1902 even the idealists on the Highways Committee were showing signs of regretting their high-minded committment to the conduit — that the LCCT hoped eventually to electrify the line from Kennington change-pit on the overhead, but this was not to be; by now the Borough Councils were playing the LCC at its own game.

Several events of 1902 deserve our attention. Firstly, the work of converting the line from Tooting to the Bridges — shared by Streatham cars north of Kennington — began, and in the autumn the LCCT set up its first Motor School at Telford Avenue Depot. It was estimated that 250 motormen would be required, and first choice of these jobs was offered to horse-car drivers. Two instructors and an A class car were installed, together with a small generator worked off the cable power plant. In the same year, eighty 'special' four-wheel B class cars were ordered for the Streatham services, and as they were ordered to be fitted with both plough and cable gripper apparatus it can be assumed that even in 1902 the LCCT anticipated through electric/cable services. In late 1902, also, the Board of Trade re-licensed the use of cable traction south of Kennington for a further three years. If there is anything one can deduce from these events it is that the LCCT's forward-planning was not as good as it could have been, but once the new electric services began operating to Tooting on 15th May 1903, it was realised that something would have to be done about Services 16 and 18.

1904-1926

After May 1903 it was found that the horse-drawn cars from Streatham were delaying the new electric cars, north of Kennington on the shared lines to the Bridges. This was not surprising, for electric cars — average speed, eight-and-a-half miles-per-hour — were scheduled at two miles-an-hour faster than horse cars. What was surprising was that nobody appears to have seriously anticipated this difficulty, but if the first few years of LCC tram operation are characterised by anything, it is by the Council's far-reaching lack of foresight.

There were no immediate plans to electrify the cableline at this time; indeed, as late as October 1903 a new cable was ordered. From August 1903 a few electric cars were experimentally operated over the cable line. The electric and cable conduits ran beside each other for a few feet at Kennington, where ploughs were removed from 'down' cars and grippers attached. The experiment was not a success, for electric trams were three times heavier than cable-cars, but the LCCT persevered, believing that the problem was not insoluble (which it wasn't, although success would probably have depended on the capacity of the line being restricted to about half that provided by cable-cars).

A cable car waits at the top of Brixton Road (right) while special work is installed for electric cars at Kennington in the summer of 1903. In August 1903 the conduit lines were opened to Handford Road, a short distance down Brixton Road.

The experiment ceased on October 14th, and a new service of electric cars was operated from the top of Brixton Road to the Bridges, passengers being obliged to transfer there from cable-car to electric car. Although through-tickets were issued, this system did not work well, particularly in the evening rush-hour, when passengers from London were transferring from 66-seat electric cars to 44 or 46 seat cable-cars.

The decision to electrify the cable line — now considered a matter of urgency — was taken in December 1903. The use of the cable-conduit for tee-rails was rejected because it was too small, but most of the cars which it was considered the line would require were already in stock, and power for the line could be obtained by temporarily converting the cable Power-house into a generator. At the same time, plans were drawn up for the rebuilding of Telford Avenue Depot, which it was estimated would hold eighty-two electric cars.

The contract for rebuilding the whole line was given to Messrs. J.G. White on 2nd March 1904, with the stipulation that the work should be completed by 1st July that same year. White's tender quoted £95,005 (although this included a little other work), and the LCCT estimated that the rails would cost £17,000 and the rebuilding of the depot — by direct labour — a further £35,000.

Although it was normal LCCT practice to relay in sections, one line at a time, using the second line and a temporary track for an interim horse-car service, this was considered impractical on the busy Brixton Road, despite a petition from local residents for a service of some sort to continue. There were already frequent horse-bus services on the road and more were added, and Mr. Fell — now the Chief Officer — was confident that the rejected passengers would return.

At this stage, gentle reader, a brief diversion along Camberwell New Road to number 303, at that time the **LCCT Chief Office. Since 1899, one Alfred Baker had been in charge of the LCC's tram operation, but when he was 'promoted' in 1902 to the post of Chief Officer — unfilled since it was designated in 1899, but worth £1500 pa. — the LCC General Purposes Committee refused to accept a Highways Committee recommendation that he be given the rate for the job. Had he not been happy as**

Cementing in the new electric conduit on Brixton Road, before relaying the track, 1904.

Tramways Manager at £1,000 pa ?

In July 1903, two months after driving the first electric car on the Tooting service, Alfred Baker accepted the job of managing Birmingham Corporation's trams at a salary of £1,300-£1,500 pa. So it was, then, that the new electric LCCT was without a manager until December 1903 when Mr. Fell, who had been earning £700 pa. managing Sheffield Corporation's trams, took up his duties as LCCT Chief Officer.

In the intervening period it seems that the Chairman of the Highways Committee had 'managed' the Tramways Department, with the advice of the by now distant Mr. Baker (who thereby showed remarkable charity towards a Council which had insulted him in a singularly shabby fashion). That semi-professional politicians should have handled the LCC's affairs so ineptly is perhaps not as **surprising as it should be. At this time also, two remaining senior officials of the LCCT were so 'broken down in health' as to be unable to continue with their duties.**

Meanwhile, at midnight on 5th April 1904, the Brixton Hill cable was stopped and rebuilding began. A week later the work was going on night and day with 1600 men. On May 18th the first trial car passed down the Brixton Road, under the railway bridge at Brixton — beneath which the roadway had been lowered eight inches — and on to Water Lane. Three days later a service of electric cars began running from Brixton Station to London, and on 30th May it was extended to Water Lane. Finally, on 19th June 1904, a full service of trams began operating to the terminus of the line at Streatham Library. It was considered that White's achievement was something of a record, Mr. Fell's passengers returned and multiplied, and the Chairman of the Highways Committee later averred that the electrification of the cable-road was the biggest success yet scored and further declared the receipts to be most gratifying.

For the next two years the two new electric services — from Streatham Library to the Bridges — continued unchanged. From 29th June 1904 the night-service from Water Lane to Blackfriars was restored, at first experimentally and then permanently. Two months later, a service from Water Lane to Southwark began running, but those interested in the minutae of service alterations should refer to Appendix 2.

Although the services were a success, Telford Avenue Depot did not re-open until 3rd March 1906. Even then, it seems that it was only half the old cable shed that then came into use, for there was still a temporary generator in use in one half of the shed, although this had been removed by the end of 1906. Rebuilding seems to have been limited to re-roofing the depot, laying in conduit tracks and traversers and replacing the central dividing wall with steel stanchions; at the same time a new Romanesque frontage, roof extension, and office block replaced the houses, high wall and open yard which had previously stood before the depot. It is known that the Streatham services (10, 16, 18 and Nighters) operated first from Clapham Depot (or possibly even Marius Road) and then in part from Camberwell Depot before being moved into Telford Avenue in 1906. In its formative years the LCCT operated from a number of temporary depots, including one at Kennington Cross for a short period in 1906; even after Telford Avenue Depot opened it is known that certain Extra's on Service 10 operated from Camberwell.

At first, the Brixton Road services were operated by open top B class cars; by 1906 C class trams were also on Brixton Road, and shortly afterwards Telford Avenue was putting out only the larger E and E/1 cars. The E class cars tended to be used on Service 10 until they were transferred elsewhere around 1922. Full details of the services operated in 1905 can be found at the end of Appendix one.

1906 was a good year for the LCCT. Early in that year its very own Eastern Generating Station at Greenwich came into limited use, and Mr. Fell was finally enabled to run full services after three years of frustrating dependence upon inadequate supplies of bought-in power. Some additional Extra's were added to the Brixton Hill services. At the risk of alienating the more devoted enthusiast of the LCCT, I shall not dwell on the early grandiose plan to build four mighty Power-Houses — the acquired land for one of which, in Pimlico, later became a coach station — nor on the inadequacies of the temporary transformer at Loughborough which supplied much of the LCCT's power for the first three electric years, but it is an interesting tale. For several years after 1906, the LCCT continued to buy limited amounts of electricity from private and municipal suppliers.

The second event of 1906 was the opening of a tramway from Westminster Bridge terminus to Blackfriars, via the Victoria Embankment. The London Tramways Company had first sought approval to run trams along the Embankment in 1888, and the LCC on more than one occasion since then, but always in vain. The Metropolitan Board of Works, the House of Commons and the House of Lords had at various stages prevented authorising Bills from going through Westminster — the whole scandalous story is well chronicled elsewhere — and thus for many many years thousands of Londoners had daily to walk across Blackfriars and Westminster Bridges. In 1904, the LCCT estimated that 90% of passengers to these terminii continued across the Bridges on foot. Congestion at the Bridges had brought complaints from the Commissioner of Police of the Metropolis, who had once seriously suggested to the London Tramways Company that it should turn cars short of Westminster on days when there was racing at Ascot so that the movement of carriages into Waterloo Station might not be interfered with. In 1899 he also intimated to the LCC that services be permanently cut back to York Road, but fortunately he suggested in vain. (He declared to the Royal Commissioners on London Traffic in 1903 that he was also concerned about the congestion at Blackfriars, but felt it useless to approach the LCC about this). Interestingly, at

The first electric services to Streatham in 1904 were operated by B class four-wheel cars from Clapham Depot. The motorman of car 159, above, still wears a bowler hat; the 'via' points on his car have been painted out to aid car allocation

Blackfriars terminus the LCCT had erected queuing 'pens' in the centre of the road, a device pioneered by Mr. Fell in Sheffield. By 1904 there were 74 cars per hour reversing at Westminster Bridgefoot in the rush-hours, with a further 55 trams reversing each hour at the top of Blackfriars Road, and such was the pressure on the evening rush-hour service (between 5pm and 9pm) that many people walked down Blackfriars Road and bought a half-penny ticket so that they could ride back to the terminus and retain their seats.

Trams began operating over Westminster Bridge and along the Embankment as far as New Bridge Street, on 15th December 1906, but the final link back over the Thames to Blackfriars Road had to wait another three years until 14th September 1909. For several years after 1909, most cars reversed at any one of several different turning points on the Embankment, but from 1923 a more sensible method of working became dominant and most services ran in alternate directions right round a long turning circle that began and ended — for Service 16/18 — at the Horns at Kennington.

Until 1909, trams terminated on the south side of Blackfriars Bridge, where road vehicles interfered with queuing arrangements in the middle of the road. C class car 261, **above**, waits before loading for Streatham in 1906; E/1 class car 955 crosses Blackfriars Bridge, **below**, soon after it was opened to trams.

Six weeks before trams first crossed Blackfriars Bridge, Services 16 and 18 — still two quite separate operations — were extended south from Streatham Library to the County boundary at Norbury, on 31st July 1909. There they reversed only a few feet away from the trams of Croydon Corporation which, since 1901, had been running between Purley and Norbury. Once again, this was a case of better late than never, for the LCCT had twice sought permission, in 1900 and 1902, to extend its lines to service an estate of Working Class Dwellings which it proposed to build at Norbury, using powers granted in 1900 enabling it to acquire land for housing outside the County.

The extension to Norbury required certain street widenings to be made. The need for such work had previously arisen in 1903 at the Kennington end of Brixton Road, but now expensive widenings were required immediately beyond Streatham Library. At several other points, minor alterations were made. By now, the Highways Committee's sense of aesthetic nicety had changed, and the conduit was continued only to Gleneagles Road, where there was installed a change-pit. From there to Hermitage Bridge, itself widened to take trams, overhead wires were hung above the road.

At this point it is worth looking at the LCCT conduit track. The conduit principle was rare, but not unproven in 1901, when the LCC put on display at Camberwell Depot its own pattern of conduit. It was designed by a certain Doctor Kennedy, and was roundly criticised at the time as being weak and inefficient. In fact, the design of its short yokes, slot-rails and conduit was very similar to those used on the cable-tramway.

The LCCT paid little attention to its critics, and although certain modifications were made before the Tooting lines were opened in 1903, and others were incorporated in the Streatham line, most of the inherent weaknesses remained. Put simply, the track was unstable, for the running rails were not supported by the yokes, and the three-quarter inch slot — which prevented a really strong plough-shank being used — was too easily distorted by swollen wood-blocks. The drainage arrangements were also inadequate. In 1904 the LCCT ceased to consult Doctor Kennedy.

Around 1907-1909, the original lines — including the Streatham line — were given attention; the slot was widened to one inch and every alternate (short) yoke was replaced by an extended one, which supported the running-rails and contributed much to the rigidity of the track and conduit. Thereafter the conduit worked well, but it remained an expensive and rather burdensome legacy of mis-placed idealism and even, perhaps, gullibility.

The years between 1908 and 1910 are important for tram services in Streatham, for apart from the extension to Norbury and the completion of the Embankment circle, the horse-car lines on Stockwell Road were electrified in April 1908. In November 1910 a new junction was installed at Saint Leonards Church, whereby Streatham was linked by tram direct to Tooting via Mitcham Lane and Southcroft Road. These extensions allowed trams to run from Norbury and Streatham to Victoria, and from Mitcham, via Streatham or Clapham, to Victoria, Southwark and the Embankment. The horizons of Streatham folk were greatly extended; for a short period in 1913 and 1914 they could even take a tram direct to Wandsworth and Battersea.

These extensions, however, expected too much of the limited space at Telford Avenue Depot, and it was decided that more accommodation was needed. Now one of the sound features of LCCT policy — and there were many, despite my criticisms — was that the department always tried to extend its existing depots when it needed more space, rather than build new ones; it appreciated the supposed economies of scale. So it was at Telford Avenue, for the LCCT was prepared in 1910 to seek compulsory purchase powers for land beside Telford Avenue Depot, on which it would replace a house with a car-shed. In fact, in early 1911, the LCCT bought the land for £1,500 without resort to this legal bludgeon. The Streatham (extension) car-shed was designed in an Egyptian style, and by the end of 1911 construction had started.

Unhappily, there was between the two plots owned by the LCCT, a private road, underneath which ran a main-pipe, and the Metropolitan Water Board would only allow the LCCT to link its two separate sheds with a footbridge at first floor level. However, the extension car-shed was built with an incline and tracks raised over pits, in the same way as had been the old cable-shed, and it is said that the floor levels of both sheds were at the same height to allow them to be joined if this was ever possible. In 1913 the new depot was opened, just in time for an interesting period in LCCT history.

In 1911 the LCCT had experimented with coupled-car operation in North London, hoping that this method of

Streatham Hill Station, around 1910. Car 814 is bound for Norbury.

operation might be used to improve its services through the Kingsway Tunnel, where passenger demand already exceeded the supply offered by single-deck cars. This use of coupled cars was not continued with, but two years later eight open-top horse-trams were converted into trailers, to be hauled behind Standard double-deck cars. From January 1915, 150 new trailers began entering service, and some were allocated in 1916 to Telford Avenue Depot for use on Service 16/18 in rush-hours. Although the Police cared little for trailers, they were a useful expedient at that time.

Since 1910, the LCCT had been losing (or ceasing to gain) passengers to the new motor bus; that year was also probably the undertaking's most commercially successful. By 1914, more passenger-journeys annually were being made by LGOC bus than by LCC tram, for there had been a considerable growth in the number of buses in London. In 1914 there was declared a Great War, and the LCCT's services suddenly took on a new importance. Between the summer of 1914 and the summer of 1915, 1000 of the 2900 LGOC and associated operators' buses left the road, and although the annual car-miles operated by the LCCT fell slightly between 1914 and 1915, passengers and revenue increased. Unfortunately, LCCT working expenses also rose, reflecting steep increases in the price of coal and other commodities. London's need for more tram services during the war, particularly for munitions traffic, did not coincide with the common belief that able-bodied men were most usefully and patriotically employed offering themselves up to be killed in France. Thus it was that trailer-cars were seen as a means of increasing the capacity of services without proportionately increasing either working costs or the demand for male staff, for trailers were frequently conducted by women.

From around mid-1918 there was a general reduction of LCCT services outside rush-hours, due to shortages of skilled labour and materials, and arrears of maintenance. Indeed, it is probably that between 1918 and 1920 LCCT services were at their worst, unable to provide adequately for the return to peacetime conditions.

In January 1919, additional trailer cars were transferred to Telford Avenue, for they were no longer required for munitions traffic in the Woolwich area. It is likely that there were then up to sixty trailers in use on Service 16/18, but such improvements to its operations as returning servicemen enabled the LCCT to make were not enduring; services were again reduced when the working week of tram-crews was reduced from sixty to forty-eight hours later in 1919. But not for long, for now men were coming back from France and jobs were scarce; by the end of 1919 the LCCT was employing 3100 motormen, one thousand more than two years previously.

In the summer of 1920, trailers were used for the first time on Sundays on Service 16/18, which suggests that demand for services was still outstripping supply.

Gradually, from this time, the LCCT began to respond to the new post-war world with operational changes. It was realised that the speed of services needed to be improved, and a programme of fitting more powerful motors to certain cars was begun. More new E/1's were also bought. Trailer services were slow, and they held up other services north of Streatham Library, and a point was reached when it was thought that the same number of passengers could be carried without trailers on a generally speeded up service. During three weeks in March 1923, tests were made on Service 16/18, with and without trailers, and such was the result that trailers were never returned to service. A feature of these tests was the introduction for a short period of rush-hour Extra's, numbered 16A and 18A.

During their time at Telford Avenue, the trailers were kept mainly in the extension shed, where they were shunted by two redundant C class cars (293 and 294). As the exit from the depot was down an incline, the trailers free-wheeled into service. At Norbury each car arriving left its trailer for the next tram, and continued with the trailer left by the car in front. At the Embankment the same procedure may have been used in the early years, but it is more likely that trailer sets were the first cars to regularly run in over one bridge and out over the other.

In 1919, the year in which an additional twenty trailers were allocated to Telford Avenue Depot, each LCCT tram in service was carrying, on average, 50% more passengers than it had carried five years previously. All the signs indicated continued growth in traffic, and the Highways Committee was hoping to substantially increase the size and scope of its tram network. It was decided, therefore, to erect a third tram depot at Telford Avenue, specifically to house trailer cars, and a site was acquired a few hundred yards to the north of Telford Avenue.

By 1921 the work was in hand, and on 6th March 1924 thirty-one cars began operating from what became known as Brixton Hill Depot. By that time, of course, there were no longer any trailer cars in use on Service 16/18, and as the rails in the new depot had not been bonded to provide a continuous earth return, a network of trolleybus-type overhead, with positive and negative wires, was crudely put up in the shed and extended out into the road, to enable cars to reach the change-pit outside the depot entrance. Cars 1727 — 1776 were transferred to Brixton Hill from Clapham and fitted with three-way switches so that they could operate beneath this double overhead with two poles, in the same way that certain cars had worked in the Woolwich area from 1920. That this was a rather silly way to correct an original mistake was tacitly admitted in 1927 when the depot rails were bonded, but the double overhead remained till 1951, its appearance intriguingly enhanced from the late 1930's when trolleybus twin-line hangers were put up outside the depot.

Brixton Hill Depot was never used to full capacity, for the gradual speed-up of services later in the 1920's enabled fewer cars to provide a faster service at a constant frequency. In the 1930's the spare capacity was used for storing the older cars acquired by LPTB and then for breaking up many of them.

From the time it was extended to Norbury and over Blackfriars Bridge in 1909, the pattern of service on the 16's and 18's altered little. It is probable that the combined three-minute frequency which both routes gave in 1904 remained unchanged, except in the 1918-1920 period. There were detailed alterations to the service, when the Mitcham Lane tracks were opened, for example, and such details as I have been able to trace are given on the maps in Appendix Two. One of the more obvious changes came in 1923, when for the first time the two services changed numbers in one direction according to the way in which they circled the Embankment. No longer were numbers changed on the Embankment. From 12th November 1923 all cars running 'round London' in a clockwise direction became 16's, whilst those running anti-clockwise became 18's. This sensible arrangement continued until 1951.

1926-1951

From 1909 until 1926 an insignificant bridge over the River Graveney at Norbury was the stage for one of London's longest running farces. On either side of the boundary between London and Croydon, their tracks separated by only a few inches, the trams of the LCCT and Croydon Corporation Tramways (CCT) stopped, and then returned whence they had come. Passengers wishing to cross the boundary were obliged to change cars, daily proving a point for those who argued against municipal control of transport.

That such a folly continued for so long cannot be attributed simply to civic-pride, insularity or bloody-mindedness. Croydon's stock of lightweight open-top trams was not acceptable to the LCCT, and conversely the CCT track was unsuitable for the heavier cars of the LCCT. And whilst Croydon's cars could safely pass beneath the railway bridge at Norbury Station, LCCT cars would not, although an experimental trip had been made by an LCCT car in December 1912. The initial costs of through-running would fall wholly upon the CCT, yet their investment would virtually hand over control of Croydon's main line to the LCCT.

The War delayed any action, but in 1921 the Board of Trade suggested that a through service of trams should be established. In the following year LCCT/CCT negotiations began, and in November 1923 an agreement was reached. Between April 1923 and March 1924 the tracks were relaid from Purley to Norbury, but almost two years then passed before a through service began, two years during which bus competition increased and the Southern Railway lines from London through Streatham and Norbury were electrified to Croydon and Purley. At the beginning of October 1925, work began on joining the tracks at Hermitage Bridge, and finally, on Sunday 7th February 1926, a tram service from London to Croydon began.

For many years before 1926, LCCT Service 16/18 had run from Norbury to London at three minute intervals throughout the day, and this basic service — excluding rush-hour Extra's — required about 31 trams. South of Norbury, the CCT service to Purley had operated every four minutes. From February 1926, the three-minute LCCT frequency was extended through to Purley. Although each authority was allowed to run extra cars within its own area, only the LCCT chose to do so; Croydon relied on its 'local' service from Thornton Heath to the Davis Theatre to provide additional rush-hour capacity.

The new all-day service required 52 trams, and it was agreed that the LCCT would operate 31 cars, with the CCT providing 21 new cars and four additional spare cars. But though the CCT had done all the ground-work required of it, it was not until a year after through-running began that an order was placed for ten new trams; the rest were ordered at the start of 1928. Until the CCT cars arrived, the whole service was operated with E/1's from Telford Avenue. For part of that time, CCT crews travelled daily to Telford Avenue to take out hired E/1's, and it is said that their uniforms, scarcely changed since horse tram days, caused some amusement to LCCT staff. The CCT reluctance to buy new cars at just over £2,500 each is not surprising; unification impended, and in the mid 1920's Croydon's trams were costing their rate-paying owners around £60,000 annually.

On 15th December 1927 'a new apparition burst on the eyes of the habitues of the tramway route between Streatham and London'; the first of the new CCT cars was earning money, and by September 1928 all were in service. In fact the cars were essentially E/1's — albeit a new, Pullmanised and high-powered model — for the LCCT expected its municipal collaborators in through-running to conform to its own standards in car-design. The CCT cars were coloured deep red and ivory, and they ran from Purley and Thornton Heath Depots.

From 1926 until 1933 the service was little altered, if at all. The 21 CCT cars and 31 LCCT cars ran throughout the day as 16's and 18's, and every rush-hour the LCCT flooded the line north of Norbury with Extra's numbered 16A and 18A. Later, many of these Extra's were extended to Thornton Heath Pond, certainly by and probably from 1933, when London Transport was formed. Croydon's trams had always been operated in a rather 'provincial' manner — although they did so inefficiently compared to Ilford Corporation, the undoubted masters of studious non-metropolitanism — and the 1933 Act seems to have come as something of a relief to Croydon Corporation.

In the early 1930's there was a vogue for 'speeding-up', which was applied to both buses and trams. In 1932 Clapham Depot's schedules were altered, and it is likely that Telford Avenue followed soon after July 1933; judging by what happened at Clapham, five minutes or more would have been cut from the 16/18 running-time at 'slack' times. (In 1951, 150 minutes were allowed in the morning rush-hour, Purley to Purley.) The basic service for most of the day required only fifty-one cars in November 1936, although the fifty-second still operated in the evening rush-hour to allow for a slight increase in running-time.

On 15th November 1936, trolleybuses replaced trams on the Feltham-operated tram Service 7 on the Uxbridge Road, and forty-six Feltham trams were transferred to Telford Avenue Depot. New schedules, which differentiated between Feltham and Standard cars, already operated, and Stan Collins has described the minor structural changes these forty-one-foot long leviathans imposed on the old tram-shed at Telford Avenue. Nine of the Felthams replaced Standard cars on the all-day 16/18 service (from Telford Avenue), and a further eight (two from Telford and two from Brixton Hill) were operated as rush-hour Extra's. The Felthams must have been successful, for one month later the all-day 16/18 was again 'speeded-up'; it henceforth required only 50 cars for most of the day, although the three minute service was maintained.

The rest of this first batch of Felthams was allocated to the 8/20's and 10's, while four remained in the depot as spares. In 1938, the rest of the Felthams came to Telford Avenue, around twenty in March, the rest in May. Ex-LCCT Bluebird arrived in April. Telford Avenue now had almost enough Felthams to provide all its services, but never quite enough, for although in the late 1940's an all-Feltham operation could have been managed at a pinch, in practice there was always a few E/1's or ex-Walthamstow cars running out of Telford Avenue. Three Felthams were destroyed in the Blitz, and eight were either scrapped or destroyed in 1949/1950.

From 1936 to 1951 the quality and quantity of Service 16/18 can be examined fairly accurately, for good records remain for that period. In December 1936 the all-day service was as follows:

Monday — Friday: Purley and Embankment, every three minutes; after 7 p.m., every four minutes. This required 50 cars, plus two in the evening rush-hour. All-day, 21 came from Purley Depot, 30 or 32 from Telford Avenue.
Saturday: Purley and Embankment, every three minutes. This required 52 cars all day, 20 of which came from Purley.
Sunday: Purley and Embankment, every five minutes. This required 29 cars, 16 from Purley and 13 from Telford Avenue.

Superimposed on this basic service, there operated in rush-hours (no longer labelled 16A and 18A, but 16X and 18X or simply EX) the following additional cars:
Monday — Friday: Morning, 34 cars (Telford 4, Brixton Hill 30); Evening, 21 cars (all from Brixton Hill).
Saturday: Morning, 26 cars (Telford 6, Brixton Hill 20; midday, 17 cars (Telford 1, Brixton Hill 16).

The LT tram allocation book — source of these details — shows all these Extra's operating between Norbury and the Embankment, on Mondays to Fridays at four minute intervals, but this was obviously a convenient 'shorthand', and it must be assumed that they were intended to be used flexibly by Regulators to provide such short-workings as were needed from various suburban points. (Look at the disparity between cars put out in the morning and evening peaks, and remember that 34 cars were more than Telford's contribution to the all-day three-minute service). By the late 1940's scheduling practice had gone to the other extreme, as you will see, although it is probable that Regulators quietly continued to run their cars as they thought best.

On Saturdays, at this time, the Extra's were used differently, for some stayed out between the peaks, during which time crews would have taken it in turn to enjoy their recently conceded meal-relief.

After 1936 the frequencies were altered occasionally. Every Summer until 1940 a four-minute service operated on Sundays, and although the records first show Extra's running to Thornton Heath Pond in 1937, there exists photographic evidence to suggest — as does common sense — that these had been working since 1933. In February 1938 the number of Monday to Friday rush-hour cars was increased to 37, and the whole operation in the evening peak now cost 89 trams, a record for Service 16/18.

In December 1940, during the Blitz, came the first recorded reduction in service; the evening service then operated at six-minute intervals on Mondays to Fridays and twelve-minute intervals (2½ c.p.h. on each service) on Saturdays and Sundays. It is apparent from Stan Collins' description of the Blitz, that at this time schedules counted for little in the evenings; indeed, it must also be remembered that bombing disrupted services considerably in 1940 and 1941. Full evening services were restored on 16th April 1941. From 29th October 1941, six Monday to Friday Extra's were withdrawn, leaving 31 still operating; and during the winter evenings of 1941, 1942 and 1943 reductions in service were again made.

Purley Depot had been closed in September 1937, but though it was fortuitously used only for storing surplus or damaged cars during the War — some of which reappeared, without windscreens, when bombs severed the 16/18's

From 8th June 1949, Norwood Depot operated cars on Service 16/18. E/3 car 174 was built for Leyton Corporation in 1931 at which time the LCCT operated the Leyton system. Here it leaves Norwood Depot ready to take up service at Lambeth Town Hall.

in 1940 — from 19th April 1944 Purley regularly operated three cars on the Monday to Saturday all-day service, and this continued until 1946 or 1947. From 1946 or 1947 (the allocation books for this period are not to hand) Thornton Heath Depot began putting out rush-hour Extra's on the 16/18 for the first time.

From 8th June 1949 — at a time when LT's services were under considerable pressure, and optimistic visions of future traffic levels were being dreamt — the all-day Monday — Friday Service 16/18 was inexplicably cut by 25%; thereafter it operated only at four-minute intervals, increasing to five minutes in the evenings. As a result, the all-day service now required only 40 trams, although the number of rush-hour Extra's was increased to 40 (two of which now came from Norwood, and six from Thornton Heath). On Saturdays and Sundays a four-minute service was given. It was shortly after this that the rebuilders moved into Telford Avenue Depot. On the first day of January 1950, Thornton Heath Depot was closed, in order that it might be demolished and a bus garage erected on the site; the Thornton Heath allocation of cars was simply moved to Purley Depot, which was re-opened for the purpose. In connection with this move, a curious additional Saturday afternoon working was introduced which survived until April 1951; a twelve-minute service of Extra's operated between Telford Avenue and Coombe Road, Croydon, partly perhaps to offset a lesser reduction on Service 42 at this time.

Thereafter there was little change to the service, apart from the re-allocations of cars between Norwood, Brixton Hill and Telford Avenue in 1949 and 1950 to which page 126 refers. From now on, E/3's and rehabilitated E/1's appeared on the Purley road. Around half of Telford Avenue's Felthams were withdrawn by January 1951, when the 16/18 was left the sole service from Telford Avenue, but the rest remained in use until April 7th, 1951, when Service 16/18 and its Extra's operated for the last time. The service given in those last few months is reproduced in the next column, expressed in cars-per-hour.

Bus service 109 began operating on Sunday 8th April 1951, following exactly the route of tram 16/18. On that day 28 RT's provided a five-minute service where on previous Sundays 37 trams had operated at four-minute intervals. The new Monday — Friday rush-hour service, on the other hand, required 88 buses (52 from Telford Avenue and 36 from the new garage at Thornton Heath) to replace 74 trams, for the RT sat only 56 passengers whereas the tram had seated 64 or more. The four-minute tram service through to Purley was replaced by a bus every three minutes to Thornton Heath Pond with every second bus going on to Purley. Angell Road, Water Lane and Norbury ceased to be scheduled turning points, and for most of Saturday half the off-peak service turned round at the Swan and Sugar Loaf, South Croydon. If such changes were needed — and they probably were — one wonders why they had to wait for bus conversion.

From 8th April 1951, Telford Avenue — now known as Brixton Garage — operated a maximum of 92 buses. Some — most likely the all-day allocation — now operated from the partly completed garage which was already arising on the site of the demolished extension tram-shed — the first part of Telford Avenue Depot to disappear — and a good number ran from the temporary open-air garage behind the Streatham Hill Theatre (where there were refuelling and servicing facilities). The layout of Brixton Garage suggests that much preparatory work —

Route No.	Route	Day	Trams per hour			
			am pk.	m day	pm pk.	eve nor
16	Purley & Victoria Embkmt. (via Westminster Bridge)	M-F.	7½	7½	7½	6
18	Purley & Victoria Embkmt. (via Blackfriars Bridge)		7½	7½	7½	6
16 Ex	Thornton Heath & Embkmt. (via Westminster)		10	—	5	—
16 Ex	Telford Avenue & Embkmt. (via Westminster)		2½	—	—	—
16 Ex	Brixton, Water Lane & Embkmt. (via Westminster)		4	—	—	—
16 Ex	Brixton, Angell Rd. & Embkmt. (via Westminster)		4	—	—	—
16 Ex	Norbury & Embkmt. (via Westminster)		—	—	2½	—
16 Ex	Streatham Library & Embkmt. (via Westminster)		—	—	2½	—
16 Ex	Telford Ave. & Westminster Stn.		—	—	5	—
18 Ex	Thornton Heath & Embkmt. (via Blackfriars)		10	—	5	—
18 Ex	Telford Avenue & Embkmt. (via Blackfriars)		2½	—	—	—
18 Ex	Brixton, Water Lane & Embkt. (via Blackfriars)		4	—	—	—
18 Ex	Brixton, Angell Rd. & Embkmt. (via Blackfriars)		4	—	—	—
18 Ex	Norbury & Embkmt. (via Blackfriars)		—	—	2½	—
18 Ex	Streatham Library & Embkmt. (via Blackfriars)		—	—	2½	—

This extract from the LT Allocation Book shows the Monday - Friday service operating from 8th January 1951. The morning rush-hour required 79 trams; 5 fewer were needed in the evening rush-hour. The "all-day" service needed only 39 trams until around 7 p.m.

possibly even including some demolition — could have been carried on in the back of the old cable-shed whilst the ten trams still ran from it between January and April 1951.

Certainly, the last part of the cable shed to be demolished was the facade. By 1953 the new bus garage was complete, a functional steel framed shed lying back from the road, with a nondescript two-storey office block before it. The water main-pipe which had always divided the tram sheds had been lowered, and the 'private road' disappeared.

Strangely, perhaps, Brixton Hill Depot was never used as an operational bus garage, but in the mid-1950's it became a store for surplus RT buses awaiting sale. It still stands, quite recognisable, performing some function connected with the motor trade.

It had always been assumed that the Purley road was a good money-making road, but in the late 1950's a LT study revealed, it is said, that this was not so — hardly surprisingly, considering the expensive rush-hour boosting it required. It was presumably a similar study which caused bus 95 — the replacement for tram service 10 — to become one of London's first one-man-operated double-decked services in January 1971. That one can now operate with one-man buses what were once busy tram services is an interesting indication of changing demand for transport in London.

APPENDIX FOUR

WAGES AND CONDITIONS OF LCCT AND LT TRAM CREWS.

The 'top' rates quoted were normally reached after two years service. From 1915 until 1920, wage increases took the form of a 'temporary' war bonus, acknowledging increases in the cost-of-living which it was hoped would cease with the end of the War. In 1933 this bonus was consolidated into the basic wage.

LONDON TRAMWAYS CO. 1870-1898 (information is scarce, thus rates given are those operating at specified dates.)

Before 1877	Drivers : 4s. daily, Conductors : 3s. daily.	
In 1877	Both grades : 4s. 6d rising to 5s.	On introduction of Bell Punch. Older men who 'taught' were paid an extra 6d. daily. In 1884 daily working hours reduced to an average of twelve.
By 1891	Both grades : 4s. 6d. first 3 mths, 5s. next 9 mths., 5s. 6d. thereafter	Merit and length of service may have given slightly higher 'personal' rates. An extra 3d. daily was paid on the Peckham and Greenwich lines. 7 days a week, 11½ hours work daily, but regular men were stood off one day in eleven to provide work for spare men.
In 1898	Both grades : 4s. 6d. to 6s. daily.	

1899-1952 ((Until 1950, Motormen and Conductors were paid the same rates).

LONDON COUNTY COUNCIL, 1899-1933

Dates of alterations	Top Weekly Rate	War Bonus	Av. Weekly M'man's wage	Notes
1899 Mar	36s.			6 day week given, 11½ hour day continued; cost, £28,000.
1900	37s. 6d			10 hr. day, sixty-hour week, given; cost, £10,000
1907 Jan	39s.			Horse crews
1915 July	42s.	3s.	40s. (April)	First War bonus, given to male staff of 18 yrs and over.
1916 Nov	45s. 6d	6s. 6d.		
1917 May	48s.	9s.		
Sept	51s.	12s.		
1918 Mar	59s.	20s.		'Combine' tram rates equalised in 1918, probably at LCCT rates.
July	64s.	25s.		
Nov	69s.	30s.		
1919 Oct	73s.	34s.		48-hour week given without wage-cuts, but note that the actual working week had for some years been much less than 60 hours.
1920 Mar	78s.	39s.		
June (i)	79s.	40s.		
June (ii)	82s.	40s.		Top basic rate increased to 42s. pw, (up 3s.)
1921 Aug	79s.	37s.		Sliding-scale agreement introduced June 1921; war bonus went up or down according to cost-of-living index.
Nov	77s.	35s.		
1922 Feb	74s.	32s.		(LGOC driver's top rate is 100s. per week., conductor 87s.)
May	72s.	30s.		Sliding-scale agreement revised, September 1922, in employer's favour.
Oct	68s.	26s.		
1923 May	67s.	25s.		
Aug	66s.	24s.		
Nov	67s.	25s.		
1924 Apr.	73s.	25s.		Top basic rate increased to 48s pw; sliding-scale system altered.
1932 Sept	72s.	24s.		(LGOC driver's top rate is 88s. per week, conductor 80s.)
1933 Apr.	73s.	25s.		LCCT rates become the London Standard, given to all LT tram and trolleybus crews from 1933.

LONDON TRANSPORT, 1933-1952

Dates of alterations	Top Weekly Rate	War Bonus	Av. Weekly M'man's wage	Notes
1935 Jan	75s.		79s. 2d.	
Apr	76s.			
Nov	78s.			'Levelling-up' to Bus Conductors rates accepted by LT.
1936 Oct	80s.		83s.	Full meal reliefs given, with revised Union Agreement.
1938 Dec	82s.		82s. 7d.	
1939 Dec (i)	84s.		85s. 6d.	Tram-crews henceforth paid same rate as Central Bus conductors.
Dec (ii)	88s.			War Increase. Women Conductors start at a lower than male rate, taking six months longer to reach top-rate
1940 June	91s.		93s. 7d.	,,
1941 April	95s.		97s. 2d.	,,
1942 Mar	99s.		100s. 11d.	,,
1943 July	103s. 6d.		108s. 11d.	,,
1944 May	108s. 6d.		115s. 11d.	,,
1946 Jan	117s. 6d.		123s. 8d.	,,
1948 Mar	125s.		135s. 10d.	44-hour week given in 1947, with Sundays paid at 1½ time.
1950 Dec	Drivers : 134s. Cdrs : 132s.		140s. 8d.	Extra pay given for Saturdays after 1pm., from 1949.
1951 Aug	Drivers : 142s. 6d. Cdrs : 140s. 6d.		157s. 9d.	
1952	Drivers : 144s. 6d. Cdrs : 142s. 6d.			Full Central Bus rates.

Sources : Before 1933 : Tramway & Railway World, LCC Minutes, The Record. After 1933 : LT records.

Conditions and Wages of Traffic Section (London Tramways).

WAGES.

Drivers and Conductors.

To commence	... £3 7s. 0d.	per week.
After 6 months	... £3 8s. 6d.	,, ,,
,, 12 ,,	... £3 11s. 6d.	,, ,,
,, 18 ,,	... £3 14s. 6d.	,, ,,
,, 2 years	... £3 16s. 0d.	,, ,,
Assistant Regulators	... £3 5s. 0d.	,, ,,
Plough Shifters, £3 5s. to £3 10s. 0d.		,, ,,

Pointsmen, operating less than 40 cars per hour £3 2s.
,,   40 to 49   ,,   ,,   £3 3s.
,,   50 to 59   ,,   ,,   £3 4s.
,,   60 and over ,, ,,   £3 5s.

CONDITIONS.

Drivers and Conductors.—The duties schedule shall be a 48-hour week of six days, including signing on and off, Thursday to Wednesday.

Maximum daily duty, 8 hours 30 minutes exclusive of travelling time.

Minimum daily duty for calculation, 7 hours 30 minutes.

Sixty per cent. of depôt duties to be straight through; breaks of less than 45 minutes to be counted as time worked, except where by local arrangements the number of split duties exceed 40%, when only breaks not exceeding 20 minutes are paid as time worked.

Five minutes allowed for running car in. Ten minutes allowed for running car out.

Overtime of 8 minutes or more to be paid for as follows :
8 minutes to 22 minutes inclusive, equals $\frac{1}{4}$ hour
23   ,,   ,, 37   ,,   ,,   ,,   ,, $\frac{1}{2}$,,
38   ,,   ,, 52   ,,   ,,   ,,   ,, $\frac{3}{4}$,,
and so on.

Where overtime of 8 or more minutes is worked on each portion of a split duty the two spells shall be added together for the purpose of payment.

Spread-over payment is as follows :—
Schedule duties from 10 hours 15 minutes to 11 hours 44 minutes, 1/- per day ; 11 hours 45 minutes and over, 2/- per day.

Schedules shall be posted 10 days prior to operation, except on special occasions, when not less than two days' notice shall be given.

Rest Periods. One rest day in each pay-roll week. Rest day working is voluntary, and shall be paid at 25% in excess of the rate prevailing for that day.

There shall be a rest of not less than 8 hours between finishing one day's work and commencing the next day's work.

Where rest day intervenes, the rest period shall be 32 hours, except when rest day is Sunday ; due to schedule changing at week-end.

Overtime shall be paid for at time-and-quarter. (NOTE—there are some special payments for overtime on special occasions.)

Spare Men. A 48-hour week as near as possible, overtime to be paid in excess of 48-hour week. "Stand-by" time not to count for calculation of 48 hours.

No duty to be deliberately left open for "gate men." Daily spread-over not to exceed 13 hours, including "Stand-by" time.

Duties to be arranged in weeks of : Early—Mid-day—Late, as far as possible.

Alternate work shall consist of window and depôt cleaning in depôt only, also cleaning of punches and cancelling machines, etc. Outside work to be done by volunteers.

The total number of new entrants to the service who are not guaranteed a 48-hour week shall not exceed 10% of total number employed, and these shall be guaranteed a week of not less than 40 hours, to be completed in six days. The percentage to be agreed by negotiation. (The percentage agreed to is 5%.)

In the event of a man being called out, he shall be paid a minimum of two hours for each call in the day.

At least one day in a pay-roll week must be marked D.O. on output list. Output list to be posted as early as possible, and man should sign for his work. The duty having been signed for shall not be altered after 12 midnight, or if the man has finished his work and gone home.

Men called out on day marked N.W. will be paid ordinary rate.

Men called out on day marked D.O. will be paid time-and-quarter.

General. There shall be an annual holiday of 12 days with pay after 12 months continuous service. No employee shall be entitled to pay in lieu of holidays.

National holidays shall be paid for at time-and-quarter. Xmas Day—double time for time worked, with a minimum of 8 hours' pay. Sunday—time-and-quarter.

Men on all-night cars shall be paid a 1/- per night extra, and shall receive this rate for payment of annual holidays.

Clothing. Each driver and conductor shall receive two suits of uniform.

Drivers :—2 overcoats, 2 jackets, 2 pairs of trousers, 2 caps, 4 cap covers and 2 mackintoshes.

Conductors :—2 jackets, 2 pairs of trousers, 2 caps and 4 cap covers.

Issue :—Drivers, 1 overcoat every 2 years, 1 mackintosh every 2 years, 1 jacket every 2 years, 3 pairs of trousers every 2 years, 1 cap and 2 cap covers each year. Conductors, 3 jackets every 2 years, 3 pairs of trousers every 2 years, 1 cap and 2 cap covers every year.

Machinery is provided for dealing with complaints, which must be in writing and handed to the Secretary or a Committeeman.

When in doubt, consult the Secretary or a Member of the Committee, whose names and addresses are posted in the T. & G.W.U. notice case inside the depôt.

Pay your contributions regularly and thus be sure of always being in benefit.

Issued by E. D. SHEEHAN, Secretary, 1/337 Branch, New Cross Trams, Transport and General Workers' Union, for and on behalf of New Cross Branch Committee.

Printed by MATTHEWS & Co. (T.U.), 282, New Cross Road, S.E.

The negotiated wages and conditions of London tramwaymen operating from April until November 1935. DO means 'day-off'; NW means 'no work' and would apply only to those recent entrants without a full guaranteed week's work. Meal reliefs were not given until 1936. Many of the conditions are the uneasy result of past differences between men and their management.

APPENDIX FIVE

SOME NOTES ON LABOUR RELATIONS ON LONDON'S TRAMS.

Writing in 1891, Sidney Webb described the tramwayman's life thus : 'the 4000 (staff) are among the hardest worked, most cruelly treated and worst paid of London's wage slaves. Sixteen hours work for 4s. wage is no uncommon day's record; whilst Sunday's or other holidays are known to them only as times of extra traffic'. He continued; 'Nor is it possible to remedy this white slavery whilst the tramways remain in private hands'.

Hard worked and cruelly treated the tramwayman certainly was, but his job suffered from an operational feature of which urban road transport has never rid itself: the spreadover. The spreadover is a device whereby a crew works for a few hours in the morning and then has a few hours off before returning for a second spell of duty in the evening of the same day.

In the early days of London's horse trams, the traffic day ran roughly from eight in the morning to eleven or twelve at night, and it was common practice to allocate one crew to each car for the whole day. In the middle of the day, when traffics were slack, cars were sequentially withdrawn from service, a useful operational ploy which reduced horsing costs, for horses were not only more expensive to run than humans, but they also had a cash value (whereas men had none).

As time went on, the traffic day lengthened and an increased number of cars operated only in rush hours. By the 1890's, it seems, there had developed a practice of operating the 'all-day' cars with two 9 hour shifts, whilst rush-hour cars — and rush-hours lasted longer in those days — were operated by crews on spreadovers. In 1896, for example, on one company (probably the London Tramways Company) 'a period of 11¼ hours actually at work was then being spread over a working day of 17¾ hours'. Such lengthy shifts were probably rare, but it is likely that by this time around half the rostered duties were spreadovers, crews often working straight shifts and spreadovers on alternate days.

Wages were incremental, with progression up the scale to the top rate over a period of time, but there is evidence to suggest that the number of men was small who remained, or were allowed to remain on the job to reach the top rate.

Conditions on the North Metropolitan Tramways Company — the largest in the Metropolis, with lines in North and East London — are well documented in the first volume of 'A History of London Transport'. The North Metropolitan was, by the 1890's, a 'good' employer for its time; its wages were the best of any tramway company in London and it contributed to a Sports Club and Sick Club for its staff. Like most companies it levied fines on its staff, for loss or damage; but its benevolence seems to have owned much to the activities of one share-holding philanthropist and the general labour unrest in East London from 1889 onwards. From 1896, the North Metropolitan was obliged to work its staff for no more than an average of ten hours-a-day, the first useful imposition of the LCC on the London labour market. (Had it not been for the House of Lords, a similar condition would have improved the lot of staff on the Harrow Road and Paddington tramways from 1893).

Of the other companies much less is known. The London Tramways Company seems to have been considered a reasonable employer by the 1890's — its Traffic Manager, Mr. Wylie, was later described as 'a very fair man' in a Union journal — although it still worked its drivers and conductors for eighty hours a week right up to the end of 1898.

Car crews were in fact among the best paid tramwaymen, as the following table of weekly wages paid and hours worked on the London Tramways Company in 1898 will show. The last two columns show the number of days and hours worked in one week.

Drivers	31s. 6d. to 42s.	7	80
Conductors	31s. 6d. to 42s.	7	80
Stablemen	23s. to 30s.	7	77
Washers	22s. to 28s.	7	77
Farriers	33s. to 36s.	6	56½
Track Cleaners	21s. to 24s. 6d.	7	77
Pointsmen	15s. to 20s.	7	77
Trace boys	15s. to 18s.	7	77
Ticket Inspectors	40s. to 42s.	7	80
Regulators	42s.	7	80
Night Inspectors	32s. to 42s.	7	74
Foremen	36s. to 55s.	7	80
Deputy Foremen	40s.	7	80

Not all companies were as generous. The top crew rate on the South London Tramways Company at this time was 31s. 6d. for a 77 hour week, although its lines — from Wandsworth and Battersea — ran near and across those of the LT Company.

Like the North Metropolitan, the London Tramways Company fined its men for misdemeanours, and all staff had to deposit £5 with the Company when they were taken on. The loss of the deposit, the sack, and possibly the loss of your licence was the price paid by those who broke the Company's rules or damaged its property. Doubtless originally intended to ensure a high standard of staff, the deposit and fine system seems to have endured until the 1890's; certainly the LCCT continued to fine its tramwaymen until at least 1901.

If there was a point at which the fortunes of tramwaymen began to improve in the nineteenth century, it comes at the end of the 1880's, when there began to be developed general labour unions, the 'new unions' of labour history. East London at this time was the scene of considerable unrest, and it is recorded that tramwaymen of the North Metropolitan were sympathetic to the striking dockers and gas workers of 1889, but the Company's underwriting of the Sick Club can be interpreted as a policy of pre-empting unionisation.

South of the River Thames, in 1889, the staff of the London Tramways Company were also active, particularly after eight of them were sacked for asking the Company for the right to state their grievances. A night-time rally was held at a hall on the New Kent Road, addressed by Annie Besant and Tom Mann. Further meetings followed, but (as was to happen frequently thereafter) they were infiltrated by officials of the Company, and the activists were sacked. Nevertheless, certain useful concessions were later made by the Company.

This brief Union activity had at least personality links with the Amalgamated Omnibus and Tramway Workers

Union of 1891. Again, certain improvements in conditions followed, but after about a year the Union ceased to exist, and that seems to have been the end of Union activity among tramwaymen until 1899. However, in Salford in 1889, there was formed the Manchester and Salford Amalgamated Association of Tramway Employees, which after several years and two or three changes of name, became the Amalgamated Associated of Tramway and Vehicle Workers (AATVW): it was to play a significant part in the future of London tramwaymen. Two years later, in 1891, the Metropolitan Cab Drivers Society began organising cab-men in London, and this Union — enlarged to accommodate all licenced vehicle workers in 1913 — was to have an even greater importance for London tramwaymen.

It is not hard to understand why London tramwaymen were not organised before the late 1890's. They worked in pairs, rather than in large industrial groups, and like individual sticks were simply broken. Licences were easily obtained; there seems to have been no shortage of spare men, and tram-work was in part casual. When the LCC acquired the London Tramways Company in 1899 it did so with the intention not only of giving its new employees a shorter working day, but also of de-casualising the trams and giving continuous employment; job security was just what was required for the Unionisation of London tramwaymen.

A Driver and Conductor on the Brixton Hill cable-tramway, shortly after it was bought by the LCCT in 1899. Note the stool on the Driver's platform, frequently seen in photographs of horse-trams.

Shortly after the LCC Tramways Department began operating the lines of the London Tramways Company in 1899, it put its staff on a six-day week; a year later it introduced a ten-hour day. These efforts to improve the working conditions of its staff forced the LCCT to recruit 400 additional men. Although it was LCCT policy not to allow improved working conditions to reduce weekly wages, there were some minor reductions for certain grades, but, generally speaking, the employees benefitted from the Council's Progressive policies. There was criticism of the Council's generosity towards its staff, for together with the LCCT fares policy, it cost a large proportion of the profits once earned by the London Tramways Company. But there was also criticism that the Council was underpaying certain of its tramway staff; for many years horsekeepers and washers were paid less than 6d. an hour, the accepted LCC minimum wage. (Curiously, John Burns, who in 1889 had won a minimum wage of sixpence-an-hour for Dockers, defended the Council's policies here.) It is also a matter of record that the LCCT was sometimes a little slow to grant its standard wages and conditions to tramway undertakings which it later acquired.

By 1905, wages paid on the LCCT were as follows, listed in the same order as the table on page 162, and shewing hours worked each day and days worked each week in the last two columns; there were at that time 560 Motormen, 220 horse-drivers and 756 Conductors employed.

Drivers	28s. 6d. to 37s. 6d.	6	60
Conductors	28s. 6d. to 37s. 6d.	6	60
Stablemen	26s.	6	60
Washers	25s. to 30s.	6	60
Farriers	39s. to 43s. 6d.	6	54
Track Cleaners	25s.	6	60
Pointsmen	24s.	6	60
Trace boys	14s. to 18s.	6	60
Ticket Inspectors	42s.	6	60
Regulators	42s.	6	60
Night Inspectors	42s.	6	60
Foremen	42s. to 64s. 6d.	7	70
Deputy Foremen	42s.	7	70

In October 1899 a General Tram and Bus Workers Union issued a circular appealing to the LCCT to abolish the system of fines, but fines continued. In 1901 the Union again demanded the cessation of fines, together with certain improvements to wages, one of which sought to increase the top rate of drivers and conductors to 42s. per week. It was also alleged that the Council had broken the 10 hour day and six-day week arrangement. The wage increases were refused and the Council denied the rostering allegations. The Chairman of the Highways Committee justified the continuance of fines on disciplinary grounds, pointing out that they only amounted on average to 5d. per man each year as against 8d. per man under the Company; they were not "capriciously exacted". The Committee also refused to grant holidays with pay; when these were first granted a few years later they had to be taken in the winter months. It was also admitted that certain spare men were still employed, although they were practically permanent hands: there were only forty-eight of them and they worked 23 days out of 27 at 4s. 9d. each day.

The Union also asked that Drivers be allowed to smoke after 8 o'clock in the evening, but this was refused, although men on night-cars could smoke until 6 o'clock in the morning. In 1904 it was suggested that Drivers of electric cars be allowed to sit at their work, but the Highways Committee considered this quite improper and potentially unsafe, although it had long been accepted that horse tram-drivers could do so. (Horse-car crews were also allowed to eat on their cars, but this privilege was withdrawn from them when they took over electric cars.)

Shortly before he left London in October 1903, Alfred Baker, the Chief Officer of the LCCT, wrote a paper on the hours-of-labour and rates-of-pay of tramways employees. He defended the graduated scales of pay for Drivers and Conductors on the grounds that new men were more liable to accidents than long-service men, and he remarked that the LCCT and Glasgow Corporation alone paid the same rates to Drivers and Conductors. There was no legitimate reason why an electric-car Driver should receive more pay than a Conductor and he observed that in London no person under 21 was allowed a Police licence to work on trams. A comparative table of rates of pay presented with this paper showed that LCCT crews were the best paid in the country: "who shall say" he wrote "that these men are overpaid when it is remembered that in London a man, with perhaps a wife and family to support, cannot obtain decent rooms to dwell in for less than 14s. or 16s. per week?" The average weekly rate for motormen at this time was 31s. 3d. per week.

Although Sidney Webb had advocated an eight-hour-day for tramwaymen, and the Trades Union Congress had backed a general Eight-Hour-Day Bill in 1891, by 1903 municipal tramwaymen were most commonly working a ten-hour day. In certain parts of the country, tramwaymen worked for eight or nine hours on six or seven days a week; East Ham Corporation staff worked a nine-hour-day thirteen day fortnight, for example. Baker opined that the men would rebel at anything less than a sixty hour week if this involved a diminished earning capacity; if any change was desired at all, it would be rather towards increased rates of pay. (At around the time that Baker was writing, he was recommending to the Highways Committee that the rates of pay for car-washers be improved.) Mr. Baker, fair though he seems to have been, warned against allowing the 'pendulum' to swing too far. He spoke of one town — he did not name it, but it was probably Cardiff — where the men worked 54 hours each week, were paid time-and-a-half for Sunday, and double time for Bank and national holidays, and where an attempt was being made to classify Good Friday and Christmas Day as national holidays; 'besides paying the men who work on Bank Holidays double-pay,' he wrote 'the men who do not work are paid a days wages'. He also warned against preferential pay for municipal tramwaymen, as against other employees of the same Corporation. Foreseeing an increase in the number of tramway employees over the next five years, Baker advocated the formation of Friendly Societies as one way of attracting 'the most desirable class of men to the service'. (The LCCT wound-up the North Metropolitan's Sick Club shortly afterwards.)

Baker also revealed that the LCCT tramwayman's ten hours work could be spread over up to eighteen hours in one day, and that duties over ten hours daily were paid at the rate of time-and-a-half. (There is evidence that this latter claim was untrue). Half pay was granted to employees injured on duty, and an overcoat, jacket and two hats or caps were issued free to Drivers and Conductors. (In LT Company days, only Conductors wore this half-uniform, and at least as late as 1893, they had to buy it for themselves.) Thus it can be fairly said that, although the LCCT offered improved wages and working conditions 'to secure good men and an efficient service', its policy, even under the Progressives, was not one of intemperate benevolence to its staff.

Around 1903, the General Tram and Bus Workers Union was absorbed by the AATVW, by then organising in London, offering members a Sick Club; it has been said that this absorption added more anxiety than strength to the AATVW. A Sick Club was important at a time when there was no general sickness pay, and no retirement pension.

Shortly afterwards, the Highways Committee received a deputation from the AATVW seeking certain changes in working conditions. The request was considered in February 1905. The main Union claims were for a reduction in the working day to nine hours, with a maximum spreadover time of twelve hours and an increase in the top rate of pay from 5s. 9d. to 6s. 3d. daily; neither request was granted. It was explained that, in November 1904, the average working day consisted of nine hours nineteen minutes actual work,

Camberwell Depot around 1910, when manual labour was cheap. The bowler-hatted gentleman is Mr.J.H. Rider, the LCCT's Electrical Engineer.

spread over twelve hours and twenty-eight minutes. Out of a total of 1620 Drivers and Conductors then employed, 70% were already earning 6s. 3d. a day, and in view of the impending operational takeover of the leased lines in North London, the Highways Committee was unwilling to make any alteration in rates of pay. The Union also asked that spare men be paid 2s. a day when they showed up but were not given work; the Committee allowed that a minimum of a shilling should be paid to these men whether or not work was given to them. Two further requests are of interest. The Union asked that Drivers and Conductors be given one week's holiday with pay each year after two years service, and the Committee pointed out that all staff already had one day off every week. It was also asked that staff called upon to work on their "stand-off day" be paid at the rate of time-and-a-half, for at present such extra work was rewarded only with ordinary rates of pay. The Committee allowed that work done during "stand-off" times should be paid at the rate of time-and-a-quarter. The final Union request was for the formation of a board of conciliation, consisting of representatives of the men and of the Highways Committee; four years later four Conciliation Boards were set up covering all grades of employees in the Tramways Department.

Shortly before the Progressives lost control of the LCC, they granted a wage increase: from January 1907, the minimum weekly rate for Drivers and Conductors became 30s., the maximum 39s. This award was worth an extra 3d. daily to all platform staff, and these rates continued to be paid until 1915. Early in 1909 a further claim was made for improvements, but these were rejected by the Highways Committee, which was by then Conservative controlled. In February 1910 the four LCCT Conciliation Boards first met, and staff representatives promptly took their year-old claim to the Traffic Board. A month later an agreement was reached, and it was accepted by the LCCT and Highways Committee.

For the first time, tramwaymen were given a daily allowance of thirty minutes for 'signing-on' and 'signing-off' — preparing cars for service, collecting tickets and cashing up, putting cars away — and for the first time, also, it was agreed that annual leave could be taken all the year round, instead of in the Winter months only. On Sundays the average spreadover was reduced to eight hours, where it had previously been five minutes short of nine hours. Because of this improvement, the Conciliation Board was not disposed to grant the requested maximum spreadover of twelve hours throughout the week — at that time the average length was twelve hours and twenty-one minutes. Although the average working week — that is the time spent actually working — was now in the region of fifty-four hours, the Conciliation Board decided that no overtime would be paid until a man had worked his agreed sixty hours. In effect, this meant that a man would work for six hours without pay each week before receiving any extra money whatsoever.

The 1910 improvements were well worthwhile, and in the years leading up to the 1914 War, useful reductions were made in the length of the working day. From 1907, however, the cost-of-living slowly rose, and the LCCT employee was worse off in real terms when war was declared than he had been in 1907. Even worse, the LCCT had begun to lose both passengers and revenue to the motor bus after 1910, and the undertaking was no longer the profitable one it had once seemed to be. During this period I have come across evidence of only one strike, in 1912, when men at Stamford Hill Depot came out, presumably in sympathy with striking East London dockers.

The AATVW achieved little for its members during this pre-war decade, and it is perhaps not surprising that another Union began organising tramwaymen in London. The London Bus, Tram and Motor Workers Union became active from 1906, and it seems that it was this Union (or one derived from it, for comparative membership figures were similar) that amalgamated in 1913 with the London Cab Drivers Union — developed in 1894 from the Metropolitan Cab Drivers Society — to form the London and Provincial Licenced Vehicle Workers Union (L&P). Straightaway, it began actively and successfully recruiting LCCT tramwaymen on the south side of the Thames. From the start the L&P was a more militant Union than the AATVW, and some indication of its strength can be measured by the fact that it was in 1913 formally recognised by the LGOC.

Although the L&P approached the AAT with a view to amalgamation shortly after it was formed, the problems — mainly financial, concerned with the Sick Club provisions of the AAT — were insuperable, and for several years more the two unions competed for members in the ranks of the LCCT. The AAT had the advantage of a greater number of seats on the Traffic Section Conciliation Board, and after the London Bus and Tram-mens Sick Provident Society, known as Fullers Club, was wound up around 1914, the AAT was the only tramwayman's sick club in London and inevitably it appealed to older men.

In the six months after July 1914, prices rose by between 10 and 15%. During the same period the demands placed upon the LCCT and its servants increased; more mobility was required, particularly in connection with munitions production, and fewer buses remained on the streets.

The complaints of tramwaymen of those days are of interest; apart from an obvious wish for more money and shorter spreadovers they add up to a host of minor niggling grievances, a list of which Mr. Fell was appalled to be handed by an L&P deputation in December 1914. From New Cross Depot there were complaints that trams serving the Woolwich Arsenal were grossly overloaded, sometimes by more than 50%, and that running times were consequently inadequate. In some parts of London, Regulators were criticising Drivers for running a few minutes late in the first limited blackout London had ever experienced, although no extra running time was given. At Camberwell Green, a zealous night foreman from New Cross Depot spent his off duty mornings looking out for dirty trams. (The workload of car washers had been increased by 50% and they received less protective clothing than did their LGOC, 'under the capitalist', colleagues. From Clapham Depot came complaints that no extra money was granted to Drivers of trams which towed the first trailer cars in December 1914. Because many staff were joining the Colours there was an influx of new Conductors — called 'Practisers' — and the regular men training them on the road were liable for any cash or tickets which these Practisers lost.

Early in 1915 a new sick leave scheme was introduced. After a month of work, employees were invariably pronounced fit for duty by the LCCT doctor (Sir John Colley, who later examined Stan Collins). After complaints, this scheme was modified; employees returning from sick leave were handed a form headed 'Application for Re-employment'. At about the same time the L&P voiced its concern at the employment of women as tram conductors in Edinburgh; although they disliked the notion of women on trams, they strongly resented their employment at a lower wage than men were getting.

During the first few months of 1915 the tension mounted, although both unions were bound by an agreement made in June 1914, which 'froze' wages and conditions on the LCCT for one year. Notwithstanding this agreement, the AAT wrote to Fell in February 1915 asking for an all round 15% wage increase. The LCCT replied offering to pay a War Bonus of 3s. a week to all staff earning less than 30s. a week; Fell later admitted that only 12% of all LCCT staff qualified for this bonus.

In April 1915, new schedules were introduced which increased the proportion of spreadovers by reducing the number of cars in service at slack times; by now the unions were beginning to respond to what the L&P called 'shameful exploitation by a public body'. Although the LCCT's attitude to its staff at this time was indefensible, it must be remembered that few people anticipated either that the War would last for as long as it did, or that it would cause rapid and enduring inflation.

A strike was inevitable. At the beginning of May 1915 the L&P published 'a Call to Arms to the Tramwaymen of London', reminding members of the onerous conditions under which they worked, and announcing a series of meetings to be held all over London. By this time, despite suggestions that the LCCT had attempted to frustrate its development, the L&P claimed to represent the majority of employees; in fact it probably represented around half of them and it was still actively recruiting. The L&P demanded shorter spreadovers, proper overtime payments and a substantial War Bonus, and it was aware of the inequity of the all round percentage increase claimed by the AAT.

At 11.30 p.m. on Thursday, 13th May a meeting was held at the Gaiety Theatre in Brixton and this proved to be the catalyst. In the next issue of 'The Record' — the L&P journal — one of the 530 L&P members at New Cross Depot wrote thus "We have had the screws put on us for a long while . . .Walking home from Brixton . . . .we decided to call out the men, and at three o'clock we started. In an hour over a hundred men were out with us, and by seven o'clock the pavement was blocked with strikers. We began to feel a new sense of freedom and manliness come over us." By seven o'clock that morning Fell and his aide Mr. Slattery — later General Manager at West Ham — had visited New Cross and attempted unsuccessfully to halt the strike, but Fell would not negotiate unless the men returned to work forthwith. By nightfall, 2000 Southside LCCT employees were on strike, probably for the first time in their lives. On the following day practically the whole of South London was tramless but North London appeared normal. Late that night a second mass meeting of tramwaymen was held, at the Euston Theatre of Varieties, at which a resolution was passed giving notice that unless the AAT demand for an increase of 15% be conceded by the following day, "it is our intention to withhold our labour from the tramway service". They were as good as their word.

On Monday 17th May the strike was as complete as it ever would be. 6,500 LCC staff and a further 3000 from the Metropolitan Electric Tramways failed to report for duty; over 2000 London trams remained in their depots.

The LCCT, which had already posted dismissal notices in all the depots, began to arrange to break the strike, for even Fell seems to have realised that the dispute would not be resolved over-night. Throughout that week it advertised for new recruits, and many of them were employees who had previously dismissed themselves by striking. The Commissioner of Police for the Metropolis relaxed the stringent tram driving test procedure, new training schools were opened and 'a good class of intelligent men' came forward. Only those who were over military age were accepted.

For a few days the strike was almost solid, although it seems that almost every day some cars were operated in certain parts of London by LCCT officials. But it was not long before there developed disharmony between the L&P and AAT executives although a joint strike committee had been set up. Right from the start the L&P recognised the strike as official and began paying strike pay, but it was almost a fortnight before members of the AAT received any money from their Union.

The Press were generally unfriendly towards the strikers — in what transport strike are they not — for it was considered most unpatriotic to withdraw ones labour while the country was at war. The London Evening News, however, published details of three specimen spreadovers from actual time sheets; the longest lasted sixteen hours and fifty-eight minutes. Fell claimed that this was an exaggeration; although the maximum spreadover was between fourteen and fifteen hours, none were worked above that upper limit. Unfortunately, the just grievances of the tramwaymen tended to be obscured by the fact that munitions workers at Woolwich Arsenal and at Enfield Lock were particularly dependent upon trams, and munitions were a politically sensitive issue at that time.

From Wednesday 19th May, men began to return to work, particularly on the North-side where the AAT was strongest. On Saturday 22nd May, confident that full munition services were now operating and that new staff were daily applying for the strikers' jobs, Fell ordered the following notice to be posted in all depots: "All men on strike who are eligible for military or naval service are instructed to return their uniforms and badges to the tramway depots". A few days later depot officials were instructed not to allow any man to resume work who was eligible for His Majesty's Forces. There was at that time no conscription, and the unions later described Fell's action as an unwarranted attack on the rights of citizenship. By the end of May the strike was almost over and Fell, who appears to have handled the whole issue with ruthless insensitivity, magnanimously agreed that strikers who enlisted would receive favourable consideration for reinstatement after the War, and that any striker of military age who was unable to enlist, perhaps for personal family reasons, could appeal for an exception to be made. By Wednesday 2nd June "The Times" was able to report that return tickets were once again being issued on LCC trams, but it added that a number of L&P men were still on strike. On the following day the AAT notified Fell that its Union was withdrawing from the joint strike committee.

Quite what proportion of LCCT employees were new to the job after May 1915 is unknown but there is no doubt that the 1915 strike provided the LCCT with an excellent hedge against conscription — for all its new staff were above military age — and reduced its running costs.

Shortly after the strike was finished all LCCT traffic employees received their first War Bonus of 3s. weekly, but this would have come to them strike or no strike. In October 1915, as foreseen by the L&P, the Metropolitan Police agreed to grant licences to women conductors, and on 30th November the first of them began work on single deck tramway cars. From there they progressed, at the end of August 1916, to double deck trailer cars. On 31st March 1918 the LCCT employed 1521 women conductors, (roughly one for every three male employees who had gone to the War), but on 29th October 1919 the service of the last of them was terminated. Throughout their service they were paid less than male employees; not until May 1917 were they granted their first War Bonus. It was not until March 1918 that the LCCT allowed 67% of its women conductors to advance to the then full War Bonus of £1 each week. Apart from helping to solve the LCCT's shortage of staff — for several summers from 1914 a proportion of employees forewent their annual leave — it seems that women conductors stimulated the organised social life of tramwaymen, for there began to be held from about 1916, 'Concert Parties' at several depots, to several of which wounded military personnel were transported by free Special Cars.

Miss E. Claydon, an LCCT Woman Conductor at Stamford Hill Depot, was run down by a lorry on 8th September 1917, after point-changing in the blackout. Although their action was later regretted by Chief Office, local LCCT officials suspended three of Miss Claydon's colleagues who went to her funeral in Suffolk.

Most good strikes have their martyr, and this one was no exception. When the dispute began, Ted Hills was a Depot Inspector at Poplar. For some years he had been a member of the 'fighting' East London Branch of the AAT, and he had done much for tramwaymen. He had been concerned in obtaining the improvements of 1910. He believed that his union should do more for its members than make sick payments, and he was one of several like-minded members who threw their union badges into the East India Dock one night after a union meeting had endorsed this principle. Some time before 1915, Ted had been crushed between two cars while conducting in the fog, but he had pulled through and been given an 'inside' job. Early in the 1915 strike, Ted was sent to New Cross Depot to man a special munitions car — at one stage the Joint Strike Committee agreed to run such a special service for workers at the Woolwich Arsenal — but finding he was also expected to carry ordinary passengers, Ted refused and was sacked. His union would not argue for his re-instatement, and Ted Hills ended up as a docker. In the months following the strike Ted became something of a hero, and a collection was made for him, to which contributions came all over London.

If London tramwaymen learned anything from the strike of 1915, it was that 'in the vehicular trade of London there is room for only one society'. Many members of the AAT were disgusted by the actions of their non-elected Executive Committee, and membership of the L&P rose continually during the next few years. By May 1917 the L&P claimed to be 'manipulating' AAT activities in London, and there was considerable unanimity of opinion and a real desire to amalgamate in both unions in the London area. Formal amalgamation, when the two societies became the United Vehicle Workers, followed in 1920; London was finally cured of what the L&P — the 'red-button' union — called 'blue-itis', (the AAT badge was a blue button).

Although they had fallen, divided, LCCT tramwaymen continued to complain of their conditions. Among the more interesting comments made in 'The Record' after the strike, is one that the Department's finances would improve if only it would reduce the number of 'street ornaments' — Regulators — it employed. Some officials, it was said, had been paid eight pounds each week for 'black-legging' during the strike. It was also claimed that blacklegs were frequently promoted to become Regulators and Inspectors in the years after 1915, regardless of their abilities, although we must weigh this claim against one of 1917, that 95% of LCCT officials were members of the L&P.

The following 'pen-picture' appeared in 'The Record' in August 1915. Scene : The Embankment.   Time : Evening.

'A car rushes over the points, the Driver flies through the car even before it has stopped sometimes, receives the whistle, and then top-notch over the points again, and as he goes along people fly after the car like steel splinters onto a magnet. The car has picked up all intending passengers before it reaches Waterloo Bridge, so it need not wait long, then off again with one speed only, "hell-for-leather", to the suburbs, and he keeps time. Moreover it's the only way to do so'.

The writer then suggests that scrupulous attention to LCCT Rules and Board of Trade Regulations — particularly concerning speed limits, terminal procedures and the required fifty yards between cars — would paralyse the whole system within an hour. Although there were occasions when this ploy was later adopted — Hounslow trolleybus men demonstrated it very well one Saturday in 1962 — 'working-to-rule' is generally associated with railwaymen.

In 1916 came allegations — denied by the LCCT — that Chief Office was employing a score or so Belgian refugees (presumably recognisable by their unkempt appearance, tattered clothes and the pathetic bundles of possessions they carried) to spy on Conductors. This is an interesting variant of certain better known rumours. It was also seriously suggested that the only way to get a day-off at this time was to allow yourself to be caught ostentatiously smoking. In 1917 there were continual complaints that the LCCT was arbitrarily stopping money from Conductors's wages, allegedly to make up for short paying-in, although the L&P claimed that they were being charged for tickets missing from bundles, and that suitable explanations were never given. Indeed, most of the complaints of this period seem more symptomatic of thoughtlessness at Chief Office, than of anything else. More than once, the L&P recommended the LCCT to learn something of 'man-management' from the LGOC.

The LCCT took some note of the level of complaints, for in 1916 certain officers — including Mr Bruce, deputising for Fell during one of the Chief Officer's spells of illness — took to organising meetings at Depots specifically to hear complaints. Suggestion boxes were also put up. On his return, in 1917, Fell asked Conductors to volunteer for driving duties, but in such a way that the L&P felt he was offering this as an alternative to their leaving the Department. There was no love lost between Mr Fell and the L&P, although it must be said that his salaried staff had a strong regard for him.

Although there was an active branch of the L&P continously at Clapham Depot after 1915, at Telford Avenue the Union was less successful. After two brief false starts — during one of which the branch passed a resolution demanding a higher rate of pay for Motormen — Telford Avenue was organised in 1919. Certain branches — meetings were not allowed on LCCT premises — attracted members from more than one trade group; as this Appendix was being prepared, the 1917 L&P banner from Battersea Garage was discovered, embellished with a decidedly non-LCCT tram.

It was during the 1914 War that the practice ceased of running trams throughout Christmas Day. In 1915 the LCCT refused a L&P request for a cessation of service after six o'clock on Christmas Day, although it was agreed to reduce the service after that time. (Of the three Combine tram companies, a majority of cars on two systems was off the road by 3.30 pm. whilst the South Metropolitan Tramways Company had all its cars in their depots by 2.30 pm.) It is recorded that at 10 pm. on Christmas Day 1916, someone was knocked down by a tram in the Old Kent Road. In 1917, possibly following the lead of the London United and Metropolitan Electric Tramways which had both decided not to run cars after 4pm. on Christmas Day that year, the LCCT adopted a similar arrangement, which continued until 1951, and which gave tram staff one of the few advantages they had over LGOC busmen.

Throughout the War, the LCCT Traffic Conciliation Board — on which tramwaymen were represented by two AAT delegates, two L&P delegates and two 'odds-and-sods' (wages staff from Chief Office and the like, who were members of neither union) — continued to meet, but the demands of staff for improved war bonuses or conditions were generally referred to arbitration. The L&P sought to abolish the Board as early as 1916; apart from anything else, it claimed that the AAT and odds-and-sods delegates frequently voted with the management against the L&P. In 1918 — such was the degree of manipulation of AAT delegates by the L&P — all the staff representatives resigned from the Traffic Board. A year earlier, however, the Whitley Committee, responding to (or attempting to subvert, according to your viewpoint) growing wartime demands for worker's control, proposed a number of National Councils, among which was a National Joint Industrial Council for the Tramways Industry (NJIC), composed of Union nominees and employers.

In August 1918 many bus and tram workers struck after women were excluded from a nationally determined war bonus award; although many London United tram staff were involved, it seems that only five-per-cent of LCCT staff joined them. The memory of 1915 was still fresh, no doubt. A year later, in September 1919, during a national railway strike that lasted for more than a week, LCCT profits rose by £18000. Half this wind-fall was given, as a reward for their 'loyal service', to the staff, in the form of one or two extra days leave the following year.

Shortly before the NJIC was constituted in 1919, the national tram employers association of that time, after consultation with the National Transport Workers Federation — an alliance of delegates from many unions all over the Country, an embryonic Transport and General Workers (TGWU) Union — conceded a forty-eight-hour week to platform staff. For LCCT tramwaymen, this week was guaranteed, provided that they reported for work on time and were prepared, when necessary, to do other work of a temporary nature. In fact, it is probable that the average working day of LCCT staff just before this agreement was little more than forty-eight hours — in 1916 it had been eight-and-a-half hours daily — and we must assume that certain improved overtime rates and other conditions were the main reason for the LCCT estimate that implementation of the 1919 agreement would cost around £360,000 annually.

From this time forward, the LCCT ceased direct negotiations with its staff on matters not peculiar to London, simply accepting the wages and conditions agreed by the Metropolitan District Council of the NJIC, on which it had representation. But the overwhelming evidence is that London tramwaymen had by 1919 fallen far behind busmen in the matter of wages — as the table on page 160 shows — although ten years previously a rough parity had existed. It was not until the 1930's, after the formation of London Transport, that they began to catch up with their rubber-shod colleagues. In one respect only — albeit an important one in the years that followed — were LCCT staff better off than Combine employees, and that was their guaranteed week. Right up until 1933, it seems, both the LGOC and the Combine tramways were employing staff for either short weeks or during the summer months only.

On the crudest comparison of the jobs of bus and tram crews, throughout the 1920's the LCCT consistently underpaid its staff by around 15%; if you allow for the fact that a loaded LCC tram carried half as many passengers again as did an LGOC bus, and at a more complex fare structure, the rate of underpayment was even greater. By the 1920's, also, the LCCT was the acknowledged rate-setter for the Combine's tram staff, whilst its rates were those below which the suburban municipal operators paid. It can be argued that this underpayment, in turn, reacted on bus crews in the 1930's, when tram wages were being restored to a rough parity. In other respects, too, the LCCT employee was worse off than the LGOC busman when both were amalgamated into LT in 1933; his day was longer and he had no proper meal-relief, although, if he had accepted this inequity for twenty years before he retired he did get a good gratuity. The popular image of Belvedere Road as a benign and considerate employer is a false one, and the London tramwayman had everything to gain from amalgamation.

There are all sorts of questions one can ask at this point. If the strike of 1915 had been resolved differently, what effect would paying a fair wage have had on the LCCT finances? Or, indeed, on the Combine tramways? The hypotheses are many, and if you add to them the likely effects of what might have happened had Mr Baker not quit London for Birmingham in 1903, and any one of several possible results of the Morrison/Ashfield/Bevin relationship in the late 1920's and early 1930's you can indulge yourself in an endless enthusiast's daydream.

Three events of the 1920's deserve a brief mention, although they are well covered elsewhere. In 1921, the NJIC, responding to the falling cost-of-living, agreed that wage rates should be adjusted at three monthly intervals in accordance with a national index. This arrangement ceased

> **"JUSTICE FOR LONDON TRAMWAYMEN"**
>
> # Nothing But Our Full Demands!
>
> ## Stand Solid and the Board will Pay!
>
> We demand Busmen's wages and standards! We stand for equal wages for equal work for all L.P.T.B. surface workers!
>
> Can the Board afford to pay us our demands?
>
> Under the L.C.C. £761,799 was paid per year to the capitalists in interest and redemption—
> that is 21s. a week per tramwayman.
>
> The Board only pays about £450,000 in interest and redemption—
> that is 12s. 6d. a week per tramwayman.
>
> The Board has thus been saving about £300,000 a year or 8s. 6d. a week per tramwayman.
>
> So the Board can afford 8s. 6d. a week without taking into consideration the extra profits from speed-up, increased traffic or the introduction of trolleybuses.
>
> ### MILLIONS FOR BOND-HOLDERS!
>
> Between December 13th, 1933, and October 16th, 1935, the total value of L.P.T.B. shares increased by about £8,500,000 on the Stock Exchange. This nice little present for the bond-holders (on top of the interest they have received) would mean £120 for every L.P.T.B. worker if divided up.
>
> What have the bond-holders done to earn it? Nothing!
>
> The Board can afford to give every Tramwayman the same wages and standards as Busmen. But it won't unless we fight for it!
>
> ### A PITTANCE FOR US!
>
> The Board has made an offer—one which no self-respecting Tramwayman can accept. This offer of 2s. on January 1st and a little bit more later on (if we behave) is a sign of the Board's weakness. The Board is trying to tie our hands to stop us fighting and getting (as it knows we can) our just demands. If we stand together and show our readiness to take strike action to enforce our demand the Board will have to give way.
>
> ### TRAM AND BUSMEN UNITE FOR BETTER CONDITIONS!
>
> And this offer is conditional on the Busmen not going forward with their demand for a 7-hour day. What an obvious trick to split and so weaken the struggle of the L.P.T.B. workers. We will never sell out the Busmen in the interests of the Board, but we accept the Busmen's pledge that they will support us in every way in our demand for a levelling-up of Tramwaymen's wages and standards. Let us see how long the Board can fight against the united Tram and Bus Fleets! Not long, for sure!
>
> But this condition on the part of the Board admits the connection between Bus and Tram wages and opens up the path for joint negotiations for **one agreement** covering both Bus and Tramwaymen.
>
> Fight for our full demands and not a penny less!
>
> Mandate **every Delegate** to the Divisional Committee and the Trams' Council to accept nothing but the full demands!
>
> ### 7s. 6d. UP BACK AND FRONT.
>
> No portion of a duty to count less than 4 hours.
>
> All straight-through duties commencing before 6.30 a.m. not to exceed 8 hours all-in.
>
> Spread-over penalties, 10 hours 1s., 11 hours 2s.
>
> Spare-men (gate duties) 4 hours allowance instead of 2.
>
> Don't be tricked into accepting the Board's offer until you see the huge profits in the balance-sheet which will soon be issued.
>
> Resolution passed on Tuesday, October 29th, 1935:—
>
> "That this Committee of London Tramway Delegates adheres to its previous policy of Busmen's wages and conditions (in cost) and nothing less for all London Tramwaymen, and pledges its support to the London Trams' Council in its fight for this policy. In the absence of satisfaction this Committee calls upon London Tramwaymen to prepare to withdraw their labour to enforce the demand."
>
> Published by "Justice for London Tramwaymen's Committee," 41, Eltham Green Road, S.E.9. 'Phone: Eltham 3085.
>
> Printed by the Marston Printing Co. (T.U.), Nelson Pl., Cayton St., E.C.1.

A Handbill issued by the 'Justice for London Tramwaymen Committee', probably in 1935; the Committee was made up of delegates from every London tram depot.

after 1923. In 1921 also, the TGWU was formed, and (apart from inevitably supressing much information on LCCT conditions in the by then nationally circulated 'Record') took up the cudgel on behalf of London tramwaymen in 1923, after a wage-cut had been threatened for Combine tram staff. It did so with effect, and after a ten-day strike of bus and tram crews in March 1924, a six shilling award to LCCT and Combine tram crews was granted. Even before this strike, the TGWU had begun advocating unification, and when it came, in 1933, it took the form that Bevin, General Secretary of the TGWU, preferred. State capitalism offered more promise than Municipal Socialism.

It was just as well, perhaps, that LCCT staff conditions were a matter for the NJIC after 1919, for in 1920, after LCCT Motormen had for many years asked to be allowed to wear goggles on duty, the Metropolitan District Council of the NJIC agreed that they be allowed for a twelve month review period. Mr Fell was requested to authorise an appropriate pattern, the cost to be borne by Motormen. His selection — rather like the sort of goggles worn by motorists in early Punch cartoons — was not liked by staff. New Cross men thought them 'entirely unsuitable', whilst Hampstead Depot complained that they made Motormen look like bogeymen, and stopped them winking at the ladies. By mid-1923 a new design was in use, pairs of which could be bought for 3s. 6d. (3s. 3d. in quantities) from a TGWU official at Peckham. Just when, if ever, the LCCT agreed to pay for this essential eye protection, I have not discovered, nor have I found any record of official recognition of the TGWU by the LCCT.

During the General Strike of May 1926, only occasional LCCT trams operated. The conduit was vulnerable and the local strike committees that formed in various parts of London were generally effective in preventing cars leaving their depots. There were incidents at Clapham Depot — on May 7th, described by Stan Collins — and at New Cross on May 13th and 14th when volunteers attempted to bring cars out. 'Riots' were also recorded in the Walworth Road and around a convoy of trams briefly operating between Hampstead and Kings Cross. Power for these cars came from Greenwich Generating Station, which was manned by 37 Naval Ratings. Although the LCCT assisted the volunteers — beds were made up on the floor at Chief Office, for

A curious extract from a LT Traffic Circular dated June 1943; the controllers were not fitted with dead-man's-handles.

> **NOTICE TO TRAMDRIVERS**   3222
>
> Drivers are warned of the dangerous practice of turning their back to the controller whilst the car is in motion. Two police prosecutions have recently been taken against tramdrivers.

example — their belligerence seems to have been a little embarrassing to it, and at a best they merely made a tactical gesture.

When the strike finished, the Metropolitan District Council of the NJIC met to arrange a return to work. An attempt was made by the London managers to re-engage staff on new conditions, but this was squashed by the TGWU, although the prepared forms were still presented to staff to sign at at least one depot the following morning. At around midnight on 13th May, when agreement seemed almost complete, one of the East London managers announced that he intended to abandon two unprofitable services forthwith, with a number of redundancies. It is said by a TGWU delegate who attended that meeting, that his mind was only changed after the other London managers had taken him out and plied him with alcohol.

Women Conductors returned to London's trams in October 1940; a maximum of 3342, or 57% of tram conductors, were women in June 1945. The 'turban' head-scarf was the height of lower-middle-class fashion in the austere late 1940's.

The 1930's were a difficult time for London Transport. It felt obliged to level up all tram wages to those applying to ex-LCCT staff, and in 1935 accepted the principle of bringing tram crews wages up to the level of the Central bus Conductor's. It was ostensibly because of a long-term agreement based on this principle that tramwaymen did not join the 1937 bus strike. The 1930's saw the development of much left-wing activity, and the financial arrangements of the 1933 LT Act (unfavourable to the LCC) were among the criticisms of a Minority Movement that developed on the tramways, the Justice for London Tramwaymen Committee, in connection with which Telford Avenue and Clapham Depots — alone on the ex LCCT system — struck for forty-eight hours in March 1936, but with no useful effect. A year later, Bevin would not allow tramwaymen to join the bus strike. Busmen's conditions — the point of the strike — were already better than those of tramwaymen, and there was a feeling that the increasing and profitable use of trolleybuses by LT (operated at tram wages and conditions) posed something of a threat to established bus men and their services. The notional solidarity of transport workers in LT was rather tenuous at this time.

The only other strike which affected virtually all London tram services came on 1st January 1949, after a demand by crews for enhanced payment on Saturday afternoons and evenings. Even at this late stage, the differentials between bus and trams staff were maintained, for whilst bus crews were awarded an extra nine pence an hour, tram crews received only eightpence half-penny.

Labour relations on LT in the 1930's and 1940's are well documented already, and I have thought it better to concentrate on the earlier period, about which little is written. There is much more that could be said, but hopefully these notes will add something to the understanding of how and why London's trams developed as they did.

INDEX

Accidents: 38 39 58 65 105
Amal. Assn. of Tramway and Vehicle Workers: 163-167
Armistice Day: 72
Ashfield, Lord: 46 52 99

Baker, Alfred: 152 164
Baker, Juicy: 28 85
Bancroft, Mr: 23
Belvedere Road, 23: 21 22 38 39 75 77 114
Besant, Annie: 162
Bevin, Ernest: 169-170
Blackout: 104 105 165
Bluebird, (tram number 1): 99 100 126-127 157
Boat Race Day: 43
Bombing, effects of: 105-112 124 158
Braking: 57-58
Brass-boys: 72
Breakdown Gang: 60-61 64
Brixton Hill Depot,
- Map of: Back endpapers
- Opening of: 156
- Closure of: 159
- Photo's of: 90
- Services from: see Telford Avenue Depot

Bruce, J K: 33
Burnell, J B: 114
Bus, training as Driver: 120-122
Buses, conversion to: 126 131-132

Cable trams: 7-8 149-151
Camberwell Depot: 35 73
Central Repair Depot: 8 13-15 44 111 122
Change-pit, procedure at: 66-67 71
Charge Depot Inspector (CDI): 77 85 115 129
Clapham Depot,
- Map of: 48
- Services from in 1936: 34
- Photo's of: 48-49
- Motor School: 23-25 115-120
Colley, Sir John: 23 165
Collins, H (Stan's father): 7-8 14 18-20 28 69
Collins, H (Stan's brother): 8 22 85-86 134
Collins, Stan,
- birth: 7
- schooldays: 8-10
- butcher's boy: 10
- enlisting: 17
- 1914 War service: 19-21
- in India: 21
- marriage: 38
- children: 38
- in court: 57
- retirement: 135
Combine, (Ashfield): 2 46 52 169-170
Conciliation Board, LCCT Traffic Section: 165-169
Conduit,
- explanation of: 4
- laying: 9 152
- reasons for choice of: 137
- cleaning of: 96 98
Controller: 63 70 115-117 128
Croydon, through running to: 84-85 155 157

'Dead', stuck on: 53 54
Depot, procedure at: 70-71
Derailments: 64-66
Discipline: 27 70 77-81, 162-170
Dog Kennel Hill, services on: 35-36
Dog Racing Specials: 43
Driving in service: 53-66

E/1 trams,
- description of: 3
- driving: 53-56
Electric Points: 32
Evelyn Street Depot: 19

Fares, early policy towards: 137
Fell, A L F C: 33 77 152-153 165-168
Feltham trams,
- arrival at Telford Avenue: 85
- driving: 53 66 87-89 117
Fines: 162-163
Fog, driving in: 56
Fog duty: 95
Foreign Service: 30 37
Fuller's Club: 164

Gate men: see 'show-up'.
Geary, S R: 77
General Tram and Bus Worker's Union: 163-164
Goggles, Motormen, for the use of: 41 169-170

Hills, Jack: 51
Holloway Depot: 26-29
Home Guard: 113
Horns, Kennington, procedure at: 82
Hot-box: 64

Jew's Row Depot: see 'Wandsworth Depot'
Juice Money: 53

Justice for London Tramwaymen Committee: 169-170

Kennedy, Dr: 155
Kingsway Tunnel (Subway): 15-17 28-29 33 104 117-119

LRTL tour, 1951: 126
London Bus, Tram and Motor Workers Union: 165
London County Council:
- origins of: 136
- Highways Committee: 137 151-2 163-165
London County Council Tramways Department,
- early days of: 137 151-153 163-164
- finances: 22 30 46
- statistics: 30
London General Omnibus Company: 6 44 46 114 120 165-169
London & Provincial Licenced Vehicle
    Workers Union: 165-167
London Tramways Company: 7 136-137 149-151 153 162-163
London Transport,
- formation of: 44 52
- 1933 Act: 2-3
- Collection: 1 3 87
London United Tramways: 51 85
Luggage on trams: 76

Metropolitan Board of Works: 136 153
Metropolitan Cab Drivers Assn: 163 165
Metropolitan Electric Tramways: 26 166
Metropolitan Street Tramways Company: 149
Ministry of Supply: 112
Mirrors on trams: 56
Motor School,
- at Telford Avenue Depot: 151
- at Clapham Depot: 23-26 115
- at Charlton Works: 122
Motors, tram: 63
Municipal Socialism: 2

National Joint Industrial Council
    for the Tramway Industry: 168-169
National Transport Workers Federation: 168
New Cross Depot: 3 15 39 72 122-123 131 165-167
Night cars: 28 91-93 145
North Metropolitan Tramways Company: 162
Norwood Depot: 117 126 158-159

Pedestrian Crossings: 56
Petrol trams: 18
Penhall Road scrap-yard: 131
Penman, Miss E: 7-8
'Pirate' buses: 46
Plough,
- description of: 4 36 61-62
- changing a: 61-63
- carrier, broken: 60-61 63
Pointsmen: 69 107
Poplar Depot: 30-32 167
Pullman Court: 103

Rail-grinder: 95
Regulators: 31 62 64 79 83 107 109
Rehabilitated trams: 101
'Route' numbers, explanation of: 30

Saint Anne's Home, Streatham: 103
Sand, use of: 58 70 129
Services, particular mention of,
- 2/4 to Hampton Court: 51
- 16/18: 148-159
- 32: 46-47

171

- 65: 30-32
- from Telford Avenue Depot in 1936: 84
- from Clapham Depot in 1936: 34
- in Streatham and Clapham generally: 136-148
'Show-up' duties: 73-74 161
Single-line working: 64 106
Slattery, M L: 166
Somme, Battle of: 19
South London Tramways Company: 162
Snow-brooms: 93-94
Spencer, C J: 52
Stores-vans: 14 15 18
Strikes,
- generally: 112-113 and 162-170
- 1912: 165
- 1915: 18 166-167
- 1918: 168
- 1924: 169
- 1926: 39-40 169-170
- 1937: 170

Tea places: 50
Telford Avenue Depot,
- opening of for cable trams: 150
- rebuilding of for electric cars: 152
- erection of extension shed: 155
- conversion to buses: 126-131 159
- Services from in 1936: 84
- map of: back endpapers
- photo's of: 16 77 88 90 125 132
Terminus, procedure at: 58-59
Thomas, T E: 33 46 52 114
Tilston, T: 79
Towing, disabled cars: 61 63
Track, laying and maintenance of: 95-96
TUC (Trades Union Congress): 164
Trailer cars: 18 34 155-156 165

Train, GF: 149
Trams methods of operation in London: 3-6
Tramways, development of in London: 1-2
Transport and General Workers Union: 168-169
Trolleybuses: 51-52 85 104 124 170
Turnpike Trusts: 136
Twisted Magnets: 58

Uniforms: 74-75
Unions,
- general mentions: 18 28 39 40 110 112
- development of on trams: 162-170
Utting, G: 129

Vestibule screens: 40-41 55

Wages: 8 14 26 32 35 44 69 115 131 160 162-170
Wakelin, R: 121-122
Wallis, E: 115-117 121
Wandsworth Depot: 37 71 124
Washing of trams: 49 72 165
Webb, Juicy: 23 35 73
Webb, Sidney: 2 136 162 164
Wheel Club: 57
White feather: 17
Window order: 81
Winter 1947: 95
Women Conductors: 58 60 129 156 165-166
Working Class Dwellings,
- at Norbury: 137 155
- at Totterdown Fields: 137
- on Brixton Hill: 137
- in Central London: 136

Ypres: 20

SELECT BIBLIOGRAPHY

London County Council, Minutes, Staff Handbooks, Reports and Tramways Department Accounts.

'Tramway and Railway World'; from 1934, **'Transport World'.**   The Times   **'Railway World'**

'The Record', journal of the London and Provincial Licenced Vehicle Workers Union, and later of the Transport and General Workers Union.

'London Transport Magazine'

Royal Commission on London Traffic, 1903-1906

'The London Programme', Sidney Webb, Swan Sonnenschein, London 1891.

'The London Transport Scandal', A Downton, Communist Party, London 1936.

'History of London Transport', 2 Vols., T.C. Barker & M. Robbins, George Allen & Unwin, 1963 and 1974.

'Labour Relations on London Transport', H. Clegg, Basil Blackwell, Oxford 1950.

'Fabian Socialism and English Politics, 1884-1918', A.M. McBriars, CUP 1962.

'The London County Council Tramways Handbook', 'Kennington', T & LRS 1970.

'Fares Please', ed. O.J. Morris, Ian Allan, 1953.

'History of the London County Council, 1889-1939', Gibbons & Bell, Macmillan, London 1939.

In addition, there exist two books recounting something of the lives and philosophies of two Progressive Chairmen of the LCC Highways Committee:

'J. Allen Baker, a memoir', E. Baker and P. Noel-Baker, Swarthmore Press, London 1927.

'John Benn and the Progressive Movement', A.C. Gardiner, Benn, London 1925.

A fascinating account of the early days of the LCC has been written by a one-time Comptroller of the Council:

'The London County Council from Within', H. Haward, London 1932.

Standard works on **Ernest Bevin** and **Herbert Morrison,** and **George Brown's** autobiography include interesting references to the LCCT, as do several publications of the **Light Railway Transport League.** Most of the numerous books on the **1926 General Strike** include useful references to London trams.

London Tramways Coy
TELFORD AVENUE CABLE-TRAM DEPÔT & POWER HOUSE
SOURCE: THE RAILWAY WORLD, JANUARY 1896

London County Council Tramways Dept
TELFORD AVENUE ELECTRIC-TRAM DEPÔT
CORRECT FOR c.1914   SOURCE: LT REC

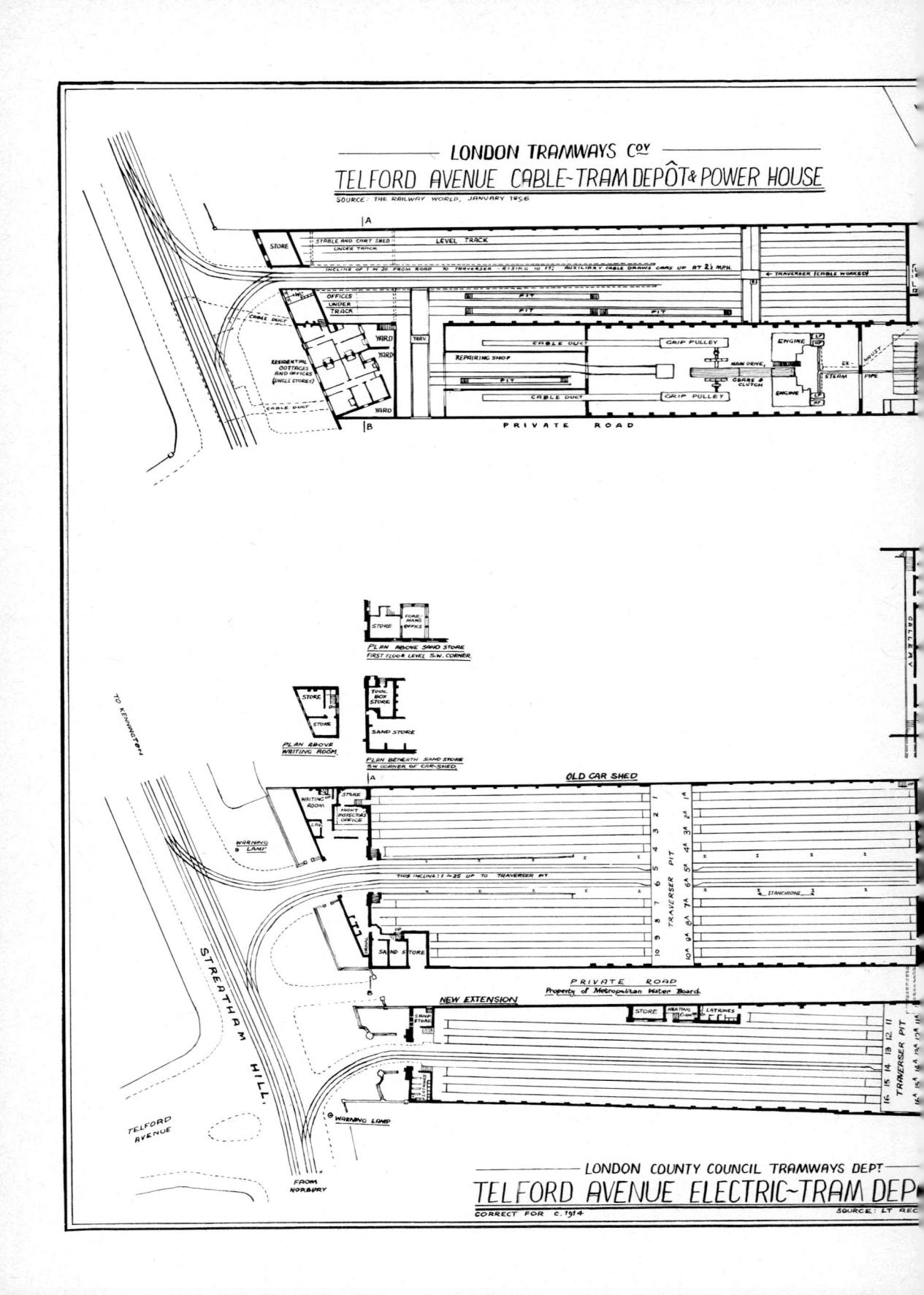

LONDON COUNTY COUNCIL, TRAMWAYS DEPT.
BRIXTON HILL TRAM DEPÔT
CORRECT FOR 1934   SOURCE: LT RECORDS

FROM NORBURY

BRIXTON HILL

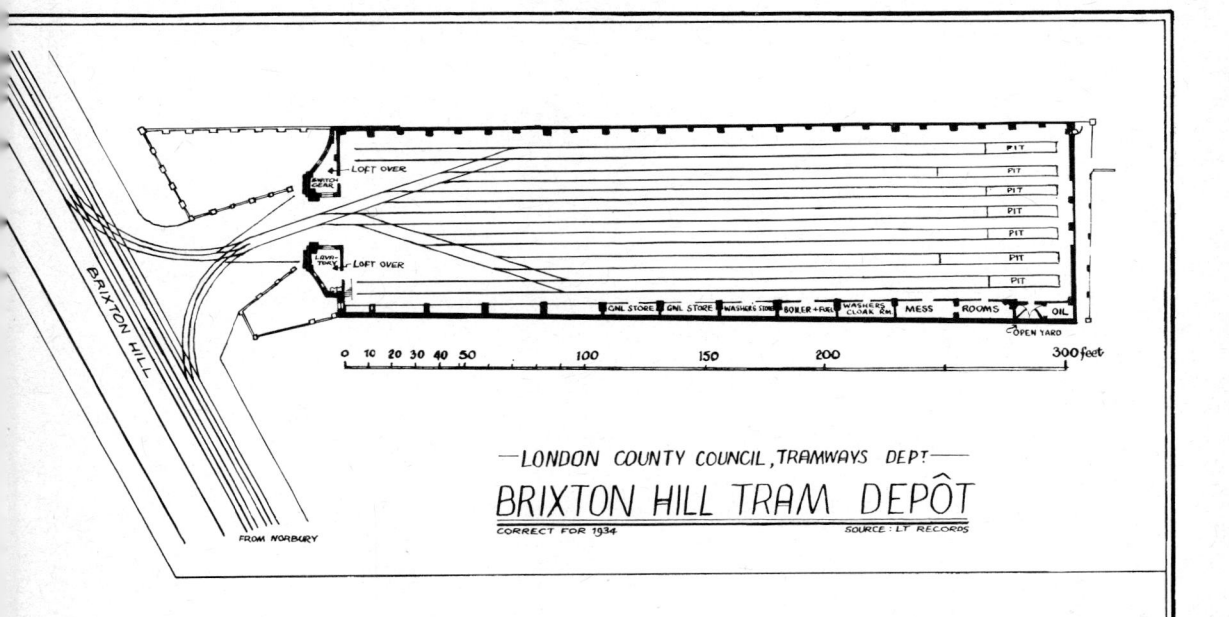

The cable-car shed (top left) was built in 1891/2, and rebuilt for electric cars between 1904/6. The 'extension' shed (bottom) was added between 1911 and 1913. Both sheds were demolished in 1951/2. Brixton Hill Depot was built between 1922 and 1924 and remains standing.

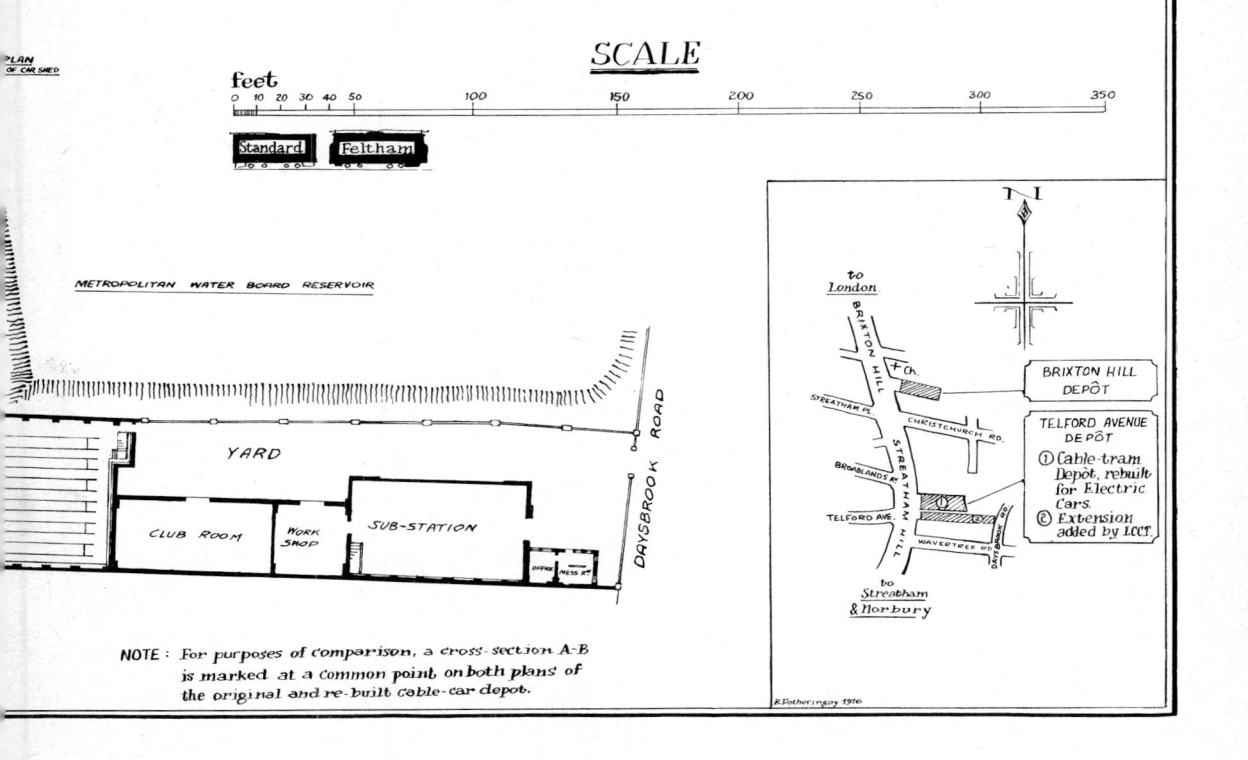

SCALE

Standard   Feltham

METROPOLITAN WATER BOARD RESERVOIR

YARD   CLUB ROOM   WORK SHOP   SUB-STATION   OFFICE   MESS Rm

DAYSBROOK ROAD

NOTE: For purposes of comparison, a cross-section A-B is marked at a common point on both plans of the original and re-built cable-car depot.

to London

BRIXTON HILL   CH.   STREATHAM PL.   CHRISTCHURCH RD.   BROADLANDS AV.   STREATHAM HILL   TELFORD AVE.   WAVERTREE RD.

BRIXTON HILL DEPÔT

TELFORD AVENUE DEPÔT
① Cable-tram Depot, rebuilt for Electric Cars.
② Extension added by LCCT.

to Streatham & Norbury

R. Fotheringay 1976